Approaches and Dilemmas in Economic Regulation

Also by Atle Midttun

ELECTRICITY MARKET REFORM IN NORWAY

EUROPEAN ELECTRICITY SYSTEMS IN TRANSITION

EUROPEAN ENERGY BUSINESS STRATEGIES

NORD POOL – ISSUES AND DILEMMAS (*with Lennart Hjalmarsson and Eirik Svindland*)

THE POLITICS OF ENERGY FORECASTING

Also by Eirik Svindland

ELEKTRONISCHE FINANZMÄRKTE

NORD POOL – ISSUES AND DILEMMAS (*with Lennart Hjalmarsson and Atle Midttun*)

Approaches and Dilemmas in Economic Regulation

Politics, Economics and Dynamics

Edited by

Atle Midttun
Professor of Economic Organisation
Norwegian School of Management

and

Eirik Svindland
Senior Research Fellow
German Institute for Economic Research

First published 2001 by
PALGRAVE
Houndmills, Basingstoke, Hampshire RG21 6XS and
175 Fifth Avenue, New York, N.Y. 10010
Companies and representatives throughout the world

PALGRAVE is the new global academic imprint of
St. Martin's Press LLC Scholarly and Reference Division and
Palgrave Publishers Ltd (formerly Macmillan Press Ltd).

ISBN 0–333–80443–0

This book is printed on paper suitable for recycling and
made from fully managed and sustained forest sources.

A catalogue record for this book is available
from the British Library.

Library of Congress Cataloging-in-Publication Data
Approaches and dilemmas in economic regulation : politics, economics,
and dynamics / edited by Atle Midttun and Eirik Svindland.
    p. cm.
Includes bibliographical references and index.
ISBN 0–333–80443–0
    1. Trade regulation. I. Midttun, Atle, 1952– II. Svindland, Eirik.

HD3612 .A67 2001
338.9—dc21
                                              2001021629

10   9   8   7   6   5   4   3   2   1
10 09 08 07 06 05 04 03 02 01

Printed and bound in Great Britain by
Antony Rowe Ltd, Chippenham, Wiltshire

Contents

Notes on the Contributors

Maarten J. Arensten is Vice Director of the Centre for Clean Technology and Environmental Policy at the University of Twente in the Netherlands.

Robert Delorme is Professor of Economics at the University of Versailles and CEPREMAP, Paris.

Alfred Haid is Senior Research Fellow at DIW-Berlin and Professor of Economics at the University of Nuremberg.

Rolf W. Künneke is Assistant Professor of Economics at the Faculty of Public Administration and Public Policy at the University of Twente in the Netherlands.

Jan-Erik Lane is Professor of Politics at the University of Geneva.

Lutz Mez is Senior Associate Professor of Politics and Vice Director of the Environmental Policy Research Unit at the Free University of Berlin.

Per Ingvar Olsen is Associate Professor at the Centre for Cooperative Studies, Institute of Innovation and Economic Organization, Norwegian School of Management.

Karen I. Vaughn is Professor of Economics at George Mason University.

Bengt-Arne Wickström is Professor of Economics at the Institut fur Finanzwissensnchaft, Humboldt-Universität zu Berlin.

Introduction

Atle Midttun and Eirik Svindland

After a post-war period with extensive use of public service models and macroeconomically orchestrated planned regimes, the 1980s and early 1990s have seen a return to more liberal styles of economic regulation in Western Europe. This increasing use of liberal market principles in the West coincides with the breakdown of Communist planned economy in Eastern Europe which gives deregulation and marketisation an even stronger momentum in Europe.

The movement from planned public service orientated systems to liberal, market orientated regulatory regimes illustrates the paradigmatic character of economic organisation and raises a need for reflection on the basic assumptions behind choice of regulatory direction. The complex interplay between sectoral and macro-orientated regulatory design points in the same direction.

The regulatory issues at this deeper level point beyond a single social science discipline. Much of the literature on economic regulation is specialised and too narrow to address this need. One way to start addressing regulation from this broader perspective may be to move out of the limited market versus hierarchy debate and its derivatives, and also to address the wider spectrum of institutional forms and functional needs that confront economic actors.

A starting point that seems analytically useful would be to enrich the classical market–hierarchy dichotomy with two additional institutional principles of economic organisation: 'network' and 'autarchy'. The inclusion of network is inspired by the current debate in organisation theory and business strategy, and is included to capture both the informal and pre-modern sides of economic organisation, as well as late-modern organisational architecture.

The inclusion of autarchy references both organisation theory literature and literature on entrepreneurship. It is included in order to capture the dynamic innovative element of economic development, indicating that designers of regulatory models must be aware of the basic need of freedom from routines and traditional practices and obligations necessary to allow for innovation.

The broadening of the institutional perspective on regulation implies a parallel broadening of functional focus. It is thus common to associate markets with efficiency, networks with trust, hierarchy with order and autarchy with creativity. These four institutional elements and their functional predispositions thereby refer to four basic goals of a system of economic regulation in a broad sense, which a broadly oriented theory of regulation and institutional infrastructure design should incorporate.

This set of institutional contexts and functions provides, it seems to us, a useful reference system for a broad social science discussion of regulation and allows us to raise a number of issues that go to the core of today's regulatory debate, such as:

- Regulation and Institutional Context
- Regulation and Complexity
- Regulation and Power
- Regulation and Economic Dynamics
- The Status of Normative Theory on Regulation

Within the theme of *regulation and institutional context*, the relationship between regulation and its political and institutional embeddedness is given central focus. This involves discussing regulation as part of the interface between markets and politics, as is done in Mez and Midttun's chapter on the politics of regulation. The chapter argues that coordination between the two levels may prove to be crucial to regulatory efficiency, in so far as the use of certain types of regulatory instruments may only work efficiently within a given institutional context.

The interrelationship between the regulation and the political and institutional level is also pursued by Arentsen and Künneke in their chapter on Dutch negotiated regulation where the authors emphasise how private associations and administrative agencies play up to each other and how networks of state, industry and societal organisations constitute a basis for regulation. This neo-corporatist perspective on regulation, typical of some small industrialised countries in Europe, is illustrated by a study of Dutch electricity regulation. However, as noted by Haid in his chapter on the Chicago school, a more cynical perspective on neo-corporatist arrangements may be put forth in the form of the so-called capture theory, where industries seek government intervention through regulation that blocks entry and prevents price competition. In his chapter Haid shows how this cynical perspective has evolved from analysis of regulation with the purpose of maximising some universal measures of economic welfare, such as consumer surplus or total surplus.

The second theme, *regulation and complexity* raises some central questions about the possibility of co-ordinating regulation between several sectors as well as between specific sectors and overarching institutional domains. The chapter *'Régulation* as an Analytical Perspective: The French Approach' by Delorme, claims that *régulation* concerns a socio-economic system of which government is a part but where governmental action alone is not decisive. *Régulation*, in this perspective, is therefore seen as the outcome of numerous interactions between components, among which the government is one. This is the main premise on which the internal differentiation of the economic system is based.

Regulation and complexity are also central to Lane's chapter 'Why Deregulation is not Reregulation'. He here argues the risk that the gains from widespread and far-reaching deregulation will be captured by the introduction of new and massive reregulation, creating an overregulation which will undermine public welfare. He shares, with Wickström, the fear that state intervention tends to be ineffective. In his chapter 'Regulation of Natural Monopoly: A Public-choice Perspective', Wickström argues that government failure may well exceed the market failure that it is supposed to correct by regulation. He here opposes the traditional neoclassical regulation theory which focuses on the efficiency of the market but not on the efficiency of the regulatory agency. Wickström, in the public-choice tradition, also questions the efficiency of the regulator. He therefore compares the welfare costs of market failure with the welfare costs of regulatory activities, and he shows that the net balance may very well be in favour of leaving the imperfect market alone. This conclusion is arrived at by consideration of the way collective decisions are being made in committees and other representative bodies, the way bureaucracies malfunction and how governments are apt to consider the self-interest of various interest groups when setting their priorities.

Like Wickström's chapter, Midttun's chapter 'Beyond Market and Hierarchy: Analytical Dilemmas in Economic Regulation' criticises the naive neoclassical view that market failures can be unproblematically solved by recursion to regulation. However, Midttun discusses the more radical choice between hierarchic governance and the regulation of decentralised markets. With a departure in organisation theory he shows that there are clear parallels between market failure and hierarchic governance failure. He describes how both worlds contain internal problems and programmes for efficiency improvements.

Several of the chapters also deal with the issue of *regulation and power*. Power is a theme in Mez and Midttun's chapter, which discusses the different payoff and organisational costs for sectoral vested interests compared with the public in general, when it comes to influencing and shaping the political mandates for economic regulation. Olsen's chapter 'Regulatory Reforms in Areas with Multilevel Politicisation' discusses functional interdependencies and power relations between different sectors of the economy and different layers of public governance. Based on the example of Norwegian electricity sector reform, he shows how changing the established balance of power triggers severe political conflicts. In this perspective, deregulation, which means opening up to market forces, may be seen as a means for the active state to overcome some of the deadlocks and conflicts of power between different levels of government and between the state government and organised sectoral interests.

Regulation and economic dynamics is treated as a central theme in Vaughn's chapter 'A Modern Austrian Approach to Economic Regulation'. She pinpoints the difference between the traditional neo-classical and the Austrian perspective on regulatory problems, and shows that by refusing to abstract from time and ignorance in human life, Austrians offer a different perspective both on the nature of markets and on the fundamental subject-matter of economics. To Austrians then, she points out, 'solving' for equilibrium conditions is something of a pointless exercise. The continually changing circumstances of and knowledge about market phenomena render even the possibility of arriving at an equilibrium beyond the pale. Hence, the Austrian refusal to abstract away from time and ignorance implies not only a positive theory of market processes, but also a critique of governmental inter-vention into market activities.

Finally, *the status of normative theory on regulation* is implicitly and partly explicitly touched upon by most authors. It follows from the insti-tutional and broader political economy perspectives in Mez and Midttun's chapter that normative statements are at best institutionally conditioned. Thus, in a Lackatoshian sense, the hard core abstract regulation theory statements must be 'cushioned' by a protective belt of institutional analysis before practical application can be made. Similar conclusions may also be derived from Delorme's and Olsen's chapters, but here based on a complexity-argument rather than on a political science analysis.

The Lane, Wickström and Vaughns chapters implicitly and to some extent also explicitly warn against strong regulatory intervention. Lane and Wickström both warn against the imperfections of the regulator as a potentially greater danger than the market-imperfections that it is supposed to cure. Vaughn's argument stresses more the challenge posed by dynamic change processes and innovations which defy strong regulatory interventionism, which is likely to be too static. Finally, Midttun's chapter points out that the lack of an overarching theory covering both organisations and markets, implies that there is no simple deductive basis for deciding on the form of regulatory intervention.

In the final chapter Eirik Svindland presents a broad reflection on some of the major regulatory issues raised in this book. Going back, in part to classical problems of economic regulation, he integrates many of the reflections presented in the previous chapters with reference to problems facing regulators today.

Finally, we would like to thank the Norwegian Research Council for generous support.

1
'Regulation' as an Analytical Perspective: The French Approach

Robert Delorme

Introduction

Regulation has several meanings. The one it receives in what has come to be known as the French 'Theory of Regulation' is specific. It is necessary to identify it unambiguously. For this reason we will use it with the French orthograph for *régulation*. According to its usual sense in economics, regulation consists of governmental actions to supervise and control the economic activities of firms with the aim of preventing private decision-making that would take inadequate account of the public interest understood as economic efficiency, fairness, health and safety. To regulate also means to cause to function accurately or to cause to conform to some standard. In general terms, regulation in the theory of systems denotes the role of feed-back mechanisms in relation to the stability of some set of interactions. In French, *réglementation* is related to the first meaning while *régulation* pertains to systems theory. However, *régulation* also means stabilisation in French, in the sense of governmental action aimed at reducing fluctuations of macroeconomic activity by means of budgetary or monetary contracyclical interventions.

Régulation in the theory of regulation is different again. It denotes the dynamic process by which production and social demand adapt to one another. It is thus much broader than mere governmental stabilisation or regulatory activities. Although regulation theoreticians are reluctant to use the terminology of the theory of systems because of the confusions

1

and the holism it may entail in economics, regulation comes close to the notion of dynamic equilibration of complex systems. *Régulation* pertains to a socio-economic system of which the government is a part, but it never boils down to governmental action alone. *Régulation* is the process and the outcome of numerous interactions between components, among which is the government. This is the main premise on which the internal differentiation of the economic system is based.

What appeared *ex post* as a rather consistent programme arising from the findings of economists sharing similar basic dissatisfactions with the then prevailing approaches in economics originated in a pragmatic and rather disseminated way among economists mainly based in Paris in the early Seventies, and became progressively perceived as the *régulation* perspective. It started practically simultaneously with the study of long-run and structural change in the French and the US economies based on a macroeconomic, sectoral and historical, empirical approach. Michel Aglietta analysed the growth of the US economy in the long run (Aglietta 1976). A simultaneous inquiry on the secular evolution of output and prices in France was conducted at CEPREMAP (Centre d'études prospectives d'économie mathématique appliquées à la planification, Paris) by several researchers. It gave rise to several publications among which are Robert Boyer and Jacques Mistral (1978) and Alain Lipietz (1979).

The then dominating approaches in France were Keynesian, neoclassical and Marxist. Keynesian-based modelling, with its emphasis on aggregate supply and demand in the short run, was felt too limited for dealing with changes in the long run, notably those concerning production. Neoclassical theory, with its emphasis on rationally substantive agents, on co-ordination obtained exclusively through markets and on equilibrium, was considered too narrow and static. Last but not least, those who engaged in the *régulation* programme shared a basic interest in the way Marx introduced an analysis of the long-run dynamics of capitalism with an emphasis on social relations and on the process of accumulation. But they rejected the mechanical and catastrophic interpretations of Marxism relying on the notion of a determinism of economic life – at the level of an economy – stemming from the methods of production, and on the idea of a predefined end state to the evolution of capitalist economies. These latter criticisms are a key to understanding what makes regulation distinctive and also what makes it belong to the broader contemporary thrust toward an open-ended evolutionary–institutional–socio-economic stance. It is these premises and the convergence of his own findings on the long-run growth of public spending in France with those of early regulationists, that made this author join the *régulation* perspective.

It is worth adding that *régulation* has diffused and raised interest among a growing number of scholars.There is today a kind of second age of the approach, after the founding period during which the main concern was with the concepts and the exploration of the possible relevance of the approach to other economies than the US and the French ones. A recent survey of the theory of *régulation* contains 54 chapters written by 46 authors (Boyer and Saillard 1995). This chapter is not intended to provide a detailed account of the theory of *régulation*. Its purpose is of assessing some of its insights and weaknesses from the perspective of economic policy-making. It is claimed that the theory of *régulation* is facing a profound challenge with respect to its lack of a normative criterion or standard of evaluation against which alternative institutional arrangements can be assessed and desirable orientations of economic policy can be defined in an operational way. This deficiency can be seen as the counterpart to its rather high capacity to describe socio-economic systems. The threat is historicism, relativism and floating eclecticism. This seems to be the main challenge to *régulation* theory.

Let it be clear at the outset that I am writing here about the theory of *régulation* from its inside. By and large I feel in agreement with most of it except for the high-floating eclecticism and the tendency toward sometimes unwarranted scientism that can be found in it. Thus, there is a diversity in methodological and theoretical views within the *régulation* perspective. Yet, despite certain differences in emphasis as well as in substance, there exists a common core built around basic concepts presented in section II. I designate here this common core by the terms 'theory of *régulation*', '*régulation* approach', '*régulation* programme' or '*régulation* perspective' indiscrimately. In the third section, I sketch some lessons from the theory of *régulation*. Indeed two main insights arise. First, macroeconomic theorising in general is often criticised for not taking institutions properly into account. What makes the theory of *régulation* truly original within economic theory is its attempt to include institutions in macroeconomic theorising and to build a framework in which institutions play an explicit and important role. A second insight comes from the open-endedness of the theory of *régulation*. It is an open-ended institutionalism. This immediately creates a challenge: how to theorise without the closure associated with the more deterministic standard ways of thinking in the economic discipline. It is well known that this is the main criticism usually addressed to what has come to be called old institutionalism by proponents of the new, mainstream institutionalism.

The institutionalism based on the heterogeneity, the diversity and the historicalness of institutions is usually downgraded on the grounds that it remained a-theoretical and unscientific. Devising an explicit theoretical core is thus the main challenge to open-ended institutionalism today.

The theory of *régulation* provides an answer through several features which appear to compose a theoretical core. Yet it can be maintained that this theoretical core is still incomplete. It lacks a body of explicit unifying foundations thanks to which the floating character of the theory of *régulation* would be eliminated and replaced by an explicit operational anchoring to founding principles. All in all, two unanswered challenges remain. One has to do with the floating eclecticism and the lack of consistency arising from research conducted under the heading of the theory of *régulation*. I do not address this issue directly here. But it pervades indirectly through a second challenge on which I shall focus. This challenge relates to economic policy-making. In order to clarify it I will rely on a comparison with the theory developed mainly in Germany under the names of Ordo liberalism or Ordnungstheorie in the fourth section.

The basic concepts

Three concepts are at the basis of *régulation*. They are the institutional forms, the regime of accumulation and the mode of *régulation*. The dynamics of *régulation* arises from their interplay.

The institutional forms

The institutional forms set a bridge between observed regularities of socio-economic life and agents' behaviour. Agents act within basic rules of interaction or institutional forms which consist in a codification of the main social relationships. It is consistent with the assumption of bounded rationality of agents. Five institutional forms are identified. First is the monetary and credit relationship. The configuration it takes depends on the type of monetary management, the kind of causality between money and credit, the structure and degree of development of national and international financial systems. The wage–labour nexus is the second institutional form. It has a key role since it is conceived as covering the main features of work organisation and the standard of living of wage-earners. Five components are distinguished by Boyer

(1988a): the organisation of the work process; the stratification of skills; workers' mobility; direct and indirect wage formation and the use of wage income. Third are the forms of competition. A basic distinction is between traditional price competition and oligopolistic competition. Fourth is the configuration of the state. It is characterised in recent work as a mode of interaction between the state and the economy (Delorme, 1995) in order to convey the idea of stabilised configurations over some periods of time with differences in history for a given country and also differences across countries. Finally there is the relationship between an economy and other economies in the world. It is the mode of interaction with the international economy or, equivalently, the type of adhesion to the international regime.

These institutional forms appear as the basic rules of the game in a capitalist, market-led, economic system. They enable variations to be depicted over time and across space within capitalism.This is the reason why the rules constituting the nature of the game (civil law, property law, and so on) are not explicitly mentioned. They are taken into acount as far as their modifications entail changes at the immediately inferior level of the institutional forms.

The regime of accumulation

The logic of accumulation is a central feature of a capitalist system. History provides evidence that accumulation is not linear: there are cumulative growth patterns separated by crises. These patterns can be viewed as stabilised configurations of the economy over some periods of time. The concept of regime of accumulation is aimed at depicting such patterns. It is defined by the set of regularities which allow a general compatibility between capital formation, production, the distribution of income and the genesis of demand. It expresses macroeconomic consistency. Given the evolution of technical coefficients, income shares, the composition of demand and time lags, it is possible to model these regularities in a dynamic setting.

A basic, simplified model is the one proposed by Boyer (1988b) with six endogenous variables.They are the productivity trend $(\overset{\circ}{PR})$ investment change $(\overset{\circ}{I})$, the households' consumption trend $(\overset{\circ}{C})$, real wage formation change $(\overset{\circ}{RW})$, the evolution of output $(\overset{\circ}{Q})$ and changes in employment $(\overset{\circ}{N})$. The six equations are, with $\circ$ denoting a rate of change and the terms in lower-case letters denoting coefficients and parameters:

(1) $\overset{\circ}{PR} = a + b.\overset{\circ}{I} + d.\overset{\circ}{Q}$ Productivity equation

(2) $\overset{\circ}{I} = f + v.\overset{\circ}{C} + u.(\overset{\circ}{PR} - \overset{\circ}{RW})$ Investment equation

(3) $\overset{\circ}{C} = c.(N.\overset{\circ}{RW}) + g$ Consumption equation
(4) $\overset{\circ}{RW} = k.\overset{\circ}{PR} + l.\overset{\circ}{N} + h$ Real wage formation
(5) $\overset{\circ}{Q} = \alpha.\overset{\circ}{C} + (1 - \alpha).\overset{\circ}{I}$ Accounting identity
(6) $\overset{\circ}{N} \approx \overset{\circ}{Q} - \overset{\circ}{PR}$ Accounting identity

Empirical investigations have revealed different regimes through history and across countries at a given period of time. A variety of regimes of accumulation exists, depending on the character and intensity of technical change and on the size and the structure of demand or, broadly speaking, on the norms of production and the norms of consumption.

The mode of *régulation*

The mode of *régulation* is a concept enabling to pass from partial regularities involving numerous agents acting autonomously to the possibility of a consistent dynamic system. Several ways of adjusting production to demand, credit to money, income distribution to demand formation are possible. Institutional forms may or may not induce a coherent adjustment process for the economy as a whole. Institutions and forms of organisation (markets, hierarchies – private firms and public units – and networks) jointly determine economic and social dynamics. Hence *régulation* depends on the behaviour of agents and of social groups in as much as it ensures the relative coherence and stability of the current regime of accumulation. Then a more specificied definition of *régulation* can be given at this point. It is a conjunction of mechanisms of adjustment associated with a configuration of institutional forms. It provides an alternative to the notion of static equilibrium. A mode of *régulation* is a set of rules and individual and collective behaviours which fulfil three requirements: they render potentially conflicting decentralised decisions mutually compatible without the need for decision units gathering the information necessary to understand the working of the entire system; in the sense defined above, they regulate the regime of accumulation; and 'They reproduce the basic social relationships through a system of historically determined institutional forms' (Boyer, 1988a).

Régulation and crises

In the theory of *régulation*, the long-run dynamics is seen as being discontinuous. Periods of relative dynamic stability, during which basic regularities prevail, reach limits and leave room for phases of change, during which the consistency among previous components vanishes, with instability and disorder until a new consistency settles. These changes can be either structural or small. This is the reason why crises play such an important role in the theory of *régulation*.

Tension and the potential for crisis are never absent from *régulation*. Indeed, although the term 'crisis' is used in many ways, it is basic to the regulation approach to distinguish two categories of crises: 'small' and 'big' crises. The former are of a rather cyclical nature. They are in the essence of *régulation*.They express the kind of self-equilibration process through which recurrent imbalances of accumulation occur within the system as a result of the necessary lags between the demand and capacity effects of investment, for instance. Variations in inventories, production, investment, employment and prices are part of these adjustments. These variations actually depict the usual business cycle. However, the institutional forms are likely to change slowly, from cycle to cycle, leaving the character of *régulation* as a whole unaffected.

The latter are of a structural nature. In structural crises the very process of accumulation becomes less and less compatible with the stability of institutional forms and the *régulation* which sustains it. In such a situation increasing doubts arise as to the long-term viability of the system. It can no longer reproduce itself in the long run on the same institutional basis. Imbalances are such that within the given mode of *régulation*, former self-correcting mechanisms become ineffective. Institutional forms become more and more questioned by the spreading of the misadjustments. Ultimately the whole combination of the mode of *régulation*, institutional forms and the regime of accumulation, which constitutes a mode of development (Figure 1.1) becomes questioned and renders necessary that strategic choices, both socio-economic and political, be made by firms, the government, the unions, in order to favour a restructuring of the economy.

This distinction is central to the *régulation* approach. Lasting high levels of unemployment in many industrialised countries are for this approach the manifestation of a structural crisis which appeared in the early 1970s.

These notions make it possible to identify varying institutional forms, regimes of accumulation and forms of *régulation* over time and across economies. Their combination constitutes a mode of development when some form of compatibility holds. Hence, post-Second World War growth is interpreted as the Fordist mode of development, combining intensive accumulation with mass consumption, modifications in the monetary regime with an increased place of credit-based money supply and primarily a shift in the wage–labour nexus (new wage norms involving the diffusion of productivity gains to wage earners on a nationwide basis, extension of social security bringing a permanent improvement in consumption norms).

A distinctive feature of the *régulation* approach is to make it possible to account endogenously for both growth and crisis. Hence, the very development of Fordism as a social, economic and technical regime led to new conflicts and imbalances which, beyond some threshold, induced tendencies toward a lasting slowdown of growth, stagnation and pressures towards changes in institutional forms.

Following R. Boyer (1988a) four tendencies of varying importance have developed as limits to Fordism. Advanced Fordism first became faced with growing imbalances in the organisation of work due to highly specialised machinery, increased specialisation of jobs, difficulties in organising assembly lines and workers' unrest enabling entire plants to be brought to a halt. These traits hampered productivity gains. Second, mass production requires ever larger markets. It intensifies competition and the overwhelming place of world markets. It may become a destabilising factor when national conditions of production do not conform with international standards, thus pushing towards the destruction of existing domestic ways of adjustment since the nation progressively loses its relevance as the space on which production standards adjust to consumption. The smaller international place of US manufacturing, together with the rising role of East Asian countries, add to internationally-based changes and to the instability of the Fordist regime. Third, Fordism leads to growing social expenditure.

Increasing needs in education, health, pensions, housing and urban infrasture cannot usually be met by mass production. Their relative costs tend to go up. The consequence is a pressure toward growing public expenditure at varying rythms according to countries and their particular ways of organising the private and public provision of services. This tendency calls for adjustments in this organisation. It is inevitably slow and difficult. A fourth factor requiring deep adjustment may be the divergence between innovations in consumption and standardised methods of production. New demands for high-quality customerised and diversified products create difficulties for traditional industrial processes based on standardisation and economies of scale. The notion of a structural crisis of the Fordist mode of development follows from these considerations.

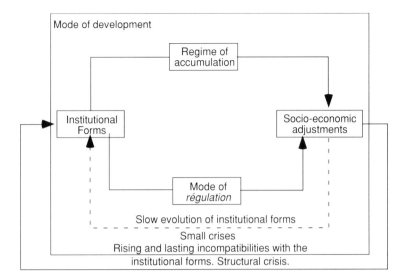

* Institutional forms: monetary regime
                             forms of competition
                             wage–labour nexus
                             place and role of the state
                             relationship with the international economy
* Regime of accumulation: dynamic compatibility between output, income dis-
                             tribution and demand.
* Mode of *régulation*:   channelling of individual and group behaviours in
                             accordance with the regime of accumulation; repro-
                             duction of institutional forms.

Source: Adapted from Boyer (Boyer and Saillard, 1995)

Figure 1.1   The basic notions of the approach of *régulation*

Lessons from *régulation*

Theory of *régulation* as macroeconomics with institutions

Let us remember that the theory of *régulation* arose from a dissatisfac-
tion with the macroeconomic theorising that prevailed in the Sixties and
Seventies, be it of a Marxist, a monetarist or even of a Keynesian style.
The engagement in historical investigation followed from it and
eventually led to identifying the basic institutional forms operating in a
market capitalist economy. It is noticeable that more than a decade later
a somewhat similar analysis could be made, but with respect also to the
theories developed in the Seventies and Eighties. In a survey done at the

beginning of the Nineties Boyer argues that none of the recent theories seems to be able to explain in a satisfactory way the major stylised facts observed during the last two decades. These stylised facts pertain to an inflationary boom followed by vigorous disinflation, to the 'paradox of productivity' due to the slowing down of growth and productivity despite a burst of innovations, to wage rigidity, to the persistence of unemployment, especially in Europe, to the polarisation of large external disequilibria and finally to the coexistence of contrasted national trajectories (Boyer 1992). The theories surveyed by Boyer are mostly, with their main authors: Keynesian (J. Tobin), monetarist (M. Friedman), disequilibrium (J.P. Benassy), new classical (R. Lucas), endogenous growth (P. Romer), new international trade (P. Krugman) and new microfoundations of macroeconomics (J. Stiglitz). Although fruitful insights were gained from these researches, Boyer contends that they remain partial and do not provide a framework which would enable the totality of the contemporary stylised facts to be articulated. The sophistication of modelling and of econometric methods goes along with often ad hoc and unsatisfactory assumptions about the institutional context of existing economies. Macroeconomic theory suffers from a deficient analysis of the impact of institutions upon individual behaviour and of the macro regularities that result from them. An example of this deficiency comes from labour. In most theories, labour is viewed as a commodity traded on a market like any other commodity. The reference is to a competitive market with constraints due to unions and the costs of moving from one job to another. Yet historical, sociological, judiciary and comparative analyses suggest that more should be done and that labour contracts are specific to institutional environments, which might contribute to an explanation of the diversity of national trajectories with respect to unemployment. Diversity would also be the key word for the other institutional forms. This observation may do harm to the idea of some canonical macroeconomic theory since the macroeconomic properties cannot but be affected by acknowledging the variety of national trajectories. In this vein, the theory of *régulation* introduces a rationale for carefully identifying national trajectories as elements of an institutional and historical macroeconomic theory.

This is one of the directions in which research is pursued in *régulation* theory. Closely related to it is a plurality of researches done at the level of the particular institutional forms. From this standpoint, the theory of *régulation* appears as federating a diversity of approaches to institutions which have an evolutionary and socio-economic perspective in common. In this sense, *régulation* theory is an open-ended institutionalism with a renewed aspect in that it relies on an explicit theoretical backbone synthesised by the notion of mode of *régulation*.

An open-ended institutionalism with a theoretical core

The theory of *régulation* is open-ended in at least two ways. First, it rejects both the idea of a predefined law of development in modern society and the notion of a predefined state of equilibrium acting as a norm thanks to which empirical situations become perceived as deviations from a non-existing situation. Second, it is transdisciplinary although the standpoint remains naturally based in the discipline of economics. But it rejects the notion that economics is necessarily self-contained as not being appropriate to the study of institutions over time and across countries. These features are among the premises which constitute the common preconception of institutional, evolutionary and socio-economic perspectives (Delorme, 1994). But on the other side of the coin arises the question of how to theorise when such important differences, both over time, as change, and across space, as heterogeneity, are present. It is worth mentioning that such founding fathers as Thorstein Veblen (1919) and the authors of the 'Ordo Manifesto' (Franz Böhm, Walter Eucken and Hans Grossmann-Doerth, 1936) all chose Gustav von Schmoller and the German historical school in general as their emblematic targets for what was to be avoided when dealing with history and institutions, namely relativistic and atheoretical discourse. This question is faced by Pasinetti (1994) and Delorme (1997) with different answers, the details of which would take us too far. Suffice it to say that there still seems to be no unified or even clarified position arising in the *régulation* approach about this issue. High eclecticism seems to be the answer.

However the overall picture is not quite so gloomy. Comparison with other approaches reveals that strong regularities on some key issues are present in the theory of *régulation*. They compose a rather consistent whole which is naturally calling for further insights but which may be considered as something akin to a theoretical core. These regularities pertain to the plurality of institutions, to their emergence, to their functioning, to the diversity of modes of *régulation* and ultimately to their potential as an alternative to general equilibrium.

Plurality, not dichotomy, of basic institutions in a market economy

The first and possibly major trait of the theory of *régulation* is the plurality of the relevant institutions, broadly defined, of a market economy. It rejects the dichotomy often postulated between market and state. This binary distinction condemns one to over-globalism. It may serve ideological purposes when the market is equated with liberty and the state with coercion. It over-simplifies issues when it is used to support state intervention as a necessary consequence of market failure and vice versa. Simply, it does not reflect the role played by other institutional and organisational forms in modern economies.This distinction considers that institutions are the rules of interactions and that forms of organisation are forms of interactions. Several forms of interactions may be compatible with given rules of the game. Markets, hierarchies (private and public), networks and alliances are such forms of organisation (Delorme, 1995). A hierarchy exists going down from the principles defining the nature of interactions (nature of the game) analogous to the constituent principles of Ordo-liberalism (Grossekettler 1989) to the rules of the game and to the forms taken by the playing of the game and players (actors, be they individuals or groups). These components depict the architecture of an economy. A corollary is that the combination of these components varies over time and across countries. Well-performing economies may combine them in different ways. Understanding economic performance and its variations requires a primary identification and understanding of what these combinations are and how they operate. What they are cannot be decided or assumed realistically beforehand by way of deductive reasoning, but only through empirical inquiry. Comparative studies conducted along these lines show that the concrete organisation of the wage–labour nexus is as crucial as are forms of competition or monetary regimes. Understanding how institutions and organisations operate and relate to the economic performance of an economy is a most difficult task remaining on the agenda. These difficulties are illustrated by the limited existing literature and by the temptation it reveals of conflating the emergence and the efficiency of institutions.

History matters

The issue of the emergence of institutions is a challenge to any theory aiming at empirical relevance. Game theory has an impressive record in showing how conventions may emerge in theory but it still seems far from explaining how institutions appear in concrete, historical life. Institutions are social constructs. They appear in historical processes. The task of explaining their emergence seems to require combining the three components of history consisting of chance, necessity and human will (Lesourne, 1992). How they combine empirically can hardly be established by deductive reasoning or even by simulation but rather through empirical investigation in a first step, as a basis for theorising in a further step.

Taking history seriously leads to rejection of the functionalism too often implied by work done in economics. An instance is O.E. Williamson's starting point according to which all economic institutions arise for the sake of economic efficiency, to minimise transaction costs. It thus conflates the questions of where institutions come from with what effect they have on economic operations (Piore 1996).

Another example is D.C. North's theory of institutional evolution (North 1990). His own evolution on this subject reveals a move from a stance in his early work in which institutional evolution assures something like optimality to a distance taken in more recent work with such functionalism. He argues that major differences in economic performance among nations are due to differences in their institutions and in their evolutions. In some countries they have evolved in ways favourable to economic progress. Cultural and political contingencies play an important part in these differences. Learning has a crucial role. This leads North to depict his own view as institutional/cognitive analysis (North 1994). One may however still wonder whether 'economic progress' is not conceived as a kind of progression towards a Western-style ideal trajectory of efficient institutions (Khalil 1993).

Thus history presents a challenge to theorising, between the two poles of efficiency and culturalism. An additional difficulty comes from the genuine many-sided nature of most institutions: both efficiency and other factors are present but in very complicated combinations. Thus an economic organisation may strive to reduce transaction costs but this is generally not its sole aim. Likewise, although markets may in some cases not be able to process all the information necessary to their operation, this does not seem enough to explain institutions exclusively with a theory of imperfect information.

Institutions arise through historical processes which combine, to various degrees, first, technical aspects of efficiency or necessity, second, tensions, conflicts between collective actors and third, chance. It is only in a second stage that every institution has to pass the test of its viability and its compatibility with economic reproduction in the medium term and in the long run. It is only *ex post* that coherence, whenever it is the case, can be observed, after a process of trial and error. Although intentionality is present *ex ante*, the *ex post* manifestations and effects are often different from what was expected.

The functioning of institutions: viability before allocative efficiency

Is it possible to assess the operational efficiency of an institution separately from its connections with other institutions? Whereas the standard analytical standpoint would maintain that decomposability is relevant here, *régulation* theory emphasises the complementarity of institutions. The very concepts of mode of *régulation* and of regime of accumulation express situations in which a sufficient degree of compatibility between the component forms is achieved, thus creating synergy and satisfactory performance which render a given configuration acceptable to people and thus confer upon it a viability in the mid-term and possibly in the long run.

The language of systems theory, which is very seldom used in the theory of *régulation*, is helpful here: viability pertains to what appears as a systemic coherence when a mode of *régulation* holds and reproduces over some historical period. It translates in empirical inquiry and international comparison in the form of national trajectories based on the combination of the five institutional forms, on constituent principles, on forms of organisation and on the interplay of actors. Boyer is thus able to distinguish between five such national trajectories or types of capitalism in the present time (Boyer 1995). According to him, they are financial market-based capitalism (USA, Canada, United Kingdom), micro-corporatism (Japan, Taïwan), social market economy (Germany, Austria), state capitalism (France) and social democratic capitalism (Sweden, Norway). For example, in the Japanese micro-corporatist system, the role of bank-financed group activities, the importance of interactive participation within the firm, cross-shareholding within and between groups, the role of informal co-operative relationships and the practice of life employment in the biggest firms might appear as nonviable habits and practices if they were considered independently.

Viability is also highlighted in other research done in the *régulation* approach. An instance is the mode of interaction between the state and the economy whereby economies as close to each other as France and Germany appear to have quite differentiated patterns of state–economy relationships although the basic components are alike (Delorme, 1995). This feature points to the fact that it would be difficult to interpret such enduring differences between national configurations otherwise than by reckoning the viability of the national patterns in their respective contexts. Such viability is naturally evolving and may eventually be endangered and disrupted. But it nevertheless suggests strongly that it does not suffice to isolate and analyse the function and the effectiveness of an institution in order to assess its viability. It is necessary to examine how a particular institution inserts itself in a network of other institutions and organisations. It is noticeable that D.C. North himself comes close to a notion of long-run viability when he states that 'it is adaptive rather than allocative efficiency which is the key to long-run growth' (North, 1994, p. 367).

A related notion is institutional isomorphism (DiMaggio and Powell 1983, 1991) or organisational isomorphism (Orrù, Biggart and Hamilton 1991) whereby technical and institutional environments shape organisations through efficiency and legitimacy pressures. This may explain why distinct institutional models, shaping differentially organisational behaviour and structure, are viable. Orrù et al. show that the institutional traits of different East Asian businesses (Japanese, Taiwanese and South-Korean) contribute to their economic success. The patterns of firm relations are uniform or isomorphic within each economy, but different from each other owing to different environments. These environments do not hamper efficiency 'but rather provide a basis for market order and for competitive relations' (Orrù et al., p. 363). Orrù et al. conclude that it is only 'if one assumes, in a Western vein, that firm individuation is the natural state of an orderly market' (p. 388) that the principles they describe can be understood as institutional obstacles to good economic performance.

The diversity of the modes of régulation

The diversity of the modes of *régulation* derives directly from the traits presented above. That economic regimes vary over time and across space within the same matrix of market-led capitalist economies is a cornerstone of *régulation* theory. Furthermore, their viability relies on varying combinations of components. One may depict the compatibility of an institutional pattern with the economic dynamics it shapes as a kind of equilibrating process in which there is no necessary convergence towards some canonical model. Convergence or divergence may occur as only specific cases among a variety of other possible paths such as autonomous evolution, partial catching up and then lagging evolution, catching up and forging ahead, collapse and imitation. This suggests that there is no one best way to becoming a market-led economy and that there is no one best market economy. One must admit that if we were to stop here, the picture given of *régulation* theory might evoke historicism and relativism. Although these threats are not absent, we think that it is through comparing various theoretical systems that their merits and deficiencies can be clarified rather than by way of a reflection developed in absolute or too general terms. This will be evoked below. It is worth adding at this point that the viability of any mode of *régulation* is defined in historical, not abstract time. This means that the very factors which led to the rise and the success of a mode of *régulation* in a first stage can lead to the destabilisation and erosion of the same institutional forms in a second stage – as is evidenced by structural crises that were mentioned above.

The theory of régulation as an alternative research programme

We started by saying that *régulation* theory is an open-ended institutionalism with a theoretical core. The open-ended aspect has been illustrated in the paragraphs above. The existence of a theoretical core can be introduced in two ways. First, it suffices to recall the connection between the mode of *régulation* and the economic regularities present in the regime of accumulation. This category provides a theoretical base. And the whole set-up of the mode of development is also itself a theoretical entity. Second, one may wonder whether there are regularities arising from the traits presented above which would enable one to draw a comparison with standard theorising in economics.

A natural way for comparing theoretical programmes in the economic discipline consists primarily in identifying their respective hypotheses on three basic issues common to any economy: how agents behave, what efficiency consists of and how co-ordination is achieved. We have developed this comparison between the evolutionary perspective and a standard perspective on transition in post-socialist countries (Delorme 1995). Let us stay here with the co-ordination and the efficiency questions. General equilibrium is naturally the standard term of comparison. We contend that the theory of *régulation* differs from it not only with respect to the usual questions of existence, uniqueness and stability, but also with respect to the cognitive and normative principles that are embodied in both programmes.

The entries in Table 1.1 are inevitably schematised. They are aimed at capturing the main differences between the two programmes. The first three criteria were evoked in the previous paragraphs. The cognitive and normative principles are those put into practice in each programme. In the equilibrium approach, equilibrium is given *ex ante* the substantive content of an optimum situation with exceptions due to market failures. This definition carries with it a powerful and simple normative principle for action and economic policy. The theory of *régulation* operates quite differently. The historical and open-ended character of *régulation* is such that the substantive content of a mode of *régulation* or of an institutional

Table 1.1 The *régulation* programme and general equilibrium theory compared

Criterion	General Equilibrum Theory	*Régulation* programme
Co-ordinating principle	Existence of an equilibrium as compatibility of economic agents' plans and actions through competitive markets	Existence of a mode of *régulation* as compatibility of institutions, of organisations and of behaviours channelled by them.
Uniqueness or not	Uniqueness of equilibrium	Diversity of modes of *régulation*
Stability or not	Market forces ensure the stability of equilibrium	Phases of evolving stabilisation alternating with recurring structural crises
Embodied cognitive principle	Substantive content of equilibrium situation defined deductively *ex ante*	Substantive content of a mode of *régulation* is the outcome of a historical process and is known *ex post*
Embodied normative principle	Optimality of equilibrium situation with local, circumscribed exceptions (market failures)	No explicit criterion Viability (of a mode of *régulation* or of an institutional configuration) as a surrogate

arrangement can be known only once it has settled, *ex post*. And *régulation* theory does not seem to contain a core normative principle enabling one to set orientations for action. Viability is only an *ex post* surrogate to it. It does not provide guidelines as easily applicable to orientations of economic policy as is the optimality of equilibrium. This deficiency may have no influence as long as the theory of *régulation* is engaged in identifying and describing *régulation* trajectories. But it may become annoying when one attempts to analyse its implications for economic policy. Naturally the theory of *régulation* is far from being silent on objectives of economic policy such as increasing the standard of living, and employment and equity considerations. Yet there still does not seem to emerge from it a norm that would be translatable into operational policy statements. This may be the main challenge to the theory of *régulation*. We discuss it through a comparison with the German conception of Ordnungstheorie in the next section.

Challenges to the theory of *régulation*

Régulation theory is an open-ended form of institutionalism with a theoretical core as we emphasised in the previous section. However this theoretical core is partial. Yet it could be argued that any theoretical system is partial. In order to gain accuracy here, let us distinguish two aspects in this issue. First, one may point to directions in which improvements would be welcome. Thus a more complete specification of regimes of accumulation may be needed. It would include considering monetary, financial and international variables. Yet, given the current macroeconomic instability, it must be acknowledged that it is an extremely difficult task. A more explicit microfoundation is also wanting. Although there is a general reference to bounded rationality in *régulation* theory, much variety arises among regulationists in the ways it influences the emergence, the functioning and changes in institutions. *Régulation* seems still far from achieving a rather unified view on this key issue and is still quite divided about the research options, be it between history and deductive reasoning or between empirically-based theorising and a more abstract reasoning.

Second, another way for assessing *régulation* theory as an alternative research programme consists in confronting it with the fundamental dimensions of any economic theory. These dimensions are agents' behaviour, mechanisms of co-ordination, efficiency and implications for economic policy. Efficiency and implications for economic policy seem to be the remaining most challenging issues to the theory of *régulation*.

Whereas general equilibrium contains a clear statement on this question, *régulation* theory is more problematic in its reliance on the viability of institutional forms or of an institutional arrangement be it called a mode of *régulation* or a national trajectory. Instead of engaging in a systematic analysis of efficiency in *régulation* theory, we introduce a brief comparison with the Ordo theory of institutions and of political economy known as Ordnungstheorie (Eucken 1948, 1950; Boehm, Eucken and Grossman-Doerth 1936; Grossekettler 1989, 1994; Peacock and Willgerodt 1989a, 1989b; Rieter and Schmolz 1993; Schmidtchen 1984; Vanberg 1988; Wagener 1992).

A detour via Ordnungstheorie

The comparison of *régulation* theory with Ordo theory is revealing of their proximity, although *régulation* theory developed in ignorance of Ordo theory. They have important similarities and differences. This mirror effect helps to highlight strong and weak aspects in both theories.

In Walter Eucken's *Foundations of Economics* the observed, historical economy is viewed as a superposition of different elementary constitutive forms of allocation, of markets and of the monetary system. The economy is determined in a two-step way, by first considering the economic order and then the economic process. The economic order is the prior determining factor. Order – Ordnung – has a specific meaning in Ordo theory. It is neither a system of institutions nor rules of the game guiding individual action, nor the regulation of the actions of economic agents. It is the commonly shared paradigm behind this set of institutions and of actions (Wagener, 1992). It consists of a 'totality of forms', of a 'morphological formation' and is practically synonymous with a system (Schmidtchen 1984). Eucken emphasised the interdependencies between the organisational forms of societies (Interdependenz der Ordnungen) i.e. between economic, legal and social orders. The economic system is thus seen in the context of the main organisational forms of societies in which it operates. Eucken states as a fundamental principle of constitutional law the striving for competitive prices. But for such a system to function properly, an active role of the state is necessary. Although there are minor variations among authors on the nature and the number of principles which appear in Eucken's work, two groups of principles for action by the state stand out: the constituent principles, which relate to the creation of rules for a competitive order, and the regulating principles, concerned with keeping the competitive order working. Eucken lists six constituent principles of a well-functioning market economy: free and open competitive markets, monetary stability, private ownership of the means of production, freedom of contract, responsibility for economic decisions and stability of economic policy.

Thus the state is responsible for maintaining the economy's constituent principles. But it should not intervene in the process, the day-to-day functioning of the economy apart from the limited list of regulating principles pertaining to market failures and to income distribution (Schmidtchen 1984, p. 59; Grossekettler 1989 p. 48, 1994; Willgerodt and Peacock in Peacock and Willgerodt 1989a, p. 7; Wagener 1992 pp. 28–9, Karsten 1992, pp. 118–21).

This leaves open the issue of anticyclical policy. However difficult the distinction between order and process may sometimes be empirically, Eucken's conception contains a clear message: it is to base the legitimacy of economic intervention on its conformity with the principles of the economic order first, and second to base the economic order on the principle of individual freedom. The so-called social market economy – an expression coined by Alfred Müller-Armack – prolongs this initial view by insisting on the social responsibility of the state although there is debate on whether the social aspect is part of order and rules or of process and outcomes (Vanberg, 1988). This ambiguity may have proved to be quite useful in providing the plasticity necessary for such a formula to resist historical changes so far. Above all, it relies on a broad but definite normative principle for the orientation of economic policy. It must be noticed at this stage that Eucken criticised laissez-faire and the notion of a spontaneous order. For him 'a liberal order requires a deliberate decision and policy efforts' (Oswalt-Eucken, 1994, p. 44). Implied in this view and other contributions from members of the 'Freiburg School' is the state's important and continuous role in providing and enforcing an appropriate framework of rules to be monitored with respect to its effects on the competitive process under changing circumstances. However it is only one part of the active role the state receives in the social market economy.

Müller-Armack puts more emphasis on social policy. Securing broad social acceptance of a market economy through a mechanism generating consensus but with a limit set by 'market conformity' defines the second role of the state. It leaves open the question of what is exactly meant by market conformity. The distinctions and debates on a process, rule-oriented perspective opposed to an outcome-oriented perspective (Vanberg, 1988) or, more generally, on 'procedural rules' liberalism and 'end state' liberalism (Barry, 1989) illustrate this ambiguity. However the other side of ambiguity may well be plasticity. And there are grounds to assume that it is thanks to this plasticity that associating the apparently opposed notions of a competitive market and of a social concern in one single formula enabled the social market economy to gain consensus as a normative principle of economic policy. Finally, it is worth noting the combination of economic efficiency and social efficiency ending in a notion of viability of an economic system understood as a humanly acceptable lifestyle (Rieter and Schmolz, 1993).

Theory of *régulation* and economic policy

Régulation theory seems to be more detailed and sophisticated analytically than Ordo theory with respect to the macroeconomic co-ordination dimension. But it lacks the normative potential that is contained in Ordo theory. This is not to say that efficiency considerations are absent in it.

Efficiency takes on several forms in the theory of *régulation*. One form is cumulative causality attached to the Fordist regime of accumulation. It is mirrored by the notion of compatibility between institutional forms. A synthesis is brought by the notion of viability of a 'national trajectory' or of a mode of development. An example of how these notions can be used is offered by the analysis of the collapse of Central and Eastern European economies (Boyer, 1995) and by the comparison with other interpretations of this collapse. One of these interpretations derives from considering that centralised planning is permanently less efficient than the market in the allocation of resources. According to another approach, political democracy and markets allow trial and error and thus adaptation of society and the economy. The crisis resulted from the inability of Eastern economics to adapt to the aspirations of the population and to the opportunities of technology. Technological and economic innovation became hindered by political inertia. It ended in a failure of economic reform in the context of a single political party. Productivity tended to stagnate. Hence, according to such an Austrian and evolutionary type of perspective, the crisis in Eastern Europe resulted largely from the inability of economic agents and of politicians to accept the emergence of decentralised innovations, to open them to competition and retain the most promising ones, through a process of trial and error. The main source of failure can be attributed to the inability of a system based upon a single political party and a centralised planned economy to give rise to a process of permanent adaptation and innovation necessary to ensure its long-term viability compared to capitalist economies, since the latter have been able to survive structural crises thanks to institutional and technological innovations operating in both private and public spheres. The conception of efficiency that arises here is different from static allocative efficiency. The ability to adapt to change in a decentralised system, the errors of some being compensated by the successes of others, is thus given a larger role in the sources of overall economic performance.

The *régulation* perspective emphasises the inability of socialist systems to move towards a 'socialist' Fordism. No mass consumption nor mass production developed. Accumulation remained mainly extensive and became pulled down by excess investment and expenditure in defence and by the Nomenklatura. The move towards political democratisation reinforced the economic crisis.

The focus in *régulation* on promoting a cumulative improvement in the standard of living taken as a good indication of welfare, complements the preceding view. Dynamic efficiency may result from the working of the market when it is fitted in a consistent set of institutions inducing agents to mobilise technological improvements to respond to – and stimulate – consumers' demands.Then the difficulties of the East may be considered as an inability to put into place a socialist Fordism, meaning by this an upward spiral between norms of production and norms of consumption. Instead, and notwithstanding several attempts at reform, the socialist system showed an equilibrium characterised by poor intensity of labour and a lack of consumer goods – but with full employment. In their application to policy making, these views point first to the institutional framework of a market-led, decentralised economy. This demarcates them from the not irrelevant, but almost one-sided views, giving absolute priority either to macroeconomic equilibrium or to unleashed markets deemed to create the right incentives. The regulationist views advocate a many-sided strategy in which all institutional forms are affected, with an emphasis on the wage–labour nexus (securing social protection and supporting mobility), on money and credit (reconstruction of a system of payments and of a supportive banking network, reorganisation of a statute for the central bank peventing an automatic financing of budget deficits), on organisation of a state of law and on more gradualist orientations of economic policy (contractual policy of prices, consolidation or cancellation of past debts).

Such advice sounds reasonable in order for Eastern European economies to become viable market-led systems. But are all market systems equivalent? How does one assess the merits and deficiencies of different institutional arrangements? Cumulative growth and viability are not only global notions, the way they are used in *régulation* theory is from an *ex post* standpoint, benefiting from hindsight. When it comes to comparing ongoing evolutions in different countries in terms of their viability one cannot but feel a difficulty coming from the fact that viability is more an *ex post* observed quality than an *ex ante* guiding principle. After all the Soviet system proved to be viable during several decades. Ordo has a clear criterion here: it is individual liberty and equating economic liberty with the functioning of a competitive market. The remaining architecture of the theory derives from this basic principle. The creators of Ordo theory – and of the social market economy – were seeking practical solutions to real problems. The creators of *régulation* theory seem to have been mainly seeking theoretical solutions to a mixture of theoretical and real problems. *Régulation* lacks an explicit binding guideline which could play the role of a clarifying and unifying principle which could be translated into economic policy-making and give the theory of *régulation* the consistency it is badly lacking.

Both Ordo and *régulation* theory are institutionalist and socio-economic. They both reject pure historicism and the idea of general laws of history. Yet they are influenced by the legacy of the Historical School in 'their urgent concern with the real world' by which F. Lutz charac-terised the Ordo liberals (Hutchison, 1981, p. 22). But their differences illustrate the importance of their respective origins. For Ordo theorists the main concern was with economic policy-making and with linking ethical, theoretical and action-directed principles. They wanted to tame both private power and state power and to build the foundations of a different kind of order from the one in which they lived. The main concern of regulationists was – and still seems to be – with theorising.

This may explain why 'Ordnung' policy occupies such an important place in Ordo thinking. One may also wonder whether the social market economy formula has a geneal bearing or is rather limited to economies in which there exist – among other favorable factors – few but strong socio-economic actors with a kind of quasi-national responsibility compelling them, so to speak, to solve tensions and conflicts by way of compromises.

All in all this comparison points to a fundamental deficiency of the theory of *régulation* with respect to a normative principle of economic policy. *Régulation* theory enables advice to be given to Central and Eastern European countries on the basic components of the institutional framework of a market economy. But its notion of compatibility or of viability of a particular configuration operates *ex post*. This deficiency reflects the absence – or the elusiveness – of a binding, unifying principle which could counterbalance its open-endedness and the impression it gives of remaining an excessively floating eclecticism. This seems to be the main challenge and a prior task on the agenda. It is the price paid for open-endedness. Research in this direction is in progress. It should not distract us from reckoning the useful insights gained thanks to the theory of *régulation* in understanding better how to depict the institutional configurations and economic systems of industrialised societies.

Bibliography

Aglietta M. (1976) *Régulation et crises du capitalisme. L'expérience des Etats-Unis*, Paris: Calmann-Lévy. Also published in English as: *Regulation and Crisis of Capitalism*. New York: Monthly Review Press, 1982.

Barry N.P. (1989) Political and Economic Thought of German Neo-Liberals, in A. Peacock and H. Willgerodt (1989b), op. cit., pp. 105–24.

Böhm F., W. Eucken and H. Grossman-Doerth (1936), [1989]) The Ordo Manifesto of 1936, in A. Peacock and H.W. Willgerodt (1989a), op. cit., pp. 15–26.

Boyer R. (1988a) (ed.) *The Search for Labour Market Flexibility*. Oxford: Clarendon Press.

Boyer R. (1988b) Technical Change and the Theory of '*Régulation*' and: Formilizing Growth Regimes, chapters 4 and 27 of Dosi G., C. Freeman, R. Nelson, G. Silverberg and L. Soete (eds), *Technical Change and Economic Theory*; London: Pinter, 1988.

Boyer R. (1992) La crise de la macroéconomie, une conséquence de la méconnaissance des institutions? *L'Actualité économique. Revue d'analyse économique* vol. 68, nos 1 and 2, pp. 43–68.

Boyer R. (1995) The Great Transformation of Eastern Europe: a 'Regulationist' Perspective; *Emergo*, vol. 2, no. 4, pp. 25–41.

Boyer R. and J. Mistral (1978) *Accumulation, inflation, crises*. Paris: PUF.

Delorme R. (1994) Economic Diversity as Cement and as a Challenge to Evolutionary Perspectives; in Delorme and Dopfer, op. cit., pp. 1–17.

Delorme R. (1995) An Alternative Theoretical Framework for State-Economy Interactions in Transforming Economies, *Emergo*, vol. 2, n. 4, pp. 5–24.

Delorme R. (1997) The case for controlled pluralism: a bottom–up approach, in Salanti A. and E. Screpanti (eds), *Pluralism in Economics*. Cheltenham: E. Elgar.

Delorme R. and K. Dopfer (1994) (eds) *Political Economy of Diversity. Evolutionary Perspectives on Economic Order and Disorder*. Cheltenham: E. Elgar.

DiMaggio P.J. and W.W. Powell (1983), [1991]) The Iron Cage Revisited: Institutional Isomorphism and Collective Rationality in

Organizational Fields, *American Journal of Sociology*, vol. 48, April, pp. 144–60, reprinted in Powell and DiMaggio (1991), op. cit.

Eucken W. (1948, 1989) What Kind of Economic and Social System? in A. Peacock and H. Willgerodt, (1989a), op. cit.

Eucken W. (1950) *The Foundations of Economics*. Edinburgh: William Hodge.

Grossekettler H.G. (1989) On Designing an Economic Order. The Contributions of the Freiburg School in D.A. Walker (ed.): *Perspectives on the History of Economic Thought*, vol. II. Aldershot: Edward Elgar.

Grossekettler H.G. (1994) On Designing an Institutional Infrastructure for Economies: The Freiburg Legacy after 50 Years. *Journal of Economic Studies* vol. 21, no. 4, 1994, pp. 9–24.

Hollingsworth J.R., P.C. Schmitter and W. Streeck (1994) (eds): *Governing Capitalist Economies. Performance and Control of Economic Sectors*. Oxford: Oxford University Press.

Hutchison T.W. (1981) *The Politics and Philosophy of Economics. Marxians, Keynesians and Austrians*. Oxford: Basil Blackwell.

Karsten S.G. (1992) Walter Eucken: Social Economist. *International Journal of Social Economics* vol.19, nos 10/11/12, 1992, pp. 111–25.

Khalil E. (1993) Review of D.C. North: Institutions, Institutional Change and Economic Performance. *Journal of Evolutionary Economics* no. 3, pp. 250–3.

Lesourne J. (1992) *The Economics of Order and Disorder*. Oxford: Oxford University Press.

Lipietz A. (1979) *Crise et inflation, pourquoi?* Paris: Maspéro.

North D.C. (1990) *Institutions, Institutional Change and Economic Performance*. Cambridge: Cambridge University Press.

North D.C. (1994) Economic Performance Through Time: *The American Economic Review*, Vol. 84, no. 3, June 1994, pp. 359–68.

Orrù M., N.W. Biggart and G.G. Hamilton (1991) Organizational Isomorphism in East Asia, in Powell and DiMaggio, op. cit., pp. 361–89.

Oswalt-Eucken I. (1994) Freedom and Economic Power: Neglected Aspects of Walter Eucken's Work. *Journal of Economic Studies* vol. 21, no. 4, 1994, pp. 38–45.

Pasinetti L. (1994) Economic Theory and Institutions, in Delorme and Dopfer, op. cit., pp. 34–45.

Peacock A. and H. Willgerodt (1989a) (eds) *Germany's Social Market Economy: Origins and Evolution*. Basingstoke: Macmillan.

Peacock A. and H. Willgerodt (1989b) (eds) *German Neo-Liberals and the Social Market Economy*. Basingstoke: Macmillan.

Piore M.J. (1996) Review of *The Handbook of Economic Sociology; Journal of Economic Literature*, June, pp. 741–54.

Powell W.W. and P.J. DiMaggio (1991) *The New Institutionalism in Organization Analysis*. Chicago: The University of Chicago Press.

Rieter H. and M. Schmolz (1993) The Ideas of German Ordoliberalism 1938–45: Pointing the Way to a New Economic Order, *The European Journal of the History of Economic Thought*, vol.1, no. 1, pp. 87–114.

Schmidtchen D. (1984) German *'Ordnungspolitik'* as Institutional Choice, *Zeitschrift für die gesamte Staats, wissenschaft* (ZgS), 140(1), pp. 54–70.

Vanberg V. (1988) 'Ordnungstheorie' as Constitutional Economics. The German Conception of a 'Social Market Economy', *ORDO Jahrbuch*, vol. 39, pp. 17–31.

Veblen T. (1919, 1990) Gustav Schmoller's Economics in *The Place of Science in Modern Civilization and Other Essays*, pp. 252–78. New Brunswick: Transaction Publishers.

Wagener H.J. (1992) Pragmatic and Organic Change of Socio-economic Institutions in B. Dallago, H. Brezinski and W. Andreff (eds): *Convergence and System Change. The Convergence Hypothesis in the Light of Transition in Eastern Europe*. Aldershot: Dartmonth, pp. 17–37.

Wiseman J. (1989) Social Policy and the Social Market Economy in A.T. Peacock and H. Willgerodt (eds) (1989b), pp. 160–78.

2
Dutch Negotiated Regulation: Conceptualisation and Illustration

Maarten J. Arentsen, Rolf W. Künneke[1]

Introduction

> [...] where administrative agencies and private associations play up to each other and consult permanently, and where it is impossible to trace where decisions are prepared and where they are taken. Where state authority is shared with private organizations ... twilight zones emerge. And concepts of consultation-democracy, coalition model or cartel-democracy are ever so many expressions of the factual limits to the power of the state.[2]

This quote from the former Dutch Prime Minister, Joop den Uyl, contrasts with the French King Louis XIV saying: 'L'etat c'est moi'. Both opinions manifest the range of 'statism' in countries. Now we are acquainted with differences in national regulation styles and the effects on state–society relationships. The French took up a more centralised tradition, nowadays known as etatism (Smith, 1978), the United States of America took up a more pluralistic perspective in a tradition of liberalism, whereas the Netherlands took up a corporatist tradition to cope with passionate societal interests by means of strong internal state structures (Lijphart, 1976; Williamson, 1985; Scholten, 1987; Van Waarden 1992).

In this chapter the Dutch model of negotiated regulation will be conceptualised and illustrated. The central question to be answered is how within the Dutch tradition of corporatism negotiated regulation can be understood conceptually. We will argue that regulation on the one hand and the instruments to realise certain objectives on the other, strongly depend on the institutional arrangements that structure economic sectors. Negotiated regulation seems to be suitable for handling circumstances of institutional uncertainties, for instance, uncertainties about the impact of specific public goals or uncertainties accompanying institutional change. Our argument is illustrated by the Dutch electricity sector as an example of dealing with uncertainty about the future institutional structure of that sector and by the typical Dutch policy instrument of convenant as an example of dealing with future uncertainty about behavioural norms and standards.

This chapter is structured as follows. The second section goes into the concept of regulation in economic and political theory. Regulation is conceptualised in accordance with the structure of economic sectors. Section three delineates regulation by negations from other approaches to regulation. Sections four and five give two different illustrations of regulation by negotiation. Paragraph four elaborates on convenants on energy conservation, whereas section five deals with the reform of the Dutch electricity sector. The chapter ends with some concluding remarks.

Conceptualising regulation

In conceptualising regulation generally two different starting points can be chosen. First, what might be entitled the 'market failure approach', i.e. governmental intervention is necessary to correct the market mechanism in order to induce a social performance which is as close as possible to the neoclassical model of complete competition. Economic literature on regulation often refers to this context.[3] Regulatory instruments are basically needed to correct the market mechanism in some way.[4] Regulation is intended to stimulate the economic performance of the system, for example in terms of cost efficiency, allocative efficiency, innovativeness and economic growth.

A second approach of regulation goes back to the ideas of social and political engineering of society. In this approach, regulation is needed to aim at public tasks and public goals, that are defined by the political system as being of 'general interest'. Examples in the case of the electricity industry are a guarantee of low tariffs for low-income consumers, the use of specific technologies for electricity production (like nuclear energy in the case of France, sustainable energy sources, or nationally produced charcoal as in Germany). Political science literature most often concentrates on these specific aspects of regulation.[5] Both approaches are not exclusive by definition. In many situations, markets might perform 'tasks of general interest' or 'public tasks' without any interference from politicians. However, it might occur that certain socially desirable goals are not realised by the autonomous behaviour of economic actors. Sustainable energy sources, for example, are generally too expensive as yet to be used on a large scale by autonomous market action.

In this chapter we will argue that both approaches to regulation – the market failure approach and the political engineering approach – have to be integrated in order to cope with the often complex relationships between public and private actors in modern societies. Although public goals are defined and legitimised within the political system, their achievement strongly depends on the efforts of private actors. In the case of Dutch negotiated regulation, private actors are given a distinctive place in the definition of the public goals and the determination of the instruments to achieve them. This specific relation can only be understood and explained if the existing structural interrelationship between private and public actors is taken as a point of departure. In the next section we will offer a scheme which makes it possible to categorise different structural configurations between private and public actors. Using this scheme we will be able to specify the kind of public–private interrelationship which is conditional for negotiated regulation.

Different co-ordination systems as context of regulation

As we have argued elsewhere,[6] there are three basic systems co-ordinating economic activities – markets, networks and hierarchies. Among others, a distinguishing criterion is the allocation mechanism, which is in the case of market co-ordination the price mechanism, in the case of the network the mutual agreement, and in the case of the hierarchy the public rule. Each of these three systems can theoretically be used to co-ordinate all economic activities with an economic entity, such as an industrial sector or a national economy. However, in reality these pure co-ordination systems have only very limited significance, since mixed co-ordination systems are clearly prevailing. In order to be able to identify different mixed systems of co-ordinating economic activities, Arentsen and Künneke made a distinction between a 'dominant co-ordination system' and an 'added co-ordination system'. In both cases markets, networks and hierarchies can be dominant and/or added co-ordination systems, which results in six mixed co-ordination systems and three pure systems, as is illustrated in Figure 2.1.

		PRICE	AGREEMENT	HIERARCHY
ADDED CO-ORDINATION MECHANISM	PRICE	**Full Free Market**	Liberalised Co-ordination	Liberalized Hierarchy
	AGREEMENT	Co-ordinated Free Market	**Full Co-ordination**	Co-ordinated Hierarchy
	HIERARCHY	Controlled Free Market	Controlled Co-ordination	**Full Hierarchy**

Figure 2.1   Pure and mixed systems for co-ordinating economic activities

This scheme can be used to characterise the interrelation between institutional arrangements and various types of regulation. Using the neo-institutional economic approach, this characterisation can be based on the following criteria:

- the allocation of the information which is needed to operate the co-ordination mechanism;
- the kind of transactional relations between economic actors;
- the position of governmental agencies in order to facilitate goal-congruent co-ordination.

The price mechanism is fundamentally a system of decentralised decision-making, in which actors determine their activities based on their subjective individual preferences or economic cost structures. In this co-ordination mechanism the information essential to economic activity is the preferences of the individual actors and the prices of the economic goods. Neo-classical economic theory demonstrates that this information is sufficient to operate a market system.

The other extreme is a hierarchical system in which the hierarchical top (for example the CEO of a firm or the government of a country) is able to delegate certain tasks to subordinated actors, in order to force a certain combination of production factors, which is in line with his preferences. In this case the information which is needed to attain the desired results is concentrated in the hierarchical top of the system.

In a co-ordination mechanism based on mutual agreement (we use the somehow ambiguous term ' network' to refer to this system) there are some elements of hierarchies and markets uniquely combined. There is some hierarchy in the sense that the group determines as a collective entity the common preferences, to which individual actors are subordinated. On the other hand, the individual actors within the network are free to agree to the common preferences. Actors generally join the network voluntarily. Moreover they are able to contribute to the formulation of the preferences of the network in a process of negotiation. In this sense, the fundamental information which is needed for a proper functioning of the network is generated by the collective entity of the members of the network.

Transactional relations within a hierarchy can be analysed in terms of principal–agent relations. The hierarchical authority can be described as a principal who possesses a certain bundle of property rights. He delegates some of these property rights to subordinated actors (the agents), whom he expects to act on his behalf. This principal–agent relation can be described in terms of possibly conflicting preferences and information asymmetry. The principal can use various instruments of monitoring or incentives to induce the agent to behave according to his preferences. These possibilities of the principal to influence the behaviour of the agent are elaborated in much detail in principal agent theory.[7]

In the case of a market, transactions are developed because actors are interested to exchange property rights in order to optimise their individual utility. The property rights are allocated with the individual actors and the transactional activities might in general be considered as voluntary. There is no hierarchical authority which forces them to trade. However an economic actor might have a superior economic position which leaves his transactional partners little economic room for choice. As a difference from hierarchical system this type of dependency derives from economic power and not from a delegation of property rights as in the case of a hierarchy. In this sense there are no principals and agents on a market, but only independent economic actors.

In a network the members of the group constitute a common economic entity which can be defined in terms of the common goals. As a common entity, the relations between the actors in the group are determined by voluntary agreement. However, once these activities are accepted by the group, there might be some method of social control to manage the enforcement.

The position of governmental agencies is quite different in each co-ordination system, because the position of the *public authority* varies per system. In systems dominated by the price mechanism, a public authority is basically subordinated by private actors. In the most ideal case of the neo-classical full-free market a public authority only provides some general framework of property rights, in which economic action takes place. In this case it can be stated that the public authority depends to a maximum degree on the responsiveness of private actor alterations of the institutional structure which are intended to correct market failures or to attain public goals. In the other extreme case of the hierarchy, a public authority is able to impose its goals on private actors, because of its dominant position within the co-ordination system. The interdependence with private actors is at a minimum. In a system dominated by the agreement, a public authority is a member of the group, with no special dominated or subordinated authority. A public authority might convince other parties to adjust its goals by means of negotiation. For these reasons, the co-ordination systems condition the ability to regulate because the mechanism, in order to be effective as a regulator, differs among the systems; and each system has its own pros and cons to combine the achievement of public and private goals.

Each co-ordination system conditions the position of a public authority and for that reason its ability to be effective as a regulator. In systems dominated by the price mechanism, effective regulation is theoretically restricted towards the general structure of an economic sector. The resulting performance basically depends on the transactional activities of individual private actors. In hierarchical systems the public authority dominates the transactional relations within the system. In this case a public authority might regulate the structure, as well as the activities of the private actors and the performance of the overall system. In systems dominated by the agreement, the information for effective systems performance is jointly shared by public and private actors. In these systems effective public regulation becomes a matter of negotiation between private and public actors. It is obvious that the co-ordination system is conditional for the achievement of various public and private goals. Market-based co-ordination systems are predominantly oriented towards economic performance. Individual actors are motivated to search for profitability and economic continuity. Hierarchical systems are serving public goals, for example 'the general interest', whereas agreement-like systems are aiming at a trade-off between public and private (economic) goals.

To conclude, the institutional context, theoretically perceived as mixed systems of co-ordination, are conditional for public regulation because the position of a public authority to other (private) actors within each co-ordination system differs. To be effective as a regulator, a public authority has to account for its position within the institutional context in which it is regulating. Accounting for the institutional context basically means choosing regulatory instruments that fit in a specific institutional context. In accordance with our scheme elaborated in Figure 2.1, three main categories of regulatory instruments can be distinguished:

- regulation by incentives, based on the price mechanism;
- negotiated regulation, based on the agreement; and
- regulation by directives based on public rules.

It can be stated that all three types of regulatory instruments fit well in both normative bases of regulation elaborated above. Incentives, negotiation and directives are suitable to attain normative public goals and to neutralise market failure. But it can be hypothesised that the effectiveness of each type of regulatory instrument is conditioned by the specific institutional arrangement in which it is operating. The basic argument is the specific position a public authority takes in each institutional arrangement, affecting the type of regulatory instrument to be chosen. But the institutional context is not only decisive for how to regulate, but also *what to regulate*. In the next section we elaborate on this point by going into the *object* of regulation.

Different objects of regulation

Theoretically, regulating sectors of the economy can take three points of departure:

- the institutional structure;
- the conduct (or activities) of economic actors;
- the performance of actors of the sector as a whole.[8]

Structure, conduct and performance can be perceived of as the *objects of regulation*. Each of these objects of regulation will be elaborated theoretically in relation to economic sectors.

Regulation of the institutional structure of an economic sector can be conceived theoretically with the help of Figure 2.1. In general a change of the institutional structure can be interpreted as a change of the dominant or the additional allocation mechanism. As such, two types of institutional evolution might be defined:

- *an institutional change*: a change of the dominant allocation mechanism; and
- *an institutional adjustment*: a change of the additional allocation mechanism.

Besides the rather broad criterion of dominant and additional allocation mechanism, there are other institutional features to characterise institutional structures. Examples of these criteria are openness of the market, the significance of social-political goals, the kind of contractual relationships and the ownership structures. However, as we have outlined elsewhere,[9] these criteria do not uniquely fit into specific allocation mechanisms. Therefore they are not suitable for the definition of specific differences between institutional structures.[10]

Conduct as the object of regulation can be defined in terms of the behaviour of economic actors. Roughly two types of conduct might be distinguished:

- economic conduct. These are results of economic activities which are necessary to guarantee the continuity. Examples are: profitability, innovativeness, employment, turnover, investment, physical output.
- social conduct, such as environmental measures, redistribution of income, creation of non-profitable employment opportunities, schooling.

Regulating performance basically means defining social and/or economic goals for the actors in a specific sector. Table 2.1 summarises the three different objects of regulation.

Obviously there is a certain hierarchy between these different objects of regulation. Regulating structure is most fundamental because this defines 'the rules of the game' by which economic activities might develop.[11] Regulating the institutional structure has specific implications for the conduct and the performance of economic actors. For example, defining an institutional structure in which the prize mechanism is

Table 2.1 Different objects of regulation

Structure	Objects of regulation Conduct	Performance
Defining and safeguarding dominant and/or additional allocation mechanism	Influencing the production and consumption activities within an economic sector	Defining political and/or economic goals of an economic sector

dominant, will result in economic conduct based on individual preferences. Safeguarding economic continuity and profitability will be the main focus, favouring economic goals as the main performance of the sector. Defining a hierarchy-based institutional structure, the main focus will be on public preferences that may consist of political goals or a mixture of political and economic goals. The same mixture of goals might result from an institutional structure based on the agreement as dominant allocation mechanism. In these systems mixed goals seem to be obvious, because of the involvement of public and private actors. Regulating the conduct of an economic system is on a more detailed level of governmental intervention. Actors might be stimulated or ordered to adjust or to change certain aspects of their behaviour. Regulating performance might be perceived as the most detailed type of governmental intervention, directly affecting the individual and collective goals to be achieved.

To sum up, theoretically, regulation might affect the structure of an economic sector, the conduct of the actors within the sector and the performance of the actors or of the sector as a whole. Although the impact of these objects on economic sectors is different, theoretically all three might serve as points of departure for regulation. Taking the position of a public authority into account, it is theoretically possible to specify the relationship between institutional organisation and preferred object of regulation.[12] Elaborating on the institutional context of regulation enables us to position negotiated regulation as a specific type of regulation within this general theoretical framework. In the next section we will go into the specific features of negotiated regulation, arguing that this type of regulation well suits circumstances of uncertainty about institutional change and about the economic and public performance of economic sectors.

Delineating regulation by negotiation

In real life public authorities often face uncertainties about the actual impact of regulation on the structure, conduct and performance of economic sectors. These uncertainties often occur when the structure, the conduct and the performance of economic sectors are to a certain degree in upheaval at the same time, resulting in a kind of institutional instability that asks for public regulation. But how to regulate when the preferred institutional structure, conduct and performance is not certain any more? Under these circumstances it is plausible to assume that there are uncertainties about the 'new equilibrium state of the world'. From an empirical point of view, under these extreme uncertainties, regulation can hardly account for specific objects of regulation. Because of the changing character of all three objects, specific outcomes of regulation become highly unpredictable. However our theoretical framework, elaborated above, offers possibilities for identifying normative preferences in *direction* (not the specific content) of change of a sector as a point of reference for regulation. The institutional arrangements summarised in Table 2.1 above all incorporate a dominant performance indicator. In price-based systems, economic goals are the dominant performance indicators, whereas in hierarchy-dominated arrangements, public goals are the dominant performance indicators. Arrangements based on co-ordination systems take a mediate position, which combines economic and public goals. Based on this notion, we state three relationships of regulation under uncertainty:

1. If the dominant preference in performance inclines towards political goals, *directives* seem to be the most effective regulation type. Here the French regulation model of the electricity industry suits well.
2. If the dominant normative preference in performance inclines towards economic goals, *incentives* seem to be the most effective regulation type. Here the British regulation model suits well.
3. If the dominant normative preference in performance inclines towards *finding* a trade-off between political and economic goals, *negotiation* seem to be the most effective regulation type. Here the Dutch regulation model suits well.

These relationships are based on principal agent theory. The information flows necessary to realise political or economic goals are different in each institutional framework. From this perspective, regulation can be perceived as an agency problem, in which the regulatory body (the principal) tries to induce the regulatee (the agent) to perform in a certain way. In the case of politically determined public tasks, the public authority takes a dominant position in the principal–agent relationship, which results in a hierarchy-oriented co-ordination system. The vital information for the functioning of this system (i.e. the definition of the public tasks) is generated by the public authority. In order to minimise goal divergence between regulatory body and regulatee, the latter is subordinated to the public authority. This system is expected to perform optimally with respect to politically defined public tasks.

If there are social preferences to emphasise the economic performance of the system, the vital information for system performance is with the regulatees (private actors). As it is known from neoclassical theory, individual action leads under certain conditions to allocative-efficient allocations. In a market-oriented system individual actors generate all relevant information to operate efficiently, according to their economic goals. Public authority is subordinated in this case.

Negotiated regulation might be a solution for the case where there is no clear social preference towards public goals or economic performance. The regulatory body and the regulatee enter into a bargaining process about the desired direction of performance of the system. More specifically, negotiated regulation seems effective to find a trade-off between political and economic performances of an economic sector. *Theoretically the equilibrium between political and economic goals might be attained without affecting the existing institutional structure, or by a change of the institutional structure itself.* In the first case, the trade-off between political and economic performance is found by negotiating the *conduct* of the actors. This kind of negotiated regulation is typical for Dutch environmental regulation by convenants. In the second case, the trade-off between political and economic performance is found by negotiating the *institutional structure* of an economic sector. This type of negotiation might result in an institutional adjustment or an institutional change, two types of institutional evolution mentioned above. The Dutch reforms of the electricity industry illustrate this type of negotiated regulation.

Negotiated regulation seems to be effective in circumstances of uncertainty about institutional performance and change. Regulation by negotiation offers possibilities for the regulatee to enter into a bargaining process in which the desired outcomes and regulatory instruments are determined. This seems to be a contradiction. Regulation usually is needed because economic action does not result in acceptable allocations by autonomous action. Why should the regulatee in this case agree voluntarily to alter his economic behaviour, if he didn't in advance?

The first explanation might be the lack of collective action. Economic actors are individually aware of the fact that their behaviour is not desirable for some reasons. However, changing individual behaviour creates serious competitive disadvantages. Only by co-ordinated collective action can these disadvantages be overcome and all actors act as they would like. A second reason is the possibility of free rider actions. A change of economic activities can result in positive external effects, which are borne by all actors and not only those who bear the costs. A co-ordinated action can be a safeguard against asymmetric distribution of costs and benefits of desirable actions. A third reason for actors to enter into negotiated regulation might be described as 'fear of worse'. There is a pressure upon actors to adjust and/or to change and they are aware of the fact that this pressure might be legally enforced, in case they do not co-operate on a voluntary basis. Negotiation might result in a favourable outcome for all. In case of enforcement, the outcome is far more unpredictable.

However, these potential advantages of regulation by negotiation can only be realised under certain conditions. First, there must be an identifiable actor within the industry, which has authority to negotiate with the public authority in the above-mentioned way. Often these are business (umbrella) organisations or some big dominating firms. Second, there must be reason to believe that actors are willing to commit themselves towards the negotiated results. In the Netherlands these commitments are often legally documented in convenants, a so-called gentlemen's agreement. Many of these agreements list goals and efforts and lately they contain a kind of monitoring programme.

Even if these preconditions are met, there is no guarantee that regulation by negotiation is effective. Actors are most probably only willing to commit themselves if they expect net benefits. In the end, regulation by negotiation seems to be effective if at least two conditions are met:

- if there is a 'win-win situation', in which every actor has something to gain, or at least everybody contributes in the same way to the common regulatory goal;[13]
- government can commit itself to the threat of introducing forced regulation, in case the actors cannot come by themselves to a satisfactory solution.

In the next two sections of this chapter negotiated regulation in the Netherlands is illustrated. Section four illustrates negotiated regulation within a given institutional framework. The convenants between Dutch public authorities and industry on environmental quality and energy conservation are taken as examples of negotiating changes of (institutional) conduct. In section five we go into the reform of the Dutch electricity industry, illustrating negotiated regulation as a change of institutional structure.

Dutch negotiated regulation: convenants on energy conservation

Negotiated regulation and the emergence of convenants between public and private actors is rooted in Dutch corporatism, which has a long historical tradition but actually came into being after the Second World War. In the second half of the nineteenth century confessional and social groups started to emancipate, asking for societal, economic and political rights (van Goor, 1985). Out of these movements four so-called pillars (in Dutch *zuilen*) developed: the Roman Catholic pillar, the Orthodox Protestants, the social democrats and the liberals (Scholten, 1987, p. 122). These pillars segmented the Dutch society vertically. This vertical segmentation was perceived as a treat for political stability. To attain political stability, the pillars integrated at the top, to overcome and to handle the segregation in Dutch society. This is in a nutshell the basic structure of the Dutch corporatist model – the *pacification model*. By controlled integration at the top (elite), political instability could be avoided in spite of the strong vertical segmentation of society.[14]

At the end of the 1980s when the limits of conventional public regulation became manifest in the Netherlands, new forms of regulation emerged, in which regulation itself became the subject of regulation. The general agreement, or the policy agreement, between government and societal groups, is the recent manifestation of this regulation style. In almost every sector of Dutch society these agreements have come into being, although this trend is more extended in some sectors such as education, culture and welfare, housing and the environment and economic affairs. These agreements or convenants have some basic features. First, an agreement takes at least two parties, willing and able to agree upon a convenant. Second, a public authority cannot enforce a convenant directly, although it can do it indirectly by threatening more restricted regulation. Third, there are no formal rules guiding the process of agreement, between the public authority and private organizations.

For that reason, the legal status of a convenant is unclear, because in most cases the convenant cannot be understood as a legally-based agreement between public and private groups.

Since 1992 the Dutch government has signed 34 agreements on energy saving with industrial and service sectors of the Dutch economy. The aim of the agreements is to formulate energy-saving goals for the year 2000. Industrial and service sectors agreed upon energy reduction in the year 2000 by some 20 to 30 per cent in comparison to 1989. The implementation of the agreements is monitored every year.[15] In 1994, 18 economic sectors realised a reduction in energy use of 9 per cent in comparison to 1989. These economic sectors covered some 73 per cent of the annual domestic industrial energy use. The improvement in 1994 in comparison to 1993 was 3 per cent, for the most part due to the energy savings of the Dutch chemical industry, the most energy-intensive part of the Dutch economy.

In general, the negotiated process to agreement upon a convenant takes different steps. The first step is to analyse and to assess the energy use of an industrial branch, by analysing production processes, means of production, efficiencies of feedstock and energy and building facilities. Next the prospects of energy conversion and energy saving are assessed. These assessments are conducted by independent companies. The results are communicated with the branch and documented in an agreement. In Dutch these agreements are called *meerjarenafspraken energiebesparing*, which means an agreement on energy saving for several years.[16] Both the minister for the environment and for economic affairs have put a lot of effort into communicating the agreements at the local level. The Dutch environmental permit has allowed for energy-saving measures since 1993. The signed agreements on energy saving have been taken as a base for standards on energy saving in the environmental permit. Every individual firm belonging to a branch that signed an agreement, is obliged to have an energy-saving plan for the whole firm, which lists the energy-saving measures to be taken by the firm, in the context of the agreement signed at the central level. These business saving plans allow for an individual and flexible response to the central agreement, enhancing the legitimacy of this kind of negotiated regulation.

In the Dutch electricity industry, convenants are common practice. In 1992, the minister for the environment signed a general agreement with the Dutch electricity sector aiming at a reduction of SO_2, NO_x and CO_2, the general agreement on acidification. In that agreement the producers and distributors of electricity committed to emission levels of 18,000 tons of SO_2 and 30,000 tons of NO_x in the year 2000. The main task of the producers was to invest in new and added technologies, whereas the distributors should contribute by initiating and stimulating energy saving by the end users of electricity and by extending the combined heat and power generation and new generating technologies, such as wind turbines, solar energy and biomass for power-generating purposes. The distributors have summarised their environmental programme in the first and second action programme for the environment.[17] Part of the agreement is the reduction of the emission of CO_2, at first by combined heat and power generation, optimising conversion processes in power plants, a partial substitution of coal by waste wood incineration, an investment programme in Eastern Europe and by investments in new forests to absorb carbon dioxide emissions. The cost of the forest investment programme is about 250 million Dutch gilders until 2010.[18] The electricity producers initiated these CO_2-reducing investments because a cost-effective technology to remove CO_2 from the emissions of the Dutch power stations is not yet available.

From a regulatory perspective, this convenant is rather unique, because it actually treats the whole Dutch geographic area as one giant bubble. The convenant only contains national emission-reduction goals. How to attain these goals is the full responsibility of the sector itself. The sector itself determined the kind of measures needed and where to implement them in the Netherlands. One reason for this nature of agreement was the differentiation in installed production technology. Apart from the gas-fired power plants, the SEP, the Dutch association of electricity producers, owned a few conventional coal-fired power plants that heavily contributed to the emission of SO_2, NO_x and CO_2. From an environmental viewpoint, investment in these conventional power plants was desirable, but from an economic point of view not very efficient. So in order to invest as cost effectively as possible, SEP was free to chose its own reduction measures across the whole nation. And indeed, they did not invest in the conventional coal-fired plants, to meet the agreed reduction figures.

The convenant with the Dutch electricity industry was agreed upon, in a period of growing institutional instability within that industry, resulting in an overall systems reform at the end of 1996. In the next section we will go into this reform process, illustrating the case of negotiated regulation as a process of change of institutional structure.

The case of regulation of Dutch public electric utilities[19]

The reform of the Dutch electricity utility industry started in the context of stable, small-scale local organisation of production and distribution before 1985. In this period the Dutch electricity sector had a stable institutional structure, which might be characterised as 'controlled co-ordination'. Regulation was mainly aimed at the conduct of the actors. From 1996 the new institutional structure primarily based on the price mechanism emerged. This institutional change has its origins in a process which began some 40 years ago. However, the most remarkable and important aspects of the process of reorientation and transformation of this sector from a network-based system into a market regime took place in the period between 1985 and 1995. These three phases of sectoral organisation will be presented as an empirical example of the way in which regulation by negotiation can contribute to sectoral change.

Before 1985: institutional stability with conduct- and performance-oriented regulation

The Dutch electricity sector has its origins in the municipal producers/distributors that emerged at the turn of the century. In this period governmental intervention was primarily oriented towards the realisation of public tasks. Electricity production and distribution have developed as a municipal task, which later became also a responsibility of the provinces. The provision of electricity was considered a public task of common economic need to be provided by public service depending on publicly owned firms.[20] Although in principle electricity could be provided by private firms – actually common practice in the very beginning of electricity production and distribution in the Netherlands[21] – there were two important reasons for public provision. Firstly the infrastructure, i.e., the grid, makes use of the municipal road network. The municipal owner of this network is thus directly involved in the development and maintenance of the electricity grid. Secondly, the electric utilities are traditionally considered as natural monopolies. To avoid destruction of capital by means of inefficient double investments in the infrastructure, it was perceived socially desirable to have one grid to which access and use is regulated by public institutions. Regulation is necessary to protect consumers from misuse of monopolistic power, in terms of extensive pricing and/or selective provision of this essential service.

Besides these primary regulatory goals, municipalities used their ownership of public utilities also for general social–economic and financial goals. For example, the city of Amsterdam had a tariff structure that favoured small domestic consumers relative to industrial consumers, related to the distribution costs of these groups of consumers. In Rotterdam a very social disconnecting policy with respect to defaulters was introduced, which led to back payments of $60 million. For the municipal owners public utilities became an important source of income, especially in the late 1970s and early 1980s, when the public budgets were cut. Individual Dutch cities introduced a system of 'normalised profits' that had to be paid in advance to the municipality.[22]

In line with the growing technical need for co-operation between the local producers/distributors and the possible cost savings because of economies of scale and scope, the number of electricity distribution companies has declined quite drastically since the beginning of the century. In 1920 there were about 550 distribution companies, declining to about 200 in 1960, 100 in 1980, to 82 in 1985.[23] Out of these 82 companies, 64 were horizontally integrated with gas and/or water and/or central antenna. During these years, all producers were integrated vertically with transport and distribution, resulting, by the mid-Eighties, in some 14 main producers,[24] which also became the biggest distributors. Of these firms ten were integrated vertically at the provincial level, the others were geographically related to the four largest cities in the urbanised western part of the Netherlands.

The first reconsideration of the role of municipalities in electricity production and distribution started in 1958. These reconsiderations initiated a process of concentration and vertical integration, to increase the professionalism and economic performance of the public utility sector. In 1970 this process was advanced by two boards advising Dutch central government.[25]

The public debate on the restructuring of the public utility sector that preceded the ongoing reform process, was actually started by the so-called CoCoNut board.[26] This board, installed by the minister for economic affairs, had to advise on the impact of concentrating public utilities. The CoCoNut board was strongly in favour of more concentration, because it was the only tool able to realise a significant cost efficiency in the public utility sector. The Dutch government took over the recommendations of the CoCoNut board and opened the dialogue with the utility sector on institutional restructuring. The utility sector, united in associations for electricity, gas and district heating, was willing to discuss the need for reconstruction, as far as the process could be governed by the sector itself, without formal intervention by the central government. The sector underlined this position by installing its own advisory board (commission Brandsma), to make an inventory of the organisational alternatives for reforming the sector in congruence with the official governmental goals on the theme. The Dutch government agreed upon the voluntary base of the reconstruction process, but thought it wise to initiate new legislation to ensure that the voluntary co-operating parties would take their job on reconstruction seriously. The Dutch government prepared a Distribution Act, to be used as a 'big stick' in case the self-regulating forces of the sector turned out to be unreliable or ineffective. The Brandsma commission started working in 1985, marking the end of an era of institutional, stable, decentralised local utility structures.

During this period, the fulfilment of public tasks, as defined by local authorities, clearly dominated the performance of electric utilities. The discussion concerning possible reorganisation can be interpreted as a first sign of an ongoing reorientation towards a more market-oriented functioning of this sector.

1985–1995: initiation of fundamental institutional change

During this transition period, regulation by negotiation was applied to initiate a change in the dominant co-ordination system of the Dutch electricity sector. There was considerable uncertainty about the future structure of the sector and about the possible benefits of different options for restructuring. In terms of the model elaborated above, this uncertainty concerned not only the institutional structure, but also the implications of a structural change with respect to the conduct of actors and the expected social and economic performance. Regulation by negotiation was used in the Netherlands to define the contours of the sector in future and to determine the common goals of the reform as anticipated by the sector and various governmental authorities.

In 1985 negotiations concerning the structure and tasks of the public utilities were opened seriously by the installation of the commission Brandsma. The participants concentrated on discussing several aspects of the structure of the future public utility. A very dominant aspect was the optimal scale of distribution companies, an extensive public discussion of which led to different points of view. The central government was opting for a minimum scale of 100,000 consumers, a number reducing the amount of horizontally integrated distributors to 20 to 25. The sector was less in favour of concentration and defended itself by arguing efficient integration scales for gas and electricity distribution of some 30,000, instead of 100,000 consumers as was proposed by central government. Distributing only electricity, efficiency could be maximised at 75,000 connections and for distributing only gas, efficiency could be maximised at between 30,000 and 50,000 connections, according to the sector. These figures resulted in a need for 60 to 70 companies to distribute electricity and gas.[27]

An important milestone in the reform process was the initiation of the Electricity Act in 1989 for the production sector, which had several consequences for the distribution companies as well. In several aspects this act governed the voluntary process of reform by the sector itself. First, a vertical disintegration between production/transport on the one hand and distribution of electricity on the other was legally enacted. At the national level, this clarified the division of tasks in the utility sector. Secondly, the act prescribed a minimum scale of electricity production at 2500 MW production capacity. This minimum capacity was perceived as necessary to achieve economies of scale. Thirdly, the act allowed production companies to optimise their production processes according to cost criteria rather than to the political considerations of the public owners.[28] The act did not attack the public ownership of the production companies.

Between 1985 and 1989, the emerging restructuring of the utility sector was a manifestation of a reorientation on the public tasks of utilities. The main question that guided the process was, how to integrate the public tasks and responsibilities of the utility sector with an effective and efficient economic performance of that sector. The sector had to meet its public responsibilities, such as reliability and security of electricity supply,[29] meanwhile improving the economic performance of the sector. This was not an easy job to do, because the production and distribution conditions had changed. The sector was facing a new challenge due to environmental considerations: improving its economic performance under more strict environmental regulations. Actually, the environmental impact of electricity production had penetrated the sector since the mid-1970s and had become a significant public issue by the end of the 1980s.

Another aspect of the public task of the utility sector is the reliability and security of supply. Security of supply had to be guaranteed by a system of central planning of the production capacity. The Electricity Act prescribed a planning system by the sector itself, based on a forecast of energy demand over a period of ten years in advance. The sector is legally obliged to actualise these plans every two years. These so-called electricity plans (in Dutch: *electriciteitsplan*) have to be approved by the minister of economic affairs.[30] This system of centrally approved production planning was meant to protect the consumers and to secure a reliable supply of electricity for the Dutch economy. The security of electricity supply became supervised by the central government between the years 1985 and 1989. This governmental involvement in the utility sector can be perceived as controlled self-regulation. The same happened with the protection of private consumers. The Dutch government agreed upon maximum tariffs with the utility sector. The production costs became pooled and compensated, according to a certain formula, for the production costs 'of reasonably efficient' producers.

Meanwhile the sector was allowed to restructure institutionally. During these years, the production sector merged into five giant production companies (after 1989 into four), united in the SEP, co-ordinating their production activities to improve the economic performance of production. After the reorganisation, the four producers had all the legal form of private stock companies, allowing public organisations only as stockholders.[31] The distributors also merged, a process that turned out to be very successful after a reticent and sloppy start. The process developed almost perfectly according to the scheme provided by the commission installed by the sector (commission Brandsma). The big provincial distributors became the most important buyers of the smaller municipal utilities. These provincial distributors, which were legally separated from their production activities by the Electricity Act, achieved good financial positions, due to the relatively high degree of accumulation of equity. The provincial stockholders only required them to pay dividends as high as the rents on the capital market plus a few percents premium, whereas the old municipal utilities had to pay 75 per cent to 100 per cent of their annual surpluses to their municipal owners. The big provincial distributors offered very attractive takeover prices to the municipal owners that many of them gladly accepted. Some municipalities also received shares in the provincial distribution company and/or seat(s) on the board of commissioners. Once the first deals were made, the followers imitated this pattern, sometimes under even better conditions, reorganising the distribution sector towards increased concentration.

After 1990, the Electric utilities developed an attitude towards self-assured business firms, trading in the special market of utility services. The Electricity Act legalised limited liberal trading and the vertical dis-integration freed the distributors from the dominance of the producers. The merging and ever-growing distribution companies strengthened their self-consciousness. Like private business firms they took the opportunities offered by the Electricity Act, starting to explore new markets, to offer new products. However, the new institutional arrangements turned out to be in some respects destabilising and threatened the existing economic order of the sector.

In the first half of the Nineties, the distributors became the dominant actor in the Dutch electricity sector – a dominance nobody expected, but embedded in the Electricity Act. Before the reorganisation, the big vertically integrated producers/distributors were the most important economic actors in the electricity market. The mostly small municipal distributors were obliged to buy all their electricity from their regional producer. These producers sometimes also decided the tariffs for consumers that 'independent' municipal distributors were allowed to charge. The reorganisation changed the market position of suppliers and buyers in several respects. Due to the concentration process, distributors got a significant market position because the number of actors was drastically reduced and the purchase volume of each of them grew significantly. The producers depend economically on the distributors, because they cannot legally sell electricity directly to consumers. Only very big industrial consumers are allowed to bypass the distribution companies. Due to the abolition of the regional monopolies of the producers, the distributors could compare prices. Shortly after the introduction of this possibility of 'horizontal shopping', all significant price differences between the producers vanished and no distributor used this new possibility of free purchase within Dutch territory.

The possibility of small-scale electricity production that was granted to distributors by the Electricity Act was consequently used by them and resulted in significant competition with the big producers, united in the SEP. Towards the end of the period the distributors invested heavily in decentralised electric power production with small-scale cogeneration units, partly as joint ventures with private industrial firms. These activities were stimulated by the Electricity Act of 1989 and received societal and political support for environmental reasons. In this way they are competing significantly with the producers. Meanwhile about 17 per cent of the national electricity production[32] is decentrally generated.[33]

In conclusion, it can be stated that after 1990, distributors took several opportunities to expand their position on the electricity market, partly owing to the position of the producers. They penetrated the production market, supported by the environmental considerations of the government. The institutional framework that was erected by the Electricity Act turned out to be hardly suitable to cope with these unforseeable developments in the market. The central planning system of the producers was seriously tackled by the production activities of the distributors. The reorganisation of the electricity market, formalised in the Electricity Act, made the distributors a dominant economic market party, a position that undermined the institutional framework and resulted in market upheaval in the 1990s.

1995–98: towards a market-oriented system

In December 1995 the Dutch government published a policy note on the prospected institutional development of the electricity sector (the 'Third Policy note on Energy Policy').[34] This policy note describes the results of the intensive negotiations and discussions with all major participants about the institutional reform. Although this note is quite general in nature and therefore leaves a lot of unsolved aspects and questions which are recently being addressed; it gives a blueprint of what has to be expected in future. Meanwhile two follow-ups of this policy note have been published, in which some of the details are elaborated.[35] The publication of this policy note might be interpreted as a way of ratifying the results of the ongoing negotiations.

The government proposes generally free access to the gas and electricity grids, based on non-discriminatory conditions. However, this right to free access will be granted to different groups of customers in different time schedules. Three groups of customers are identified:

- captive customers which consume annually less than 50,000 KWh electricity or 170,000 m^3 gas. These captives will be provided by the regional distributors as natural monopolists. They will get access to the grid as a last customer group, within a period of approximately ten years.
- an 'intermediate group' of customers, with electricity consumption between 50,000 KWh and 10 million KWh per year, or between 170,000m^3 and 10 million m^3 natural gas. This group will be captive for a maximum period of five years. Exemptions for earlier access might be possible in the coming period.
- very big industrial consumers with more than 10 million KWh electricity consumption and more than 10 million m^3 gas. This group will have immediate access to the grids.

Free access customers have a completely free choice of energy producers or traders. In this market segment, the price mechanism will be assumed to guide economic activities.

The captive customers and the 'intermediate group' are provided with electricity by the existing distribution companies, which have the legal obligation to serve them. Distribution companies are free in their choice of electricity supplier, and thus might also get involved in direct international trade. Captive customers will be protected in several aspects. In order to guarantee safety of supply, distribution companies have to prove to government that they have contracted sufficient capacity to meet demand. Also, the tariffs charged to these consumers have to be approved by the minister of economic affairs. In this market segment the controlled self-regulation of the present system will basically be continued. However, the government intends to reduce this market segment, and finally grant all consumers free access.

The four existing electricity producers are intended to merge together into one big firm. This concentration process is thought to be necessary to afford Dutch electricity production a stronger position in the anticipated liberal European market. Competition from the much bigger French and German companies will appear less threatening if there is one large-scale producer.

The national electricity producer will be organised as a private law stock company, with distribution companies and some big municipalities as the only shareholders. Thus, there is some vertical integration by way of the ownership structure. This point of independence of the electricity producer is at the moment under political discussion. It remains to be seen how independent producers and distributors might act on the liberal market share. It might be possible in the future for electricity production to be privatised in the sense that private investors are allowed to buy shares in this firm. It is intended to maintain the vertical disintegration between production, transport, distribution, and in future, trade.[36]

The dominant instrument of central governmental energy policy, the Elektriciteitsplan, will be abolished in the new regime. Instead of this it is planned to offer an Energy Report every four years to parliament, in which important developments in the electricity and gas markets are presented and analysed.

As a general conclusion it can be stated that there is a common interest in Dutch government and the main players to enter into a market-oriented institutional regime. This is the outcome of a long process of negotiations which started in 1958, but became significant more than 25 years later, in 1985. Within the following 10-year period decisions were taken and important actions developed towards a market-oriented regime. It is expected that the process of shaping the market will take another 10 years, although some insiders anticipate much speedier completion of this reform.

Conclusion

In this chapter we positioned regulation by negotiation in a general framework of regulation. We started our argument by positioning regulation in general within the institutional context of economic sectors. To be effective in regulation, a public authority should account for the institutional context of which it is part and in which it is operating. The type of co-ordination system is decisive for the position a public regulator takes within the institutional framework, conditioning the *style of regulation*. Next we distinguished negotiated regulation as a style of regulation that well suits circumstances of uncertainty about trade-offs between political and (private) economic goals. Regulation by negotiation turned out to be a suitable tool for managing institutional change and institutional adjustment. In this respect some general conclusions can be drawn.

1. In the Netherlands regulation by negotiation builds on a political culture of interaction and communication between public and private actors. It is the way the Dutch manage political, economic and social questions. Negotiation is a 'way of regulation' to account for all the interests involved, preparing for outcomes and results without losers. It is not a confrontational style of regulation, but, almost by definition, a consensus-building style of regulation. Results are attained in a step-by-step process, in which the participants are experiencing to commit themselves to the results of the negotiation, even if they are not legally enforceable.
2. For that reason, regulation by negotiation is apparently not a regulation style to achieve certain goals overnight. As was illustrated by the reforms of the Dutch electricity industry, the process might take several decades, until a structural institutional change is realised. The ongoing discussion in the EU on the liberalisation of the European electricity market is but another illustration of the viscosity of a negotiated process.
3. Regulation by negotiation minimises the risk of taking inappropriate actions. Negotiation is a process of searching for solutions which are satisfying for most actors, but these solutions are not always the best or the most optimal. It can be assumed that the consequences for all the actors involved are clearly considered. For that reason, it is very difficult for a public regulator to manifest a kind of 'public entrepeneurship'. High public expectations of attainable goals do not fit well in the process of negotiation.

4. The active participation of the different interests in the process of negotiation enhances the legitimisation of the outcomes, although the best outcomes will always be compromises. For that reason, negotiated regulation is a continuing process of regulation, that has to be learned individually and, as the Dutch have experienced, collectively.

Notes

1. Our thanks to dr. Piet de Vries (University of Twente) for his most helpful comments on earlier versions of this chapter.
2. Den Uyl, J. 'De tijd komt nooit meer terug' in: Wirardi Beckman Stichting (ed), *En toch beweegt het*, Kluwer, Deventer 1977. See also: Van Waarden, F. 'The historical institutionalization of typical national patterns in policy networks between state and industry. A comparison of the USA and The Netherlands' in: *European Journal of Political Research*, vol. 21, no. 1–2, 1992, pp. 131–62.
3. Sugden (1993), p. xi.
4. Other authors are less decisive with respect to the role of government in the regulatory process. See for example Train 1994. However the definition given by Sugden is useful as a reference in order to emphasise the specific aspects of regulation by negotiation.
5. T.R. Dye, Understanding Public Policy, Eaglewood Cliffs, 1975. A. Hoogerwerf (ed.), Overheidsbeleid, Alphen aan den Rijn, 1993 (1978).
6. Arentsen, M.J., Künneke, R.W., *Economic Organization and Liberalization of the Electricity Sector: In Search of Conceptualization*, Energy Policy, 1996, vol. 24, no. 6, pp. 541–52.
7. For an introduction see for example Eggertsson (1990).
8. These points of departure are taken from the neo-classical structure–conduct–performance paradigm.
9. Arentsen and Künneke 1996.
10. A related question is of course how different institutional structures can be described empirically in terms of dominant and additional allocation mechanisms. Which specific transactions would have to be considered, when are they considered as being dominant or additional? In general it is possible to identify the core activities within an economic sector or an economic system. It can be argued that allocation mechanism which is used to co-ordinate these core activities can be defined as being the dominant allocation mechanism. Of course, the identification and definition of core

activities within an economic sector are at the end an empirical problem.

11. North, 1990.
12. In our article in Energy Policy we have elaborated the argument for this proposition.
13. See Robert Axelrod, *The Evolution of Cooperation*, Basic Books, New York, 1984.
14. According to van Waarden (1992) Dutch corporatism is rooted well before the second half of the nineteenth century. In explaining Dutch corporatism one has to point to the combination of a strong state with strong societal interests in his view: 'Corporatism ... is often the outcome of a combination of a strong state and a strong civil society' (p. 141).
15. See for example, Ministry for Economic Affairs, *Meerjarenafspraken over energie-efficiëntie. Resultaten 1994 (Mid-term agreements on energy efficiency. Results 1994)*, The Hague, 1996.
16. Contrary to the ministry for the environment, the ministry for economic affairs labels agreements with industry as 'agreement' and not as a convenant.
17. Energiened, Milieuactieplan van de energiedistributiesector, Arnhem, 1991 en 1994. Dutch distributors of energy, Action programme for the Environment I and II.
18. The Dutch association of producers (SEP) has initiated a Forest Absorbing Carbondioxide Emission programme (FACE) to invest in new forests to absorb CO_2 emissions.
19. This section is drawn from Arentsen, Künneke and Moll (1996).
20. For example Simons in his dissertation on Dutch municipal services from 1939.
21. The first electricity producer/distributor was a private firm in the city of Rotterdam in 1883.
22. Baake, H. (1988), *Normalisering van bedrijfswinst, winstpunt?* s' Gravenhage.
23. Brandsma (1985), *Reorganisatie nutsbedrijven*, Arnhem, p. 9.
24. Besides these 14 companies there is a small electricity producer, called GKN, in which (mainly on a scientific basis) a small nuclear power plant is exploited. This firm is not vertically integrated.
25. Commissions Hupkes 1958 and Rietveld 1970.
26. Commission concentration public utilities (in Dutch **CO**mmissie **CO**ncentratie **Nut**sbedrijven).
27. Brandsma, pp. 14 and 15.

28. Out of the 15 original production companies, about 7 were organised as provincial or municipal service departments and the others as stock companies, with provinces and municipalities as the only stockholders.
29. See for example article 2 of the Electricity Act 1989.
30. This right of approval was already agreed upon between the sector and the minister of economic affairs in a convenant in 1975. This is another example of the Dutch consultation economy.
31. Stockholders are provinces, municipalities and distribution companies. Not all distribution companies are stockholders of electricity producers.
32. Elektriciteitsplan 1993–2002, Arnhem, pp. 14–18.
33. Distributors are allowed to install decentral small-scale production units according to the Electricity Act 1989.
34. Tweede Kamer der Staten Generaal, Derde Energienota 1996.
35. Dutch Ministry of Economic Affairs, *Current Lines 1996*.
36. The gas market will be liberalised along roughly the same lines.

Bibliography

Arentsen, M.J., Künneke, R.W. (1996) Economic organization and liberalization of the electricity sector: In search of conceptualization, in *Energy Policy*, Vol. 24, No. 6, pp. 541–52.

Arentsen, M.J., Künneke, R.W., Moll H.C. (1997) The Dutch electricity reform: Reorganization by negotiation, in Midttun, A. (ed.), *European Electricity Systems in Transition*, Elsevier Science.

Axelrod, R. (1984) *The Evolution of Cooperation*, Basic Books, New York.

Baake, H. (1988) *Normering van bedrijfswinst, winstpunt?*, s'Gravenhage.

Brandsma, (1985) *Reorganisatie nutsbedrijven*, Arnhem.

Dutch General Account Council, *Convenanten van het Rijk met bedrijven en instellingen*, Tweede Kamer, 1995–1996, 24 480, Nos 1–2.

Dutch Ministry of Economic Affairs, *Current Lines*, Structures of a new Electricity Act in The Netherlands, discussion paper, The Hague, July 1996.

Dye, T.R. (1975) *Understanding Public Policy*, Eaglewood Cliffs.

EnergieNed, *Milieuactieplan van de energiedistributiesector, EnergieNed*, Arnhem, 1991 en 1994.

Eggertsson, T. (1990) *Economic Behavior and Institutions*, Cambridge University Press, Cambridge.

Goor, H. van, (1985) Politieke participatie van collectiviteiten: pressiegroepen, in R. Andeweg, A. Hoogerwerf en J. Thomassen, *Politiek in Nederland*, Alphen aan den Rijn.

Hoogerwerf, A. (ed.), 1993 (1978) *Overheidsbeleid*, Samson, Alphen aan den Rijn.

Lijphart, A. (1976) *Verzuiling, pacificatie en kentering in de Nederlandse politiek*, Amsterdam.

North, D.C. (1990) *Institutions, Institutional Change, and Economic Performance*, Cambridge University Press, Cambridge.

Scholten, I. (1987) Corporatism and the neo-liberal backlash in the Netherlands, in Scholten (ed.), *Political Stability and Neo-Corporatism*, London.

Simons, D. (1939) *Gemeentebedrijven*, Dissertation Rijksuniversiteit Leiden.

Smith, G. (1978) *Politics in Western Europe*, London.

Sugden, R. (ed) (1993) *Industrial Economic regulation*, London.

Train, K.E. (1994) *Optimal Regulation*, Cambridge (Mass).

Uyl, J. den (1977) En toch beweegt het, in Wiardi Beckman Stichting (ed.), *Die tijd komt nooit meer terug*, Kluwer, Deventer.

Waarden, F van (1992) The historical institutionalization of typical national patterns in policy networks between state and industry. A comparison of the USA and the Netherlands, in *European Journal of Political Research*, Vol. 21, Nos 1–2, pp. 131–63.

Williamson, P. (1985) *Varieties in Corporatism*, Cambridge.

3
Regulation of Natural Monopoly: A Public-choice Perspective

Bengt-Arne Wickström

Introduction

The traditional theory of regulation studies the possibilities of correcting market failures through public action. The goal of the public sector is thereby, as a rule, described by some welfare measure, usually involving efficiency and sometimes some form of equality. Rules or direct regulation, optimising the welfare measure under various information and other constraints on the public sector, are then characterised (see for instance Bös, 1986).

The public-choice school, on the other hand, through its focusing on government failure has cast some doubts on the relevance of the traditional theory of market failure and its remedies through regulation. Here, instead, the focus is on the functioning of representative government, and its different branches are studied in some detail. This includes the way collective decisions are being made in committees and other representative bodies, the way bureaucracies (mal)function, and how governments are apt to consider the self-interest of various interest groups when setting their priorities.

Needless to say, governments as a rule have no clear incentives to maximise any reasonable welfare function. Re-election chances might be a much more realistic goal, which can be furthered through myopic policies or selective support to various interest groups. However, any policy has to be carried out by a bureaucracy, and public servants, in addition to serving the public, also have an interest in serving themselves which might be neither in the interest of the elected politicians of the government, nor in the public interest, however defined. Furthermore, whenever the public sector interferes with the working of the economy, there are, in addition to possible efficiency gains, as a rule, redistributional effects. That is, public policies give rise to rents, creating incentives for interest groups to organise rent-seeking activities. For a general overview of the public-choice literature, see Mueller (1989).

A classical case of public regulation is that of a natural monopoly. A natural monopoly is characterised by a production technology with falling average costs (usually as a result of high fixed and low variable costs), implying that marginal costs lie below average costs. Because of these increasing returns to scale, an unregulated market will result in a monopoly, which, of course, also is the cost-efficient market form, minimising average costs for any given market output level. On the other hand, the overall Pareto-efficient output level determined by marginal-cost pricing leads to losses. The traditional form of regulation then consists of marginal-cost pricing and subsidies covering the deficits. Other 'solutions' are various two-tier pricing systems and different forms of price discrimination. In this chapter we will, however, limit ourselves to a one-price regulation model and, with the aid of a simple example, investigate how the introduction of bureaucracy theory and rent seeking in its simplest forms alter the results of traditional regulation theory.

The benchmark case

We assume that some good or service is being produced with fixed costs f and constant marginal costs c. The good is sold in quantity q to the consumers in the market place at price p. The demand function is given by $q = Q(p)$ and the inverse demand function by $p = Q^{-1}(q) =: P(q)$. For illustrative purposes, we will assume that the inverse demand function takes the linear form $p = a-bq$.

Under these assumptions, the sum of consumer surplus,

$$u = \frac{bq^2}{2},$$

and producer surplus,

$$\pi = (a - c)q - bq^2 - f,$$

is given by

$$s := u + \pi = (a - c)q - \frac{bq^2}{2} - f.$$

This sum is maximised for

$$q = \frac{a - c}{b}$$

or

$$p = c,$$

taking the value

$$s^{\max} = \frac{(a - c)^2}{2b} - f.$$

This is our benchmark welfare level, and we define the welfare deficit, λ, of the various solutions as the deviation of the sum of the surpluses from this value:

$$\lambda = \frac{(a - c)^2}{2b} - (a - c)q + \frac{bq^2}{2}.$$

An unregulated market

In an unregulated market, a monopoly will emerge where the produced quantity q_m is found by equating marginal revenue $MR = p(1+1/\varepsilon)$ to marginal cost c, where the price elasticity of demand $\varepsilon := Q'(p)\, p/q$. The price is given by $p_m = P(q_m)$. Since the price is higher than marginal costs, a certain efficiency loss occurs. Using the linear demand curve, we find the following values for price, quantity, consumer and producer surplus:

$$p_m = \frac{a + c}{2},$$

$$q_m = \frac{a - c}{2b},$$

$$u_m = \frac{(a - c)^2}{8b},$$

and

$$\pi_m = \frac{(a - c)^2}{4b} - f.$$

These profits, of course, have to be non-negative for the production to take place at all.

Comparing these values with the benchmark values, we find the efficiency deficit in relation to a welfare optimum to be given by

$$\lambda_m = \frac{(a - c)^2}{8b}.$$

Welfare-maximising regulation

First best efficient public production

The traditional remedy for this loss of efficiency is to transfer the production to the public sector. A welfare-maximising bureaucracy would determine the output level such that price equals marginal costs and then cover the fixed costs through lump-sum taxation subject to the condition that total surplus is greater than zero. In our example, we find

$$p_p = c,$$

$$q_p = \frac{a - c}{b},$$

$$u_p = \frac{(a - c)^2}{2b},$$

$$\pi_p = -f,$$

and, of course,

$$\lambda_p = 0,$$

since this is our benchmark case.

Total surplus is positive if the fixed costs are smaller than the consumer surplus:

$$u_p = \frac{(a-c)^2}{2b} > f.$$

Regulated zero-profit public utility

An alternative to this is to let the production take place in the private sector with a regulatory board regulating the price. Here we assume that the objective of the regulatory board is to prevent losses, i.e., the board will attempt to set the price equal to average cost. This leads to the following values in our example:

$$p_r = \frac{a+c}{2} - \sqrt{\frac{(a-c)^2}{4} - bf},$$

$$q_r = \frac{a-c}{2b} + \frac{1}{b}\sqrt{\frac{(a-c)^2}{4} - bf},$$

$$u_r = \frac{(a-c)^2}{4b} - \frac{f}{2} + \frac{a-c}{2b}\sqrt{\frac{(a-c)^2}{4} - bf},$$

$$\pi_r = 0,$$

and

$$\lambda_r = \frac{(a-c)^2}{4b} - \frac{f}{2} - \frac{a-c}{2b}\sqrt{\frac{(a-c)^2}{4} - bf}.$$

It is readily seen that as f varies from zero to $(a - c)^2/4b$, the highest possible value of the fixed costs compatible with non-negative profits, the consumer surplus varies between $(a - c)^2/2b$ and $(a - c)^2/8b$, the production varies between the welfare optimal one and that of an unregulated monopoly and hence the efficiency deficit varies between zero and that of a monopoly.

That is, the zero-profit regulation always outperforms the unregulated monopoly on efficiency grounds, and public production with marginal-cost pricing always outperforms zero-profit regulation.

Politico-economic aspects of regulation

It is obvious that the models of regulation outlined above are far too simple. In the public-production model, non-distortionary taxation is assumed. This is hardly a realistic possibility. Hence, a welfare loss due to the dead-weight loss of the taxation necessary to cover the fixed costs would have to be accounted for. This might make the zero-profit regulation more attractive than the public-production alternative.

In the zero-profit model, however, it must be assumed that the regulator knows the cost structure in order to regulate the public utility. This is normally not the case, and we have a problem of asymmetric information. A principal–agent structure would have to be assumed.

In the unregulated case, we have assumed that price discrimination does not take place. Various forms of price discrimination would, of course, increase profits and reduce the efficiency loss, as well as the consumer surplus. This would make the unregulated alternative more attractive on efficiency grounds, but more unattractive from a distributional viewpoint.

All these and many other aspects would have to be considered in a complete traditional welfare-economic analysis of the problem. Here, however, we want to concentrate on another side of the problem, namely, what happens when the regulator does not attempt to maximise welfare, but follows his own objectives. Two central themes in the public-choice literature will be treated, bureaucracy theory and rent seeking.

In the bureaucracy theory going back to Niskanen (1971), the prime objective of the bureaucrat is to maximise his budget or the budget of his agency or of the sector of the economy that he controls. The rationale behind this is that the bureaucrat's promotion possibilities are positively correlated to the importance of his bureau, and this importance is measured in budget terms. Also, various fringe benefits are correlated with the size of the bureau.

It is further assumed that the bureaucrat, the agent, is the agenda setter *vis-à-vis* the political authorities, his principal, and, hence, is only restricted to set an agenda that offers the political authorities an improvement on *status quo*, but not an optimum (see for instance Romer and Rosenthal (1978)). The justification for this lies in asymmetric information. The bureaucrat is assumed to have an information advantage over the political authorities. If the *status quo* is no production at all, this assumption implies that the relevant constraint on the bureaucrat is that the total surplus be non-negative. The government is prepared to support its bureaucracy as long as it contributes non-negatively to welfare. The problem of asymmetric information between the bureaucracy and the government also extends to the production technology. Hence, through misrepresentation of the true costs, the bureaucracy can increase its budget by producing technically ineffi-ciently (X-inefficiency). Although the assumptions are extreme, the model is useful as a polar case to the welfare maximiser.

In the rent-seeking literature (see for instance Buchanan, Tollison and Tullock, 1980), it is assumed that individuals and organisations allocate resources to lobbying and other activities with the goal of influencing public decision-makers to allocate rents from public activities to the individuals in question. Such rents can for instance come from the profits from operating a public utility or a natural monopoly. Hence, an operating licence for such an enterprise has a value and in order to obtain this licence potential operators are willing to use resources.

Public production and a budget-maximising bureaucracy

The budget is here given by the production costs:

$$B = cq + f$$

The goal of the bureaucrat is then the greatest possible output q. We assume, in line with the discussion above, that the bureaucracy is only constrained by the restrictions that the expenditure over the public budget should not exceed the total welfare generated, and that the price should not be negative:

$$u \geq f + cq - pq$$

and

$$p \geq 0$$

Production costs are common knowledge

If the production costs are common knowledge, the bureaucracy takes the two constraints as given and maximises the budget. It is then readily seen that at least one of the constraints will be binding. If the second one is binding, we find in our example:

$$p_n = 0,$$

$$q_n = \frac{a}{b},$$

$$u_n = \frac{a^2}{2b},$$

$$\pi_n = -(f + \frac{ca}{b}),$$

and

$$\lambda_n = \frac{c^2}{2b}.$$

If $a < 3c$, we find that the efficiency deficit in this case is greater than in an unregulated market. If we in addition consider the dead-weight loss due to the necessary taxation to cover the public budget this restriction becomes even less strict. That is, public production, the 'best' case when we did not consider the behaviour of the bureaucracy, becomes worse than an unregulated monopoly, the 'worst' traditional case when bureaucratic behaviour is taken into account if marginal costs are sufficiently high.

If the first constraint is binding, we similarly find:

$$p_b = c - \sqrt{(a - c)^2 - 2bf},$$

$$q_b = \frac{a - c}{b} + \frac{1}{b}\sqrt{(a - c)^2 - 2bf},$$

$$u_b = \frac{(a-c)^2}{b} - f + \frac{a-c}{b}\sqrt{(a-c)^2 - 2bf},$$

$$\pi_b = -\frac{(a-c)^2}{b} + f - \frac{a-c}{b}\sqrt{(a-c)^2 - 2bf},$$

and

$$\lambda_b = \frac{(a-c)^2}{2b} - f.$$

Of course, here the efficiency loss is maximal. The public production adds no welfare. If we in addition consider the dead-weight loss of the taxation needed to finance the public budget, we, in this case, have a net loss from the public production.

In the public production case, we hence find that the efficiency performance is worse than that of an unregulated monopoly if the first constraint is binding or if $a < 3c$. In other words, public production is preferred to an unregulated monopoly if and only if

$$c < \min\left\{\frac{a}{2} - \frac{bf}{a}, \frac{a}{3}\right\}.$$

Public production and a budget-maximising bureaucracy with X-inefficiency

If the second constraint in the previous section is binding (i.e., if the consumer surplus at a price equal to zero exceeds the production costs), and if production costs are not commonly known, the bureaucracy can use its information monopoly on production costs and organise the production technically inefficiently, thereby increasing the budget until the first constraint becomes binding, too. We find:

$$p_x = 0,$$

$$q_x = \frac{a}{b},$$

$$u_x = \frac{a^2}{2b},$$

$$\pi_x = -\frac{a^2}{2b},$$

and again the efficiency loss is at the maximum:

$$\lambda_x = \frac{(a-c)^2}{2b} - f.$$

In this case, public production is never desired.

Regulation through a sector-revenue-maximising bureaucracy

We assume that the bureaucracy is interested in maximising the revenue in the sector under its jurisdiction with the constraint that the regulated industry cannot make a loss. That is, the bureaucracy wants the industry to maximise pq under the restriction that $pq \geq cq + f$. Again there are two possibilities, the constraint can be binding or not. If the constraint is binding, we have the case analysed above in the section 'Regulated zero-profit public utility' (p. 59) without consideration of the bureaucratic behaviour. The efficiency deficit is then less than in the unregulated case. How it performs relative to the model with public production is uncertain. It is readily seen that λ_r is a decreasing function of $(a - c)$ ranging between $\frac{1}{2}f$ and zero and hence bigger than λ_n if c is sufficiently small.

Positive profits and no rent seeking

If the constraint is not binding, profits will be positive, and revenue is maximised when the marginal revenue equals zero. In our example, this implies:

$$p_c = \frac{a}{2},$$

$$q_c = \frac{a}{2b},$$

$$u_c = \frac{a^2}{8b},$$

$$\pi_c = \frac{a(a - 2c)}{4b} - f,$$

and

$$\lambda_c = \frac{(a - 2c)^2}{8b} > \frac{2bf^2}{a^2}.$$

The last inequality follows from the fact that the constraint is not binding. In comparison with the case of an unregulated market, we see that the efficiency deficit would be greater under regulation when we consider the behaviour of the bureaucracy, if

$$a < \frac{3c}{2}.$$

This, however, contradicts the constraint for positive profits which implies that

$$c < \frac{a}{2} - \frac{2bf}{a}.$$

That is, a revenue-maximising bureaucracy would always perform better on efficiency grounds than a monopoly in an unregulated market.

Comparing the performance of the revenue-maximising bureaucracy with public production, we find that $\lambda_c < \lambda_n$ if and only if

$$c > \frac{a}{4}.$$

We can distinguish three different regimes depending on the value of the parameters of the demand function in comparison to the fixed costs:

(i) $a^2 \le 8bf$

In this case, a revenue-maximising bureaucracy with positive profits will never outperform public production, since the relevant condition contradicts the constraint for positive profits. That is, if

$$c < \frac{a}{2} - \frac{2b}{a},$$

public production has the smallest efficiency deficit.

Under the condition

$$c > \min\left\{\frac{a}{2} - \frac{bf}{a}, \frac{a}{3}\right\},$$

on the other hand, public production, as we have seen in the section 'Production costs are common knowledge' (p. 62), is inferior to an unregulated market, which in turn is inferior to revenue maximisation (in this case with zero profits). If

$$\frac{a}{2} - \frac{2b}{a} \le c \le \min\left\{\frac{a}{2} - \frac{bf}{a}, \frac{a}{3}\right\},$$

the revenue-maximising monopoly would still make zero profits, and we cannot unambiguously chose between public production and revenue maximisation.

(ii) $8bf < a^2 \le 12bf$

Here, the revenue-maximising bureaucracy (with positive profits) has the best performance on efficiency grounds (better than an unregulated market and better than public production) if

$$\frac{a}{4} < c < \frac{a}{2} - \frac{2bf}{a}$$

and, since sector-revenue maximisation outperforms the unregulated market, if

$$c > \min\left\{\frac{a}{2} - \frac{bf}{a}, \frac{a}{3}\right\} = \frac{a}{3}.$$

Public production is best if

$$c < \frac{a}{4}.$$

If

$$\frac{a}{2} - \frac{2bf}{a} < c < \min\left\{\frac{a}{2} - \frac{bf}{a}, \frac{a}{3}\right\} = \frac{a}{3},$$

the comparison of public production and revenue maximisation is again ambiguous.

(iii) $a^2 > 12bf$

In this case the ambiguous region disappears and public production is preferable if

$$c < \frac{a}{4}.$$

Revenue-maximising bureaucracy has the lowest efficiency loss and is making positive profits if

$$\frac{a}{4} < c < \frac{a}{2} - \frac{2bf}{a}$$

and is making zero profits if

$$c \geq \frac{a}{2} - \frac{2bf}{a}.$$

In conclusion, regulation or public production always performs better than the unregulated market – also when we take bureaucratic behaviour in this extreme form into account. The welfare-optimal case of public production, however, loses some of its importance and revenue-maximising regulation becomes more efficient if marginal costs are high enough.

For the even more extreme case of X-inefficient public production, of course, the result is clear. Revenue-maximising regulation outperforms both the unregulated market and public production.

Regulation through a sector-revenue-maximising bureaucracy with rent seeking

This favourable result for regulation, however, might disappear when we consider rent seeking. In some of the cases above, the operator of the public utility receives a positive profit π_c. That signifies that many different potential operators will attempt to receive the operating licence. Under the assumption that one can influence the probability of receiving such a licence through the use of resources, all potential operators will consider such activities. The resources thus spent are assumed not to contribute to the economic welfare. Hence they have to be added to the efficiency deficit. In the following, we model the rent-seeking game as in Wickström (1993).

The probability of potential operator i receiving the operating licence is given by δ_i and the amount of resources expended by him is l_i. It is assumed that the probability is influenced by the amount of expended resources by the potential operators in such a way that

$$\frac{\delta_i}{\delta_j} = \frac{g(l_i)}{g(l_j)},$$

where g is some concave function. This implies that

$$\delta_i = \frac{g(l_i)}{\sum_j g(l_j)}.$$

The expected rent of a potential operator is

$$R_i = \delta_i \pi_c - l_i = \frac{g(l_i)}{\sum_j g(l_j)} \pi_c - l_i.$$

We assume that each potential operator attempts to maximise this expected rent under the assumption that his behaviour does not influence the behaviour of the others, that is, we assume a Nash strategy. The first-order condition for a maximum is given by

$$l_i = \pi_c \eta_i (1 - \delta_i) \delta_i,$$

where the elasticity

$$\eta_i = \frac{g'(l_i) l_i}{g(l_i)}.$$

It can be shown (see Wickström, 1993) that a unique Nash equilibrium exists. Since we have assumed that the functions g are the same for all individuals, it is also symmetric. That is, each δ equals $1/N$, where N is the number of potential operators. From the expression above, we then find that the amount of resources expended on rent-seeking activities equals

$$L := \sum_i l_i = \pi_c \eta (1 - \frac{1}{N}).$$

This expression shows that the amount of resources lost to rent-seeking activities is a fraction of the total profits. For a large number N, this fraction equals the elasticity of the function g and can range between zero and one. Basically, this elasticity shows how receptive the bureaucracy is to rent-seeking activities.

In order to find the efficiency deficit of the regulation, we hence have to add L to λ_c:

$$\lambda_l = \lambda_c + L = \frac{(a - 2c)^2}{8b} + \left[\frac{a(a - 2c)}{4b} - f \right] \alpha,$$

where we have defined

$$\alpha := \eta(1 - \frac{1}{N}).$$

Comparing revenue maximisation with the unregulated monopoly and public production, we find that public production performs better if

$$c < \frac{a^2(1 + 2\alpha) - 8bf\alpha}{4a(1 + \alpha)}$$

and that the unregulated monopoly is outperformed by revenue maximisation if

$$\frac{a(1 + 2\alpha)}{3} - \frac{1}{3}\sqrt{a^2(1 + 2\alpha)^2 - 6a^2\alpha + 24bf\alpha} < c <$$
$$\frac{a(1 + 2\alpha)}{3} + \frac{1}{3}\sqrt{a^2(1 + 2\alpha)^2 - 6a^2\alpha + 24bf\alpha}.$$

For the relevant parameter range the second inequality conflicts with the constraint for positive profit, hence we only have to consider the first inequality. In the extreme case with N infinite and η equal to one, that is, α equal to one, these conditions reduce to

$$c < \frac{3a}{8} - bf$$

and

$$c > a - \frac{1}{3}\sqrt{3a^2 + 24bf}.$$

That is, if we take rent seeking into account and if the marginal costs are sufficiently small the unregulated monopoly is more efficient than revenue maximisation.

Of the three cases considered in the section 'Positive profits and no rent seeking' (p. 64), the last two have to be modified. The first one is unaltered, since public production is most efficient for the parameter constellations that would give positive profits by revenue maximisation.

The second case has to be modified for the values of c where revenue maximisation gives positive profits and dominates public production. Here, for sufficiently high values of α, public production becomes more efficient. Finally, in the third case, in the corresponding range of values of c (where revenue maximisation gives rise to positive profits and revenue maximisation is more efficient than public production) in addition to public production becoming the most efficient alternative, also the unregulated monopoly can be the best alternative. This is the case if a is sufficiently big and if $c > a/3$.

Also the case of X-inefficiency has to be modified. Here, the remaining most efficient alternatives are revenue maximisation and unregulated monopoly. If the marginal costs are sufficiently small and rent seeking sufficiently strong, this will make revenue maximisation with positive profits less efficient than the unregulated market.

Conclusion

With the help of an example, we have shown that the traditional results of public-utility regulation can be reversed under reasonable assumptions, when the behaviour of bureaucrats and rent seekers is taken into account. We illustrate the results in four diagrams, corresponding to the three cases in the section 'Positive profits and no rent seeking' (p. 64), as well as X-inefficiency. In the various regions the most efficient alternative is indicated: PP for public production, RM for revenue-maximising bureaucratic regulation, UM for unregulated monopoly, and AM for ambiguous (either PP or RM).

If $a^2 \leq 8bf$, rent seeking does not influence the result. If marginal costs are small enough, public production is most efficient; if marginal costs are high enough, revenue maximisation is the best alternative.

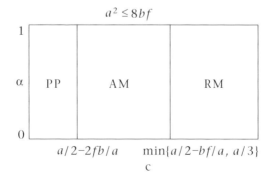

If $8bf < a^2 \le 12bf$, rent seeking matters and can extend the region where public production is optimal at the cost of revenue maximisation, and if $a^2 > 12bf$, rent seeking might even make the unregulated monopoly the most efficient alternative. Even if this is possible, it must be noted that for most parameter values some form of public action is still most efficient, either as public production or as regulation in spite of the revenue-maximising preferences of the bureaucracy. It should also be noted that we have made the most extreme assumptions about the behaviour of the bureaucracy. Less selfish behaviour on behalf of the bureaucracy will, of course, weaken the results and make public action more efficient.

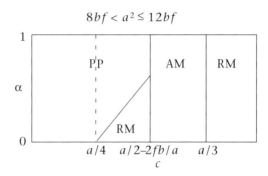

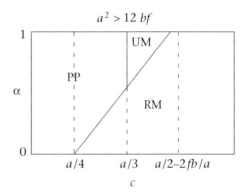

The even more extreme assumption of X-inefficiency in the public sector, however, is necessary in order to make the unregulated monopoly the most efficient alternative for a wide range of parameter values. If α is sufficiently big, this is indeed the case for sufficiently small marginal costs.

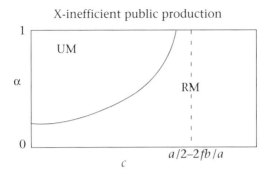

X-inefficient public production

Bibliography

Bös, Dieter (1986). *Public Enterprise Economics.* Amsterdam: North-Holland.

Buchanan, James M., Robert D. Tollison, and Gordon Tullock (1980). *Towards a Theory of the Rent-Seeking Society.* College Station: Texas A&M University Press.

Mueller, Dennis C. (1989). *Public Choice II.* Cambridge: Cambridge University Press.

Niskanen, William A. (1971). *Bureaucracy and Representative Government.* New York: Aldine Atherton.

Romer, Thomas, and Howard Rosenthal (1978). 'Political resource allocation, controlled agendas, and the status quo'. *Public Choice* 33: 27–43.

Wickström, Bengt-Arne (1993). 'Rent-seeking in different political environments'. In: Peder Andersen, Vibeke Jensen, and Jørgen Birk Mortensen, eds. *Governance by Legal and Economic Measures.* Copenhagen: G.E.C. Gad.

4
The Chicago School of Regulatory Theory

Alfred Haid

Evolution of Regulatory Thought

One of the objectives of a theory of regulation is to answer the question, why is there regulation? There have been three stages in the evolution of thought which address this question. A variety of market failures (natural monopoly, externalities, or some other source) constituted the first hypothesis, called the *public interest theory*. This normative theory of regulation, more recently referred to as *normative analysis as a positive theory* had great appeal among economists until the 1960s. The essence of this 'theory' is that one begins an analysis of a regulatory process with the assumption that its purpose is to maximise some universal measure of economic welfare, such as consumers' surplus or total surplus (Joskow and Noll 1981, p. 36). Understanding when regulation *should* occur is normative analysis. Positive theory explains when regulation *does occur*. *Normative analysis as a positive theory* uses normative analysis to generate a positive theory in that regulation is supplied because of the demand of the public for the correction of market failures. In a natural monopoly market, regulation will be the result of the public's demand if a first-best solution is not achieved in the absence of regulation. Unconstrained competition would result in either too many suppliers or a price above its social optimum. As a by-product of regulation, net welfare gains result. These potential welfare gains generate the public's demand for regulation. Hence, normative analysis (when should regulation occur?)

is used by public interest theory to produce a positive theory (when does regulation occur?). Thus, the hypothesis is put forth that regulation *occurs* when it *should* occur because the potential for a net social welfare gain generates public demand for regulation. The mechanism that allows the public to bring this about is not described. The issue of how the potential for net social welfare gains induces legislators to pass regulatory legislation and regulators to pursue the proper actions is not addressed. There are at least two reasons for the failure of the normative theory as a theory of regulation. First, individuals' various objectives (guarantees of procedural fairness, pleasant human relations, and so on) are affected by regulatory actions. Second, political agents being economic actors (like consumers and producers), respond to incentives created by political institutions and administrative processes. Thus, rational regulators would be unlikely to seek to maximise conventional measures of economic welfare. There is no testable prediction that regulation occurs to correct a market failure, instead regulation is rather assumed. Empirical evidence shows, however, that many industries have been regulated that were neither natural monopolies nor plagued by externalities; notable examples in the US were price and entry regulation in the trucking, taxicab and securities industries. 'Some fifteen years of theoretical and empirical research, conducted mainly by economists, have demonstrated that regulation is not positively correlated with the presence of external economies or diseconomies or with monopolistic market structure' (Posner, 1974, p. 336).

One empirical regularity was that regulation is pro-producer in that it tended to raise industry profit. In the US, in potentially competitive industries like trucking and taxicabs, regulation supported prices being above cost and prevented entry from dissipating rents. On the other side, in naturally monopolistic industries like electric utilities, there was some evidence that regulation had little effect on price, generating above-normal profits. Hence, regulation seemed to be inherently pro-producer (Jordan, 1972).

Due to numerous inconsistencies of this normative approach with empirical evidence and the observation that the regulatory agency comes to be controlled by the industry over time, economists and political scientists developed the second hypothesis, the *capture theory*. It stated that either regulation is supplied in response to the industry's demand for regulation, that is legislators are captured by the industry, or the regulatory agency comes to be controlled by the industry over time, that is regulators are captured by the industry (see Bernstein's (1955) life cycle hypothesis for a regulatory agency).

Capture theory does not explain how regulation comes to be controlled by the industry. In light of there being several interest groups affected by regulation, including consumer and labour groups as well as firms, why should regulation be controlled by the industry rather than these other interest groups? In its original form, capture theory did not provide an explanation, it rather states the hypothesis that regulation is pro-producer. Despite empirical evidence supportive of the capture theory, there are a number of empirical observations that are inconsistent with it. One of them is cross subsidisation, which is inconsistent with profit maximisation and thus cannot be considered pro-producer. Another common property of regulation was that regulation was often biased toward small producers. Small producers were allowed to earn greater profits relative to larger firms under regulation than they would have earned in an unregulated market. This was true of small oil refiners under oil price controls. There is a long list of regulations that were not supported by the industry and have resulted in lower profits, for example oil and natural gas price regulation, as well as social regulation over the environment, product safety, and worker safety. Capture theory, too, could not explain both why many industries were regulated and why they were later deregulated.

Normative analysis as a positive theory and capture theory

Both were actually not theories in the proper sense because they did not generate testable hypotheses as logical implications from a set of assumptions. Thus, Posner (1971) and subsequently Stigler (1971) introduced the idea that some industries seek government intervention either in the form of subsidies, protection, or in the form of regulation which reduces or blocks entry and prevents price competition. This third stage in the evolution of thought has been called the Chicago School of regulation, the outstanding proponents of which are Posner (1971, 1974), Peltzman (1976), and Becker (1983, 1985). Publication of Stigler's 'Theory of Economic Regulation' (1971) was the 'watershed event' in regulatory theory in that it forced 'a fundamental change in the way important problems are analysed' (Peltzman, 1976, p. 211). His approach may be called a theory because a set of assumptions was put forth and predictions were generated about which industries would be regulated and what form regulation would take.

Chicago School Theory

The objectives for a theory of regulation were laid out by Stigler (1971). Its central tasks are 'to explain who will receive the benefits or burdens of regulation, what form regulation will take, and the effects of regulation upon the allocation of resources' (Stigler, 1971, p. 3). According to Joskow and Noll (1981, p. 36), general theories of regulation are either legislative or bureaucratic, in that they select either the electoral process and the incentives operating on politicians or the bureaucratic process and the incentives operating on regulators as the focus of analysis. In the first category is the Chicago School theory. The essence of this theory is that 'regulation is a device for transferring income to well-organised groups if the groups will return the favour with votes and contributions to politicians' (Joskow and Noll, 1981, p. 36). Regulators generally use their power to transfer income from those with less political power to those with more.

Stigler–Peltzman Model

Stigler's analysis rests on two basic premises. First, that the state has a resource which 'is not shared with even the mightiest of its citizens: the power to coerce' (Stigler, 1971, p. 4). This power provides the possibility for the utilisation of the state by an industry to increase its profitability. Second, that agents are rational in the sense of choosing actions that are utility-maximising. A group or industry can increase its income by having the state redistribute wealth from other parts of the society to that group or industry. There are a number of obvious contributions that a group or industry may seek of the government: direct subsidies of money; policies which affect substitutes and complements of their own product; price-fixing; and regulation by seeking control over price or control over entry by new rivals. Thus, regulation is just one way by which wealth of an interest group can be increased. Stigler's analysis has been formalised by a later paper by Peltzman (1976).[1]

The Stigler–Peltzman model rests on three assumptions. First, regulatory processes redistribute wealth. The transfer of wealth will mostly be not in cash, but rather in the form of a regulated price, an entry restriction, and so on. Second, legislators choose policy so as to maximise political support, because their behaviour is driven by the desire to remain in office. Third, interest groups compete and pay with both votes and dollars in exchange for favourable legislation thereby assuming 'that the productivity of the dollars to a politician lies in mitigation of opposition' (Peltzman, 1976, p. 214). In a more general model 'dollars' might be made a source of direct as well as indirect utility to the regulator (for example employment of a former regulator). Peltzman's (1976, p. 222) generalisation of Stigler's model of political transfers assumes the objective function of the politician as

$$m = M(W_1, W_2), \tag{1}$$

where W_i = wealth of group i, and $M_i > 0$, and $M_{12} = 0$, that is to say that no intergroup dependencies exist. The objective function is then maximised subject to a constraint on total wealth (V)

$$V = W_1 + W_2 = V (W_1, W_2),$$

where $V_i > 0$ and $V_{12} < 0$. That is, one group's wealth can be increased only by decreasing the wealth of the other group. Peltzman addresses in detail the issue of price-entry regulation and derives implications for the price-profits outcome and the demand for new regulation, but the principle could equally well applied to policies other than price-entry regulation.

The two groups vying to achieve benefits from the political process are consumers and producers. Assuming the majority generating function (1) as

$$M = M (p, (\pi),$$

where p is price and π is industry profit, $M_p < 0$, $M_\pi > 0$, $M_{pp} < 0$, and $M_{\pi\pi}$, < 0. That is, M (p, π) is assumed to be decreasing in price because consumers increase their political opposition when price is higher. On the other side, $M (p, \pi)$ is increasing in profit because firms will respond with greater support when price is higher. Furthermore, political returns to higher π or lower p are diminishing. It is also assumed that no intergroup political effects (envy, vindictiveness) exist, so $M_{\pi p} = 0$. The relevant constraint is given by cost and demand conditions, summarised by the profit function

$$\pi = f (p, c)$$

where $c = c(Q)$ is production costs as a function of quantity (Q). It is assumed that $f_p \geq 0$, $f_{pp} < 0$, and $f_c < 0$. Profit π is increasing in p for prices less than monopoly price p^m and is decreasing in p for all prices above p^m. The formal problem for the regulator is to maximise the Lagrangian

$$L = M (P, \pi) + \lambda (n - f (p,c)),$$

with respect to p, π and λ. This yields (Fig. 4.1):

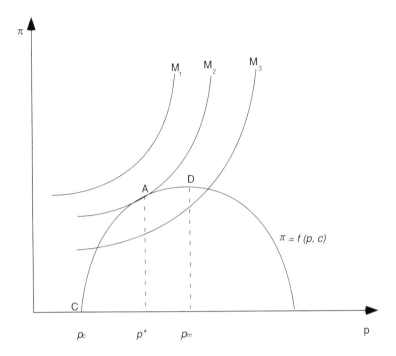

Figure 4.1   Optimal Regulatory Policy: Stigler–Peltzman Model

The optimisation condition (2) says that the marginal political product of a dollar of profits (M_π) must equal the marginal political product of a price cut ($- M_p$) that also costs a dollar of profits, whereby f_p is the dollar profit loss per dollar price reduction (Peltzman, 1976, p. 223). The solution is shown graphically in Figure 4.1. The curves labelled M_1, M_2 and M_3 are a portion of a regulator's indifference map, whereby $M_1 < M_2 < M_3$, that is, support is increasing in the direction north of west. M_1 represents all combinations of price and profit yielding the level M_1 of political support. The slope of the indifference curve is positive. reflecting the fact that if price is higher (reducing consumer support) then profit must be higher (hence raising industry support) if a constant level of political support is to be achieved. For given production costs, the profit function depends on price and is illustrated as $f(p, c)$. For a maximum $f_p > 0$ is required since $- M_p$, $M_\pi > 0$. Hence, 'political equilibrium will not result in the monopoly or cartel-profit maximising price ($f_p = 0$). Political equilibrium occurs at tangency (A) between the profit hill and an iso-majority curve' (Peltzman, 1976, p. 223). The optimal price, p*, is that which achieves the highest level of political support, subject to the constraint that profit equals $\pi = f(p, c)$. It is higher p than the competitive price, p^c, where profit is zero (point C) but lower than the monopoly price, p^m, where the slope of the profit function becomes horizontal, that is $f_p = 0$ (point D). Point D (pure producer protection) would be rational only in the absence of any consumer opposition. The optimal solution (point A) provides important insight into which industries are likely to gain the most from government regulation. If, in the absence of regulation, the equilibrium price of the industry were close to the price which could be achieved under regulation, then regulation is unlikely to occur. The interest group would not gain enough, such that it would not warrant the investment of resources to get the industry regulated. Thus (Peltzman, 1976, pp. 223–4)

> either naturally monopolistic or naturally competitive industries are more politically attractive to regulate than an oligopolistic hybrid. The inducement to regulate is the change in the level of M_i occasioned thereby. For an oligopoly with a price already intermediate between the competitive and monopoly price, the political gain from moving to A will be smaller in general than if the pre-regulation price is either at the top or bottom of the profit hill. This may help explain such phenomena as the concurrence of regulation of ostensible 'natural monopolies' like railroads, utilities and telephones with that of seemingly competitive industries like trucking, airlines, taxicabs, barbers, and agriculture. It may also rationalise the twin focus of antitrust on reducing concentration and protecting small businessmen, and the delay until comparatively recent times in applying the Sherman Act to less than the most concentrated industries.

Empirical observations underline that it is indeed these two extremes that tend to be subject to regulation. In both cases, some interest groups would gain more than trivially from regulation.

Becker Model

Whereas the Stigler–Peltzman Model rests on the assumption of a regulator maximising political support, the Becker modelling focuses on competition between interest groups instead (Becker 1983). In his approach the role of the regulator is suppressed by assuming that 'Politicians, political parties, and voters transmit the pressure of active groups' (Becker, 1983, p. 372). According to Becker, regulation is used to increase the welfare of more influential interest groups. Assuming two interest groups denoted by group 1 and group 2, each group can raise its welfare by influencing regulatory policy. The higher the pressure that group 1 exerts on the regulator, denoted by p_1, the higher will be the wealth transfer, denoted by T. However, the wealth transfer that group 1 gets also depends on the pressure exerted by group 2, denoted by p_2. The amount of pressure exerted by one group is determined by the number of members in the group and the amount of resources used. Thus wealth transfer to group 1, T, depends on the influence function I (p_1, p_2), whereby I is an increasing function of the pressure applied by group 1, p_1, and a decreasing function of the pressure of group 2, p_2. In order to transfer wealth of amount T to group 1, wealth of group 2 must be reduced by $(1 + x)T$, where $x \geq 0$. In case of $x > 0$, more wealth is taken from group 2 than is transferred to group 1. Thus, there is a dead-weight loss of amount xT from regulation.

In the Becker model it is assumed that aggregate influence is fixed. Hence, what counts is the influence of one group *relative* to the influence of the other group. Greater pressure uses up a group's resources. Thus, no one group will want to apply too much pressure. Taking into account the benefits and costs of pressure, the optimal value of p_1, may be derived, given any value for p_2. Let us denote this optimal level of pressure for group 1 by $\psi_1 (p_2)$. This function may be called group 1's 'best response function' or 'reaction function' and is illustrated in Figure 4.2. It is increasing in p_2, because in order to offset a higher pressure of group 2, group 1 has to apply more pressure, too. The same applies for the derivation of group 2's reaction function, denoted by $\psi_2 (p_1)$. The political equilibrium (P_1, P_2) is defined by the intersection of the two reaction functions at (point A).

From Figure 4.2, the effect of an increase of the marginal dead-weight loss from regulation, x can be derived. In that case, group 2 would forego an even bigger loss for any given transfer received by group 1. This, in turn, would cause group 2 to exert more pressure given any pressure level of group 1. As a consequence, group 2's best response function would shift from $\psi_2 (p_1)$ to $\psi'_2 (p_1)$. The implication of a higher value of x is that group 1 will get a smaller wealth transfer for any given tax of group 2 causing, in turn, group 1 to apply less pressure because now group 1 has less incentive to invest resources in order to increase regulatory actions. This effect is illustrated in Figure 4.2 by a shift of group 1's best response function from $\psi_1 (p_2)$ to $\psi'_1 (p_2)$. The new equilibrium will be at (p_1, p_2) – point B – which entails more pressure by group 2 and less

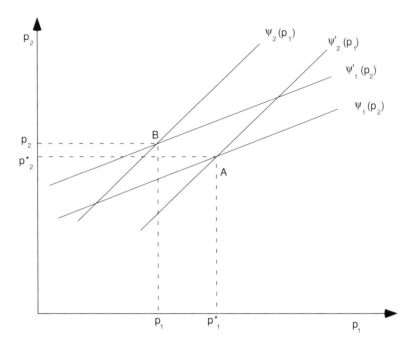

Figure 4.2   Political Equilibrium in the Becker Model

pressure by group 1. Because of $T = I(p_1, p_2)$, that is, transfer is a function of influence which in turn is increasing in p_1 and decreasing in p_2, it follows that $I(p_1, p_2) < I(p_1^*, p_2^*)$. Thus, as a consequence of an increase in the marginal dead-weight loss, in the new equilibrium there will be reduced regulatory activities as measured by the amount of wealth transfer.

The Becker model might be used to generate testable hypotheses concerning the properties of regulation. According to the above result, regulatory policies that are welfare-improving are more likely to be implemented than policies that are not. Hence, industries plagued by market failures and thus having low (or negative) dead-weight loss from regulation are more likely to be regulated than competitive industries which are already achieving a welfare optimum.

Posner Model

One common property of regulation is cross-subsidisation. Cross-subsidisation in regulated industries like railroads, airlines, and inter-city telecommunications often took the form of uniform prices being charged to different consumers even though the marginal cost of supplying these consumers differed considerably. Such pricing behaviour is inconsistent with both profit maximisation and welfare maximisation. In Posner's paper 'Taxation by Regulation' (Posner, 1971) an explanation for cross-subsidisation was provided. In light of his theory, cross-subsidisation may be interpreted as a means of redistributing wealth from one group of individuals to a second one, thereby assisting the government in its role of redistributing resources. His analysis fits in with the Becker model if the outcome of cross-subsidisation is interpreted as revealing that some individuals (consumers) have relatively more influence on the political process than others. Cross-subsidisation thus can be explained as the result of competition among 'different interest groups' (Viscusi, Vernon and Harrington, 1996).

Evaluation and critique

In contrast to older hypotheses put forth, Chicago School theory generated testable hypotheses, predicting the form of regulation and which industries were to be regulated. It was an important advance and explained a number of observed regulatory actions. It postulated that there is a tendency for regulation to benefit relatively small groups with strong preferences over regulation at the cost of relatively large groups with weak preferences over regulation. This implies that regulation, in many cases, will be pro-producer. Although regulation might be pro-producer, policy will not be maximising industry profits because of constraining influences of consumers. Furthermore, it is postulated that regulation is most likely in relative competitive or relative monopolistic industries. In those industries regulation will have the strongest impact on some groups' welfare. Finally, in markets with market failure, regulation is more likely than in competitive markets because of relatively large gains to some groups. However, a lot of evidence is inconsistent with Chicago Theory.

One of the basic assumptions of Chicago School theory is that regulatory policies are directly influenced by interest groups. However, in the regulatory process numerous actors are involved. Theory predicts that regulators will use their power to transfer income from individuals with less political power to individuals with more political power. However, predictions of the direction of this income distribution are difficult to achieve. The effects depend on the costs and benefits of regulation as perceived by competing groups and their ability to exert pressure in the political arena. Voters determine who the legislators are, legislators in turn determine the kind of regulatory legislation, whereby the actual policy is influenced by the regulators at work. To have an impact on regulatory policy, interest groups must be sure that the political process works the right way. Legislators are not 'puppets of their interest groups' and regulators need not be 'puppets of legislators' (Viscusi, Vernon and Harrington, 1996). First, the impact of interest groups on the outcome of elections should be sufficiently strong. Second, the (elected) legislators should be constrained to implement the kind of policy supported by the interest groups. Third, regulators in office should be under control in order to prevent deviations from the desired policy. By assuming that interest groups adequately control legislators and legislators adequately control regulators, these important elements of the regulatory process are widely ignored.

It is agreed that legislators wish to remain in office and thus care about being re-elected, but they also care about other things. That is, legislators have preferences – sometimes referred to as an ideology[2] – over issues. Hence, interest groups face a principal–agent problem in that they cannot perfectly control or monitor the legislators' activities. As a consequence, legislators can be expected to 'shirk' their responsibilities to their interest group and instead pursue their own ideology, probably in conflict with the interest group's desires. Legislators also face a principal–agent problem: regulators are difficult to control in case they have access to information not available to the legislator. This implies that regulators can have considerable discretion in implementing policy (Spiller, 1990; Laffont and Tirole, 1993). On the other side, the ability of Congress to control regulators has been stressed (Weingast and Moran, 1983). There is another major conceptual difficulty with Chicago Theory: it is difficult to separate from more general positive theories of representative democracy. Regulation is typical of government policies in that regulatory actions affect both economic efficiency and the distribution of income, in that an important part of both effects is on some well-organised groups, and in that regulation is carried out by a bureaucracy according to the tenets of administrative law. Chicago Theories cannot explain why politicians sometimes choose regulation but at other times choose other instruments of public policy to distribute the favours of a pluralistic democracy, nor why the inefficiencies of a regulatory bureaucracy differ from those of bureaucracy generally. There is an empirical problem as well. The pluralist theories are built upon comparisons of the economic stakes, the degree of organisation, and the resources of the interest groups, yet these variables have proved especially difficult to measure. Empirical tests of interest-group theories inevitably boil down to an estimate of the distribution of costs and benefits of an interventionist policy that is based on the departure of regulated equilibrium from perfect competition. Examples include the study of railroads by Spann and Erickson (1970) and Stigler's (1971) empirical tests of his initial statement of the Chicago School theory.

The way in which Chicago School theory has evolved makes rejection of the null hypothesis virtually impossible. All the empirical information that is used to test the theory is also the information available to identify the successful interest groups. If there is no clear way to reject the hypotheses to be tested, the theories can easily become tautological. A non-tautological test of interest-group theories would require one to go one step farther. Measures of the *ex ante* political influence of a group should be correlated with its *ex post* net benefits from regulation. Influence measures could be used to explain the absence of regulation where that is the case (Joskow and Noll, 1981, p. 39).

A central challenge to every theory of regulation would be to explain both the regulation and deregulation of such industries as railroads, telecommunications, and so on. Chicago theory of regulation would predict deregulation when the relative influence of interest groups that are benefited by regulation is reduced. Reviewing the recent deregulatory movement in the US suggests that the evidence is mixed (for surveys see Keeler, 1984; Peltzman, 1989). The deregulation of the US railroad industry in 1976–1980 would appear to be broadly consistent with it. The original regulation of the industry is explained by the industry being more influential in the political process. Originally, regulation allowed even above-normal profits. Later, firm profitability were reduced. In response, one would expect the industry to pressure for deregulation. This indeed happened in 1950s. But why did it take so long for significant deregulation to take place? The deregulation of US trucking appears, however, to be quite inconsistent with theory. At the time of its deregulation, the trucking industry due to regulation was earning above-normal profits. Further, why should consumers of trucking services have become relatively more influential in the political process than trucking firms? Finally, what can be argued to be supportive of the theory is the deregulation of the inter-city telecommunications market. What complicates matters is that the FCC allowed very limited entry and was steadfastly against allowing entry into certain segments of the market (in particular, the long-distance telephone service). This policy could be explained by the theory in that technological changes brought forth a new interest group in the form of prospective firms (for example MCI).

This interest group was influential enough to pressure the Federal Communication Commission to allow partial entry, but AT&T was too influential to allow full entry. The institution which eventually expanded entry was the US Court of Appeals.

A review of direct empirical tests (see for example Becker, 1986; Delorme, Kamerschen and Thompson, 1994; Kaserman, Mayo and Pacey, 1993) reveals that while Chicago School theory is an important advance in understanding government intervention, there is still much empirical evidence that would seem to be inconsistent with it.

Economists have not yet demonstrated convincingly that they understand what political purposes are served by regulation, why some industries are regulated and others are not, and why regulatory controls rather than other policy instruments are selected. Until answers to questions like these are forthcoming, the theory of regulation serves as a convenient way of organising historical material, but not one that is particularly rich in predictive value.

Despite a number of reservations about the theory of regulation, this research has played a significant part in shaping our conceptions of regulation. We are reminded that there is no free lunch. Curing a market failure by regulatory activities generates both benefits and costs. Regulators cannot be expected to stop just at curing the market failure.

> General theories also raise issues that must be faced by those who would reform, rather than abolish, regulation. Presumably, only by asking fairly general questions about regulation can scholars ascertain what purposes regulation serves from the viewpoint of political and bureaucratic actors. Understanding these purposes is a prerequisite to predicting the effect on policy outcomes of a change in the instruments of policy. (Joskow and Noll, 1981, p. 40).

Notes

1. Notable antecedents of their work are Bemstein (1955), Downs (1957), Caves (1962), Kolko (1965), MacAvoy (1965), Olson (1965), and Buchanan and Tullock (1962).
2. 'Ideologies are more or less consistent sets of normative statements as to best or preferred states of the world' (Kalt and Zupan, 1984).

Bibliography

Becker, G.S. (1983) A Theory of Competition Among Pressure Groups for Political Influence, *Quarterly Journal of Economics* 98 (August): 371–400.

Becker, G.S. (1985) Public Policies, Pressure Groups, and Dead Weight Costs, *Journal of Public Economics*, 28: 329–47.

Becker, G.S. (1986) The Public Interest Hypothesis Revisited: A New Test of Peltzman's Theory of Regulation, *Public Choice* 49: 223–34.

Bemstein, M.S. (1955) *Regulating Business by Independent Commission.* Princeton: Princeton University Press.

Buchanan, J.G. and Tullock, G. (1962) *The Calculus of Consent.* Ann Arbor: University of Michigan Press.

Caves, R.E. (1962) *Air Transport and its Regulators.* Cambridge (Mass.): Harvard University Press.

Delorme, Jr, Ch.D., D.R. Kamerschen and H.G. Thompson, Jr (1994) Pricing in the Nuclear Power Industry: Public or Private Interest? *Public Choice* 73 (June): 385–96.

Downs, A. (1957) *An Economic Theory of Democracy.* New York: Harper and Row.

Jordan, W.A. (1972) Producer Protection, Prior Market Structure and the Effects of Government Regulation, *Journal of Law and Economics* 15 (April): 151–76.

Joskow, P.L. and R. G. Noll (1981) Regulation in Theory and Practice: An Overview, in Gary Fromm (ed.), *Studies in Public Regulation.* Cambridge (Mass.): MIT Press.

Kalt J.P. and M.A. Zupan (1984) Capture and Ideology in the Economic Theory of Politics, *American Economic Review* 74 (June): 279–300.

Kaserman, D.L., J. W. Mayo, and P.L. Pacey (1993) The Political Economy of Deregulation: The Case of Intrastate Long Distance, *Journal of Regulatory Economics* 5 (March): 49–63.

Keeler, Th.E. (1984) Theories of Regulation and the Deregulation Movement, *Public Choice*, 44: 103–45.

Kolko, G. (1965) *Railroads and Regulation, 1877–1916.* New York: Norton.

Laffont, J.-J. and J. Tirole (1993) *A Theory of Incentives in Procurement and Regulation.* Cambridge (Mass.): The MIT Press.

MacAvoy, P.W. (1965) *The Economic Effects of Regulation. The Trunkline Railroad Cartels and the ICC before 1900.* Cambridge (Mass.): MIT Press.

Olson, M. (1965) *The Logic of Collective Action.* Cambridge (Mass.): Harvard University Press.

Peltzman, S. (1976) Toward a More General Theory of Regulation, *Journal of Law and Economics* 19 (August): 211–40.

Peltzman, S. (1989) The Economic Theory of Regulation after a Decade of Deregulation, in Martin Neil Baily and Clifford Winston (eds), *Brookings Papers on Economic Activity: Microeconomics 1989.* Washington, DC: Brookings Institution.

Posner, R.A. (1971) Taxation by Regulation, *Bell Journal of Economics and Management Science* 2 (Spring): 22–50.

Posner, R.A. (1974) Theories of Economic Regulation, *Bell Journal of Economics and Management Science* 5 (Autumn): 335–58.

Spann, R., and E.W. Erickson (1970) The Economics of Railroading: The Beginning of Cartelization and Regulation, *Bell Journal of Economics and Management Science*: 227–44.

Spiller, P.T. (1990) Politicians, Interest Groups, and Regulators: A Multiple-Principals Agency Theory of Regulation, or 'Let Them Be Bribed', *Journal of Law and Economics* 22 (April): 65–101.

Stigler, G.J. (1971) The Theory of Economic Regulation, *Bell Journal of Economics and Management Science* 2 (Spring): 3–21.

Viscusi, W.K., J.M. Vernon, and J.E. Harrington, jr. (1996) Economics of Regulation and Antitrust, Cambridge (Mass.): The MIT Press.

Weingast, B.R. and M.J. Moran (1983) Bureaucratic Discretion or Congressional Control? Regulatory Policymaking by the Federal Trade Commission, Journal of Political Economy 5 (October): 765–800.

5
Beyond Market and Hierarchy: Analytical Dilemmas in Economic Regulation

Atle Midttun

Introduction

Much of the debate on economic regulation has revolved around the relative role of markets and hierarchies and the juxtaposition of those two modes of governance *vis à vis* each other. The advanced Western market economies have generally taken the market as the basic mode of economic organisation based on arguments of efficiency, flexibility, contestability and freedom of choice. The reference has traditionally been to idealised resource optimisation under free trade generalised to a whole market system in general equilibrium theory.

However, hierarchic formal organisation also plays an important role in economic governance and regulation[1] in several respects. It is traditionally ascribed a vital role in the framesetting, or organisation of boundaries to economic activity. Hierarchy is also seen as an important device for aggregation and representation of collective interests.

Traditionally, a basic orientation in economic regulation has been to unproblematically assume that functioning hierarchic governance was available when markets failed. Hierarchy was, for instance traditionally ascribed a vital role by the early public finance literature as a substitute for market transactions in cases of inherent market failure.

In the strong rationality sometimes explicitly, but mostly implicitly attributed to hierarchy, the economic regulation literature, whether at the meso- or macro-level, has neglected a vast organisational theory and politological literature questioning the feasibility of the idealised model of hierarchical bureaucracy and the representativity of modern democratic governance. More recently, the growing influence of public choice theory in economic analysis, has corroborated many of the insights of the above-mentioned literature phrased in an economic conceptual terminology. The joint effect of this critique is that traditional hierarchic solutions have fallen more and more into disrepute.

With the critique of idealised hierarchy economic regulation theory finds itself in a dilemma, torn between imperfections of two worlds. On the one hand, the old arguments for the need for regulatory intervention against market failures and economic imbalances of market systems still remain. On the other hand, one of the principal instruments in such market regulation – hierarchical governance – also seems to have major flaws.

The effect of bringing in the organisational dimension by adding the discussion of hierarchic failure to the discussion of market failure, is thus to severely complicate the regulatory task (Table 5.1). The extreme cases of market failure and hierarchic/state success (3) as well as market success and hierarchical/state failure (2) of course remain simple to handle, as one regulatory model stands out as the optimal solution.

The dilemma of choice of regulatory regimes arises when both market and hierarchy are successful (1) or when neither of the two regulatory modes can be prescribed (4). In the first case (1) the dilemma is not problematic, as the choice stands between two ideal options. In the second case (4), when the choice stands between two unattractive options and where the model gives no prescription, the dilemma is more serious.

Table 5.1 Market, hierarchy, success and failure

	Public hierarchy/ state success	Public hierarchy/ state failure
Private market success	1	2
Private market failure	3	4

We shall proceed to discuss this regulatory dilemma in four steps: firstly, we shall briefly review some of the central critique of hierarchy, which must be established as a parallel to the aforementioned critique of the market. Secondly, we shall expand on external and internal incentive-based approaches to move out of the regulatory dilemma by refining respectively market-based or hierarchic-based regulation. Thirdly, we shall discuss the problem of establishing a conceptual apparatus for comparing hierarchic and market-based refinements as a way to determine when the one and when the other provide the optimal way out of the dilemma. We shall here argue that, in spite of partial attempts, the lack of a bridging theory across economic and organisation theory creates a reducibility problem where organisational and economic regulatory solutions cannot be systematically evaluated against each other. Fourthly, therefore, in a final section we shall discuss the problems of complexity arising by having to handle two theoretically irreducible worlds. We will show how this necessitates a transition to procedural rationality and how cultural/institutional embeddedness may be brought in to decrease the regulatory indeterminacy.

This chapter restricts the discussion to market and hierarchy and thereby leaves out a major set of regulatory options based on network-governance. Although we recognise this as a major omission, we have consciously made this restriction for the sake of simplicity and analytical clarity. To those who see network-governance as an intermediary form – between market and hierarchy – this omission is perhaps not so serious. To those who, with Powell (1981), see network-governance as a distinct governance form, the omission is more serious. Especially in the latter case this chapter should only be seen as a preliminary discussion, leading up to a later broader analysis of all three forms.

The critique of hierarchy and the myth of a perfect alternative to market failure

The basis for the analytical dilemma addressed in this chapter is, as already mentioned, the problem of hierarchy failure and thereby the lack of a perfect governance alternative when the market fails. More specifically, we may here distinguish between a problem related to the 'internal' operation of hierarchical governance, as well as a selection problem related to establishing the criteria for selecting between hierarchic and market governance.

The dilemma for a theory of regulation, if these two problems are not solved, is quite serious, as the internal hierarchic failure problem leads to a serious questioning of one of the major remedies to cure the 'disease' of market failure, and the selection problem prevents us from giving the right 'diagnosis'.

We shall here briefly review some of the core issues in the literature on both selection and 'internal' hierarchy failure. The external selection discussion has largely been conducted within the public finance literature, and thus constitutes a rather 'endogenous' debate. The issue of 'internal' failure, however, refers extensively outside the economic literature on regulation and draws more broadly on general organisation theory, and institutional economics.

The problem of selection failure or the demarcation problem

A core issue in economic regulation is, of course, the basic choice of regulatory regime, or more specifically between market-based or hierarchy-based governance. The problem of selection between the two modes of economic governance is generally discussed as a 'demarcation problem' in the public finance literature. The demarcation criteria between market-based and hierarchically-based regulation in the early public finance literature included both *consumption side* and *production side* elements (Samuelson, 1954; Musgrave and Peacock, 1967; Lane, 1993). In line with its basic liberalist position, this literature assumed the market to be the 'default option' and the question was when the market failed, in which case hierarchic governance had to be brought in.

In its traditional formulation, one of the central *consumption side* arguments for hierarchic intervention was the inexcludability argument, meaning that the good cannot be 'fenced in' from collective consumption under a market-based regime. A second prominent consumption side argument for hierarchic intervention was the public welfare argument stating that it is desirable to allow open access to a good even though it can be 'fenced in' if the marginal cost of adding another consumer is extremely small.

On the *production side* the argument of scale advantages has traditionally been the cornerstone reason for public hierarchic intervention (Musgrave, 1959). The argument was here that if a given consumer segment can be more efficiently served by one than by many producers because of falling costs in large co-ordinated production systems, then producer competition was impossible to maintain. Given the greater efficiency and hence the competitive advantage of the large producer, the argument is that a free trade market would degenerate into monopoly, and there would be no endogenous market incentives to evade monopoly profits, hence the need for public hierarchic control.

The elegance of these demarcation criteria was that they apparently relied on rather clear-cut objective criteria, and gave simple rules for when to apply hierarchic governance in accordance with technical–economic characteristics of the production process in question. However, closer analysis has revealed that very few goods are, in fact, characterised by inexcludability or non-subtractability in a strict sense (Lane, 1993). Rather, it is argued, non-excludability or non-subtractability very often refers to the social construction (Berger and Luckman, 1967) of the market system and not to the inherent technical character of the good. Toll roads, for instance, are a mechanism by which excludability can be organisationally designed even within a market context. To save the theory's empirical relevance, a less absolute delineation, based on economic criteria, therefore, had to be introduced. In this delineation the costs of constructing excludability mechanisms, for instance, would have to be taken into account and the demarcation would take on a gradualist character.

There has also been a critique of the so-called natural monopoly concept based on technically inherent production characteristics. Firstly, it has been shown that the natural monopoly element often only concerns certain parts of the sector, for instance the electricity or gas transport and not the whole electricity or gas systems. Within the electricity or gas grid management, again, only the planning and co-ordination functions may actually constitute the problematic natural monopoly core. Furthermore, there may be institutional/organisational solutions that transcend the simple market–hierarchy dichotomy.

The consequence of the so-called demarcation problem, or the problem of selecting basic governance regimes has been to introduce far more complexity into regulation theory. When complex economic cost analysis of various excludability-mechanisms are to be compared instead of a simple excludability rule; and when careful sectoral decomposition substitutes en block binary divisions of sectoral production systems into natural monopolies and potentially competitive markets, then the effect is to make the theory much less sharply applicable.

The problem of internal hierarchic failure

The problem of 'internal' hierarchic failure provides a direct parallel to the market failure literature which has been largely overlooked in the early public finance tradition. Given the extensive literature, we cannot here examine the problem of hierarchic failure in its full extension. The main point in this chapter is to bring out some of the most central arguments in order to document the existence and consequences of hierarchic failure which, juxtaposed with market failure, allows us to focus more sharply and realistically on the regulatory dilemma addressed in this chapter.

Within organisation theory there are at least three major arguments for hierarchic failure: (1) the *goal displacement* argument, (2) the argument of *tension between formal and informal* structure and (3) the *lack of flexibility* argument.

The *goal displacement argument* has been forcefully advanced already by Selznick (1949) and Merton (1957). Merton calls attention to the fact that structural devices established to ensure reliability and adequacy of performance in the classical Weberian hierarchy such as rules, discipline, graded career and so on (Weber 1964), can also lead to an over-concern with strict adherence to regulations and thereby induce timidity, conservatism and technicism. In Merton's own words: 'When adherence to rules, originally conceived as a means, becomes transformed into an end-in-itself; there occurs the familiar process of displacement of goals whereby an instrumental value becomes a terminal value' (Merton, 1957, p. 199). Simon (1957) has added to the goal-displacement discussion by emphasising its cognitive aspects. He argues that since goals are subdivided and factored among different individuals and groups, goal displacement may be encouraged by such cognitive factors as selective perception and attention processes among individuals, the selective content of in-group communication, and the selective exposure to information occasioned by the division of labour within the larger organisation.

The *tension between formal structure and informal process-argument* has been most forcefully emphasised by the so-called human relations school in organisation theory (Mayo, 1945; Rothlisberger and Dickson, 1939; Perrow, 1970). The recognition that organisations also are informal systems, and that organisational activities are extensively shaped by their informal characteristics (Mayo, 1945; Lysgaard, 1967) implies that there is a need to address the informal system as a fundamental dimension of formal organisational order. In this line of research it has been documented that group norms and informal standards are influential modifiers of formal standards of conduct (Lysgaard, 1967; Scott, 1981). Later formulations of related perspectives emphasised the importance of organisational culture as a crucial element of hierarchic performance (Schein, 1985; Martin and Frost, 1996; Schneider, 1990; Smirchich, 1983).

The *lack of flexibility argument* argues that hierarchic failure may arise as a consequence of change of environmental conditions and the lack of organisational adaptation to this change (Pfeffer and Salancik 1978). Rapid change in hierarchic governance may be difficult to achieve, since internal hierarchic excellence is traditionally reached through measures that tend to rigidify the organisation. We are here faced with a potential conflict between internal effectiveness and external efficiency of hierarchic governance when exposed to dynamically evolving markets.

In addition to the three critical perspectives within classical organisa-tion theory comes a critique of hierarchy, within law and economic organisation theory, or more specifically within *principal agency theory*, and *public choice theory*. The legal–economic discussion of principal–agency relations focuses on the general problem of delegation where the agent is generally better informed than the principal on whose behalf he is acting, and when the agent may exploit this information to further his own ends against the interests of the principal (Barney and Ouchi, 1986). Since hierarchic governance is fundamentally reliant upon delegation, the principal–agent problem is of critical importance to this mode of economic co-ordination.

The public choice tradition has applied tools and motives from economic analysis to politics and bureaucratic–hierarchic behaviour, and thereby waged critique against the tendency to assume that the behaviour from politically instructed and hierarchically organised administrative bodies will be in accordance with public welfare. If politicians are vote maximisers (Downs, 1967) and bureaucrats are bureau maximisers (Niskanen, 1971) they will only serve the public good if subjected to strong checks and balances which, according to public choice theorists, hardly exist.

Taken together, the demarcation problem and the internal failure problem of formal organisation weaken the case for strong a priori deductive arguments for hierarchic solutions to market failure. Instead they suggest that choices of regulatory regimes or economic governance mechanisms must rely on careful empirical experimentation, where the strengths and weaknesses of the two regulatory approaches are carefully balanced off against each other.

Improving markets and hierarchies: unilateral approaches out of the regulatory dilemma

Adding hierarchic failure to the repertoire of regulation theory alongside market-based failure illustrates that economic regulation in many cases faces a true dilemma of choosing among imperfect governance regimes. Solving market imperfections by reversal to hierarchy, or hierarchic imperfections by reversal to markets, may therefore involve replacing one imperfection with another.

One way out of the dilemma of choosing between two defective alter-natives would logically be to improve on both the market and hierarchy alternatives from within. Much of the modern literature on governance, organisation and regulation has in fact taken this approach, thereby reducing the need for reverting to the opposite ideal-type to solve endogenous problems.

The core question within *economically-based regulation theory* has thus changed from *when to substitute* unsuccessful market governance with hierarchy to *how to modify* unsuccessful market governance with *supplementary means*. This approach, which we may call *external incentive-based regulation* implies working indirectly, by stimulating the market actors to change behaviour in a desired direction, by supplementing the market with additional control and incentive structures, rather than to substitute the market with administered regimes. This approach has been widely applied in general market regulation, for instance by internalising environmental externalities. By adding supplementary external incentives, for instance, through taxes or tradable permits, it has been possible to add new and more specific regulatory targets without doing away with the basic market mechanism and competitive behaviour. Adding supplementary external incentives has even made it possible to maintain elements of market competition in so-called natural monopolies.

Similarly, *hierarchically-based regulation theory* focuses on improvement through development of *internal incentives* where efficiency is furthered through positive and negative sanctions built into organisational structures and processes. In the process of organisational refinement, therefore, the internal organisation of the market actors themselves is the target and instrument of regulation. By, for instance adding supplementary internal incentives, such as divisionalisation and profit centre-responsibility, a hierarchic organisation may seek to develop some of the flexibility and cost-effectiveness of the market, yet embedded within a wider hierarchic framework, which secures the overall guidance towards collectively defined goals.

We shall briefly expand on both the 'internal' and 'external' incentive problems before returing to assess how far this takes us in solving the basic dilemma of regulation.

External incentive improvements

The task of external incentive-based regulation is to move the resource allocation as close as possible to the social optimum, by creating an incentive environment that leads the firm to seek such solutions while acting in its own interest.

The answer to the regulatory challenge of market failure is not to revert to public hierarchy, but to make use of the market mechanism as far as possible, and where this mechanism does not work in its pure form, to introduce market-like rivalry through use of tendering and auctioning systems. The Chicago school (Blaug, 1992; Stigler, 1968, 1988; Demsetz, 1968), with later public choice extensions, has given major impulses to this approach to regulation, thus emphasising the possibility of, for instance, splitting up institutional hierarchies motivated by natural monopoly problems into functional components that may subsequently be subjected to decentral market rule (Savas, 1987). In some cases such decoupled functions may be directly market-exposed. In other cases it will be necessary to establish different forms of quasi-market solutions where public authorities auction out functions. There seem to be few limits as to how far one may go in outsourcing an activity within the Chicago school paradigm, except for transaction costs (Savas, 1987).

In line with this thinking there has been an extensive redirection of traditional hierarchic governance of so-called natural monopolies in grid-based systems such as electricity, telecommunication and transport towards external incentive models such as rate of return regulation, price cap regulation, yardstick regulation and menu of contracts regulation. Common to all these models is that they seek to minimise the hierarchic input by not reverting to full hierarchic substitution of the market, but instead rely on modified market incentives, directed at commercially-oriented firms.

Among these regimes, *Rate of return regulation* is the external incentive regime that needs the most extensive hierarchic intervention (Spulber, 1989). This regime allows a firm an 'acceptable' return on invested capital, but does not allow it to gain a surplus beyond this. Within these boundaries the firm is allowed to choose technology and input factors, and to decide production quantum and prices. Rate of return regulation has been widely applied in many countries, but perhaps most prominently in the USA where it is applied to the utilities.

Price cap regulation is a rather new addition to the incentive-based regulation repertoire. It has enjoyed great popularity in Great Britain, where it is applied to gas and electricity regulation following the infrastructure reforms of the late 1980s and 1990s. The basic characteristic of this mode of regulation is that the regulatory authorities specify a maximum price for the product. This maximum price can also be adjustable with a general factor, for instance referring to the factor prices of the input factors of the regulated industry in order to promote productivity (Littlechild, 1982). The British formula RPI-x, for instance, has an inbuilt productivity factor x which pushes the firm to increase is productivity beyond the retail price index (RPI).

Yardstick regulation builds on comparisons between firms or between firms and a model firm for regulation (Schleifer, 1985). The economic results of a firm are compared to those of other comparable firms and the firm is regulated on this basis. If the regulation is not based on comparison with a norm-model, this method presupposes that a sufficient number of comparable firms exist to allow the method to be applied on an empirical basis. The so-called Data Envelopment Analysis method is a more sophisticated method of yardstick competition. This method focuses on the performance of entities in a multidimensional analysis of, for instance, capital and labour productivity. For each dimension as well as for the whole set of dimensions, the analysis allows us to specify the productivity 'front' and to compare each entity to it (Norman and Stoker, 1991).

With roots in modern information economics, Laffont and Tirole (1993) have formulated a regulatory regime where the firm is faced with a *menu of regulation contracts* allowing it to choose among different combinations of cost-sharing and rewards. Contracts with low rewards will typically be associated with the firm wishing to take on a small share of future variations in cost. On the other hand, the firm may choose to take on contract alternatives with high rewards, but which subject the firm to take responsibility for cost variations. The first type of regulation contracts will closely resemble rate of return-based regulation, while the other will be closer to price cap models.

There is a certain integrity among various regulatory approaches within the market-based external incentive literature in their orientation towards market competition as a fundamental point of departure. Although several of the new incentive models have to be administrated by advanced administrated regulatory intervention, they still aim at automating regulatory decisions as much as possible, and at leaving considerable scope for autonomous firm adaptation on commercial terms.

However there is considerable diversity both in rationality assumptions and focus of market-based regulation. A strong mainstream neoclassical tradition focuses essentially on marginalistic adaptations to static efficiency where regulation faces well-known problems and targets definable end-states. This tradition is, however, challenged by the Austrian school (Hayek, 1948; Kirzner, 1973; Ioannides, 1992), which claims that the ability to further dynamic innovation and industrial restructuration is far more important for economic growth and welfare than the marginalistic resource optimisation, focused in the static perspective. As dynamic innovation presents the regulator with radical uncertainty, the Austrian tradition is less willing than neoclassics to take up strong deductively-based regulatory positions, where industrial processes, for instance, are split up by administrative decrees to facilitate more targeted regulation.

The radical uncertainty and the dynamic focus makes the Austrian approach more process-oriented and concerned with innovation and learning as part also of regulatory practice. More specifically, regulatory implications of the Austrian position have been drawn in two directions: on the one side, towards a laissez faire position, where the regulation is reduced to a legal-state minimum. The argument for this position is the lack of sufficient knowledge of dynamic growth processes on which to base regulatory intervention. On the other side, arguments have been made for industrial policy-oriented regulation, where the regulator does not figure as an external controller, but rather co-operates with industry in building competitive clusters to further innovation, market positioning and economic growth. This position is taken by the influential business strategist Michael Porter (1990).

Internal incentive improvements

The orientation towards supplementary incentives to market-based governance has its parallel in organisation theory where we may speak of a strategy of regulatory refinement through *'internal' incentives.*

The move towards more advanced models of internal incentives has taken several paths. One path has been to develop *formal* internal incentive structures that further desired goals both at the societal and enterprise levels. Another path has sought to supplement the formal organisation with additional *informal* incentive structures. This tradition has sought to evade organisational failure stemming from incongruence between formal and informal structures within the organisation. In addition, organisation theorists have come to focus on the organisations' *external relations* as a major premise for organisational efficiency.

Richard Scott summarises the main lines in the development of internal, incentive-based, regulation in a two-dimensional model. He combines along the one axis a shift from formal to organic or natural systems and along the other axis a shift from closed to open systems (Table 5.2).

Table 5.2   Developments in organisational design

	Formal rational model	Natural/Organic model
Closed system	I	II
Open system	III	IV

Source: adapted from Scott 1981

The first, *closed, formal rational model* (type I) builds on the idealised Weberian hierarchy discussed in the previous section and seeks to refine and develop its principles of hierarchical regulation, thereby strengthening the internal incentive mechanisms within the Weberian bureaucracy (Taylor, 1911; Fayol, 1949). Some of the thrust in this approach has been to strengthen the internal incentives by:

- clarifying the goal structure of the organisation
- strengthening routines for goal implementation
- strengthening the unity of leadership and clarifying authority relations
- tailoring organisational units and subunits to tasks so that homogeneous or related activities take place within the same organisational unit.

The complexity of carefully tuning a large set of interrelated rules and routines towards a common purpose probably makes hierarchic regulation most suitable for tasks characterised by high predictability.

The *closed natural systems model* (type II) focuses on the informal dimension, and included it systematically into the repertoire of internal incentives for regulation. Given the assumption that informal behaviour patterns are crucial for the capacity of the organisation to operate successfully, the key to organisational and regulatory efficiency in this tradition is seen to lie in various improvements of the social and psychological milieu. The human relation school (Mayo, 1945), and later research following in its trail, like Trist et al. (1963), Crozier (1964) and Clark (1960) thus came to emphasise factors like personal motivation and satisfaction, group integration and identification and democratic leadership as core instruments for improved organisational and regulatory efficiency. The regulation–design implications of this tradition are obviously to target not only the formal, but also the informal incentives of the organisation towards the regulatory tasks. At the sectoral level this might, for instance, imply stepping up measures to create worker-involvement and designing interactive processes to unleash creativity within the regulated industry to be channelled into fulfilment of organisational goals.

Strong external dependencies often characterise regulated sectors. In such cases the relationship between the sector-organisation and external elements becomes an important focus of regulatory design. The open systems literature has focused on a large variety of external conditional variables, including size, technology and uncertainty, and has been concerned with how organisations, or regulatory systems, may respond rationally by choosing adequate formal structures which take the external conditional variables into account.[2] The implication for regulatory design is that the strive to develop efficient regulatory structures must relate to specific types of environments, in other words that choice of regulatory models is context-dependent.

Scott lists two variants of the open systems perspective: the first is a rationalist position which assumes that the external conditioning variables are known and that adequate regulatory responses can be designed through formal organisational means. Herein lies the rationale for Scott's labelling of this position as a rational open systems approach. The second open system position is what Scott calls the *open natural systems approach*. This position maintains the focus on external conditions but abandons the strong rationality assumption of the formal, rational approach.[3]

Some organisational theorists go so far as to argue that the whole question of rational adaptation to external circumstances is irrelevant. The population ecology perspective thus argues for environmental determinism where organisational forms are picked by 'natural' market selection (Hannan and Freeman, 1977). However, more moderate theories bring some degree of internal organisational discretion back in. Resource dependency theory (Pfeffer and Salancik, 1978) or theory focusing on loosely coupled relationships between internal and external factors (Weick, 1969) are examples of this.

The idea of loose coupling implies that environmental selection of regulatory strategies may take place over a very long period of time, or that there may be several niche possibilities that allow survival of several organisational responses to the same regulation problem. This introduces a certain degree of indeterminism into the regulatory analysis, and indicates, like the Austrian position in economics, that regulatory responses may in part be process-dependent. Various regulatory solutions may thereby stabilise around several equilibrium points, dependent on the chosen trajectory.

In spite of the common reliance on internal organisational incentives, the organisation theory repertoire provides a vast menu for regulatory improvement with considerable differences in theoretical and method-ological underpinnings. The range across closed and open system approaches is perhaps the most easy to handle: the choice may here be a pragmatic one. Closed system perspectives serve well when the regulated sector is relatively autonomous. The open system perspective serves better when the regulated industry is more strongly integrated with other systems.

The range from formal to natural systems involves less easily reconcilable assumptions, which to some extent are competing perspectives on regulation: the one focused on static rationality, while the other is dynamically process-oriented, somewhat parallel to the neoclassical and Austrian schism in economics. However, they could also be interpreted as complementary, assuming that characteristics of the regulated sector in focus would determine which model to apply. Yet assessing this complemetarity and determining which model to apply to a given sector would not be a trivial task.

The (ir)reducibility problem and the lack of a bridging theory

In spite of the strategies to improve on markets and hierarchies respectively, through external market incentives and through internal hierarchic incentives, the regulatory dilemma of handling analytically both market and hierarchy failure still remains.

Firstly, the improvement within both external market and internal hierarchic regulation does not take us all the way. A certain need for supplementary hierarchic governance remains in spite of the external incentive improvement of market governance. Similarly, a certain need for supplementary market-based co-ordination remains, in spite of the internal incentive improvement of hierarchy.

Secondly, neither the market- nor the hierarchy-improvement literature is able to answer when the one or the other improvement strategy is best. We are, in other words, left with two alternative strategies, to a large extent based on two different theoretical worlds which, as we have seen, even among themselves contain large internal analytical tensions.

What motivates the difficult task of theoretical integration is that an extended regulatory menu provided by both external, market-based modifications, and internal, incentive modifications of the hierarchy ideal type, provides opportunities for a tighter fit between regulatory problems and regulatory design. However, such integration also faces regulatory analysis with more complex choices.

Overlapping domains

With a large set of modified market and modified hierarchy models the demarcation between the two basic approaches to regulation becomes far less clear. Rather than two distinct regulatory models, we may talk about two core ideal types, where each ideal type may be modified by a set of auxiliary elements (such as introducing external incentive elements into markets and internal incentive elements into hierarchies). The 'domains' of market- and hierarchy-based regulation can thus be seen as a set of partially overlapping spheres, with the ideal type in the core and modified variants based on advanced incentive or co-ordinating mechanisms or other auxiliary elements further out in the periphery (Figure 5.1).

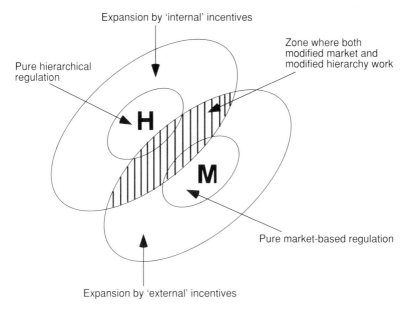

Figure 5.1 Regulatory approaches and domains

Presumably, the further out from the core one moves, the less cost-efficient becomes the regulation, because of the complexity of administrating the auxiliary mechanisms to employ the regulatory models outside of their primary domain. Thus we would expect that hierarchical approaches in the core of the market domain (for instance under ideal free trade conditions) and market-based approaches in the core of the organisational domain (for instance under situations with extensive problems of collective action) to be relatively costly compared to the other regulatory form.

The complexity of delineating the boundaries more sharply between the two approaches, however, takes us beyond the specification of simple demarcation criteria, to address the extremely complex issue of integrating market theory and organisation theory in a more general bridging theory. In the case of natural monopoly, for instance: a market-based external incentive solution might involve establishment of incentive systems such as menu of contracts regulation to combine public control over tariffs at the same time as one seeks to maintain efficiency incentives to the market actors. However, even such external incentive-based regulation would imply the establishment of a regulatory body with specialised regulatory competence, and thereby an imposition of strong hierarchic elements in the market.

Alternatively, the natural monopoly problem might be handled within a hierarchic system, where public co-ordination would be provided through the goal-structure and internal authority/task delegation in the organisation. Within this framework, the pure hierarchic model might be extensively modified by internal incentive mechanisms to promote efficiency within the decision-making pyramid. This could, for instance, include measures such as the construction of profit centres and increased use of transfer pricing, thereby allowing for more market-like flexibility and efficiency pressure, but still open to strategic, higher level hierarchical co-ordination.

A third alternative would be to pursue a combination of market-based and hierarchical solutions to the natural monopoly problem through extensive subcontracting. To the extent that the subcontracting was done by an agent representing the public interest, such a subcontracting system could be seen as a part of a hierarchic/internal incentive approach. Seen from the side of the firms competing for the tender, however, the subcontracting approach might be seen as a modified market system. In this perspective, the hierarchic elements would be defined as part of a regulatory function.

Moving from natural monopoly regulation to regulation of distributive justice, such as in health care, there is again the possibility of proceeding both along the modified hierarchic and the modified market route. The first approach implies that collective choices are made by political decisions, and implemented through a set of delegation procedures within the administrative system. However, as in the natural monopoly case, there is ample scope for modifying the administrative hierarchies through extensive use of internal incentive mechanisms that provide flexibility and imply efficiency pressures, as long as the overall distributive concerns are secured.

Again, as in the natural monopoly case, a modified market solution is also possible, for instance by supplementing the market mechanism with public subsidies to underprivileged consumers. In addition, the unequal distribution of health problems, and the immense costs of curing or limiting them for the unfortunate few who get seriously ill, creates a distribution problem over time and luck even for middle-class consumers. Special arrangements therefore have to be made for insurance, and public intervention may be necessary to secure a minimum level of insurance even within an overall market design. However, such intervention could be minimised and defined as a regulatory function.

Complementarity and incompatible mixes

A certain complementarity between hierarchic and market-based regulation obviously exists. In fact a certain element of hierarchic order is, so to speak, a premise for most market systems, and vice versa. Complementarity at this level exists 'per definition'. Such complementarity is in fact fundamental to the main thrust of the previously mentioned Chicago-approach with its use of tender and other types of quasi markets and hybrid means to design market-solutions to evade full hierarchic co-ordination. Both the specification of terms of tender as well as the implementation of the tendering, for instance, demand highly competent and co-ordinated hierarchic intervention. Most quasi-market arrangements, in fact, need specific hierarchic regulation.

Similarly, many of the attempts to make formal organisations more flexible, in organisation theory, make use of markets or market-like arrangements. The previously presented open systems approach, for instance, takes external challenges – for instance competitive pressures – as a central premise for organisational adaptation. Similarly, the creation of internal markets within hierarchies is often taken into use by organisational designers as a means to create flexibility, controllability and cost sensitivity in large hierarchies.

However, there are obviously also cases of incompatibility between market-based and hierarchy-based regulation. Much of the literature cited under the previous discussion of hierarchic failure documents this. A core problem in many such cases is that some of the checks and balances included in full hierarchic or full market-based governance are eroded, while the substituting mechanism from the other mode of regulation is not sufficiently in place. Furthermore, some combinations of market and hierarchy are obviously irreconcilable, at least if the goal is to maximise public welfare. A market must, for instance, imply a certain degree of freedom for the market players, and cannot be too authoritatively hierarchically controlled in case the efficiency-effects of competitive market behaviour be undermined. Likewise, a hierarchically-based implementation of collective interest does not allow too extensive marketisation, unless the collective interest be undermined by rent seeking or other forms of private exploitation.

More specifically, regulatory failure due to an incompatible mixture of market and hierarchy elements may, for instance, arise as a result of taking organisational models from private company law into use in public companies, giving them more flexibility and freedom to pursue their own commercial strategies while these companies are not properly exposed to market competition. When such 'liberalised' public companies are backed up by special public transfers so that their commercial exposure remains more or less fictitious, they may effectively escape both market-based and hierarchy-based regulation. On the one side the disciplining force of market competition is absent, since they are not realistically competitively exposed. On the other side, the private law-oriented commercial organisation of these companies does not provide public authorities with governance rights and inside budgetary information that is customarily provided to core public sector activities. Transfers to such companies are therefore not properly under public hierarchic control and are not systematically weighed up against other public activities in the regular budgetary process. The risk is that such companies get controlled by their administration and/or by trade unions.

Unfortunate mixes of market- and hierarchic-based regulation can also be found in sectors dominated by private firms operating under private law and fully market exposed, when these markets are supplemented by certain types of hierarchic regulatory intervention. Intensive lobbying and/or neocorporatist policy relations may, in fact, lead to a retrial of market outcomes on the political arena, securing these private firms the same de facto sheltering from market-exposition that characterised the public firms referred to above (Hernes, 1978). Politics thus becomes a supplementary arena for negotiating special compensation for losses incurred under market-competition. The special form and procedure of lobbyist and neocorporatist policy-making implies that these types of negotiated relations may remain largely outside regular democratic control. Regulatory regimes that include large subsidy programmes to the coal and steel industry or shipbuilding industry are cases in point.

The lack of a bridging theory

Both the question of choice between market- and hierarchy-based regulation and the issue of identifying irreconcilable mixes of market–hierarchy elements call for a bridging theory overarching economic and organisation theory. Such a bridging theory should, for a given regulatory problem, indicate an optimal choice of incentives/ authority mechanisms, drawing on both the market-based and organisation-based repertoire. In the difficult overlapping grey zone, where both modified market-based and modified hierarchy-based regulation are possible, the bridging theory would have to indicate the relative advantage of both models and the supremacy of one model over the other.

Transaction cost theory is today commonly put forward as a candidate for playing such a bridging role. In the words of its most well-known proponent Oliver Williamson: 'transaction cost economics is an interdisciplinary undertaking that joins economics with aspects of organisation theory and overlaps extensively with contract law' (Williamson, 1979). Compared to other perspectives on regulation, the transaction cost perspective has an advantage: it offers a conceptual apparatus that subsumes the discussion of specific transaction costs under hierarchic governance under a more general analysis, where these costs and imperfections can be discussed against similar costs on the market side.

Transaction cost theory recommends market-based governance when transaction costs are negligible. The standardised character of the transaction, in this case, makes alternative purchase and supply arrangements easy to work out in an open market. Market-based regulation, when transaction costs are negligible, may allow scale economies to be more fully exhausted. In addition, suppliers who aggregate uncorrelated demands may also realise collective pooling benefits as well.

Transaction cost theory recommends hierarchic governance as transactions become progressively more idiosyncratic, implying that the specialised human and physical assets become more oriented to a single use and hence less transferable to other uses in the market. In such situations, economies of scale can be as fully realised by the buyer as by an outside supplier under hierarchic governance. In addition to this, comes the advantage that under hierarchic governance adaptations can be made in a sequential way without the need to consult, complete or revise interfirm agreements.

Transaction cost theory is traditionally applied at the firm-level. However, the same line of reasoning may arguably be transposed to sectoral regulation or governance, where transaction costs of regulating through market mechanisms or formal organisation would be determined quite similarly to the individual firm. If the transaction costs of governing through external incentive mechanisms exceed those of regulation through internal incentives, then hierarchic regulation is prescribed, and inversely, if the transaction costs of governing through internal incentives exceed those of regulation through external incentives, this indicates market-based regulation.

At first sight the transaction cost theory, therefore, seems to offer a promising tool to bridge the gap between economics and organisational theory. It gives a consistent set of criteria for choice of institutional forms of regulation, offering a much broader perspective than the early public finance literature on market failure. It also offers criteria for specifying intermediate forms of organisation, implying that various forms of external and internal incentive modifications and mixes of such modifications may be judged up against the same criteria.

However, the transaction cost theory also has severe limitations as a bridging theory. Crucial to Williamson's argument is his focus on opportunistic behaviour (Williamson, 1993). However, the identification of control of opportunism as the core focus for economic regulation does not do justice to a large part of the organisational literature that suggests a more complicated and ambiguous relationship between formal control and behaviour.

Admittedly, in many situations control increases the costs to the individual of certain types of opportunistic behaviour, and thereby reduces such behaviour. However, with a basis, for instance in the human relations school of organisation theory referred to before, one could also argue that hierarchic control may have a number of other effects that work in the opposite direction: hierarchical control may, for instance, create negative feeling within and for the regulatory entity, which in turn increases the propensity to act opportunistically (Goshal and Morah, 1996). In line with Etzioni's well-known typology of control-types fostering different types of employee behaviour, one may argue that control is not only a question of degree, but also of quality. In Etzioni's analysis, therefore, coercive control fosters alienative employee behaviour; remunerative control fosters calculative employee behaviour; and normative control fosters moral behaviour.

Consequently, the net effect of hierarchic control on opportunistic behaviour will depend not only on the quantity, but also on the quality of control and it will depend on the effects of control directly on individual opportunism in the short run, but also on the indirect effects of control on organisational relations and organisational culture in the long run. Both the qualitative dimension and the indirect aspects are lacking in Williamson's transaction cost theory.

Much can be said for the simplicity of Williamson's transaction cost approach. However, its severe limitations *vis à vis* a large part of the research agenda within organisation theory as well as some of the research agenda, even within parts of economics, clearly make it too narrow to serve as a bridging theory to close the gap between external and internal incentive-based approaches to industrial regulation. From an organisation theory point of view it may be argued that an integrative bridging theory must have a richer repertoire of actor orientations and motivation mechanisms than the essentially opportunism-control orientation of Williamson's transaction cost theory. In this repertoire should enter such elements as purpose, trust and learning. As pointed out by Barnard already in 1938 the 'moral factor' – the efficacy of co-operation, co-ordinated by shared purpose – is an essential element in changing the preferences and utilities of the members of the organisation in order for it to achieve its ends. Barnard here voices concerns that come close to those of the human relations school previously referred to, for whom personal motivation, satisfaction, group integration and identification are major concerns in economic organisation.

Within this wider framework, it is also possible to understand why so many economic transactions are governed by organisational and not by market-based regulation in spite of the seeming lack of strong opportunistic transaction cost reasons. In the words of Simon (1991) much of the modern world's business is carried out in an 'organisational economy' and not through traditional market transactions, as Williamson's transaction cost theory would lead us to believe.

However, good candidates for a bridging theory from the organisation theory side are hardly available, and the development of a broader bridging theory, capable of incorporating this broad synthetic integration of theoretical elements across economic and organisational theory remains a difficult task on the future research agenda.

Complexity, path dependency and procedural ways out of the regulatory dilemma

Theoretical multidimensionality and the complexity problem

The extensive menu of external and internal modifications of the market- and hierarchy-ideal types leaves us with a wide set of regulatory options. However, the failure to devise an integrating bridging theory has left us with an irreconcilable multidimensionality and a complexity problem. On the one hand, the wide array of market-based and hierarchy-based regulatory options should, in principle, allow us to target complex regulatory problems far better than if only supplied with hierarchy- or market-based regulation, or modifications of only one of the two ideal types. The variety of regulatory options and dimensions potentially leaves us with the possibility of a tighter fit between regulatory tasks and regulatory means.

On the other hand the failure to develop a bridging theory across organisation and economic theory implies that we do not have theoretical tools to handle this variety and to apply the potential regulatory complementarities that are offered on a systematic deductive basis. One may therefore easily arrive at conclusions where several regulatory options are available, without being able to point out the optimal one. Or, one may risk proposing irreconcilable mixes of internal and external incentive elements, without being able to spot this beforehand.

It may be argued, on methodological grounds, that the complexity raised by the variety of regulatory combinations and the irreducible multiplicity cannot in principle be solved by deductive analytical means. By complexity we here imply, with Delorme (1994), that the subject-matter comprises numerous distinct components with strong interdependencies between them, which renders it irreducible to some tractable analytical representation. The problem of integrating economic and organisation theory of regulation is here clearly a case in point.

It has been shown by Simon (1976), Delorme (1994) and others that decision-making under such conditions cannot build exclusively on substantive rationality where the standpoint is finding the optimal solution based on end-state-driven, deductive, algorithmic reasoning. Instead, regulation under complexity must build on procedural rationality where the focus is also on the decision-making itself, and how the regulator may proceed to reach satisfactory knowledge. With satisficing, learning is an essential part of the decision-process, and hence the utility function of the regulator/decision-maker is no longer necessarily consistent over time. Given the complexity problem, the solution to the inconsistency and irreducibility problem that has been pointed out between organisation theory and economic theory of regulation can therefore, according to Simon (1976) and Delorme (1994) only be found in procedural terms.

Reflexive complexity and path dependent historical conditioning

Procedural rationality necessarily brings focus not only on the industry to be regulated, but also on the regulating agent itself, as the concept of satisficing is a cognitive notion relating an observer to the world (Simon, 1976; Delorme, 1994). It therefore puts on the regulatory agenda not only issues related to the complexity of the object of regulation – so-called objectal complexity – but also the relationship between this object and the regulatory body itself, thereby thematising *reflexive complexity*.

The concept of path dependency focuses on a major implication of reflexivity which applies to regulation both at the national and sectoral level. The term 'path dependency' refers to the fact that decisions tend to be 'historically embedded' in the sense that they are anchored in cultural and cognitive predispositions. Such predispositions imply statistically that, in a given culture, certain types of decisions are more likely to occur (David, 1993).

Given the selectivity embedded in the evaluatory process by national decision-makers and regulators, path-specific values and choices may in fact drive self-reinforcing processes towards the development and refinement of national or sectoral-specific regulatory styles and practices. The indeterminacy due to lack of an integrating theory, overarching organisation theory and economic theory of regulation may thus find its solution through subjective or nation-specific predispositions for a basic standpoint in one of the two theoretical worlds. In so far as this selection builds on nation-specific competencies and predispositions it is conceivable that a self-reinforcing build-up of diverging path-dependent regulatory strategies in two countries or regions – for instance one hierarchy-based and one market-based – may nevertheless lead to successful development in both cases.

This analytical conclusion is supported by broad empirical evidence including a large socio-economic literature which discusses national styles in industrial organisation under several labels: business systems (Whitley, 1992), social systems of production (Campbell, Hollingsworth and Lindblom, 1991) and modes of capitalist organisation (Orrù, 1994). The essence of this literature is that industrial development proceeds differently in different countries, as national industrial 'milieus' draw on specific traditions and competence in their national surroundings.

In line with this path-dependent reasoning a number of researchers have pointed out that different countries and sectors have had commercial success with widely differing developing models. On the one hand, the American car industry at the beginning of this century is brought in to illustrate great success with large-scale industrial organisation. On the other hand Italian manufacturing industry is brought in to illustrate the success of flexible specialisation based on traditional family and village networks (Piore and Sabel, 1984).

At a more aggregate level, path dependency is illustrated through different models of 'capitalist' development in major industrial countries: competitive capitalism in the USA and Great Britain; alliance capitalism in Germany and Japan; and state directed capitalism in France; all of which, in certain respects, have their advantages.

The complexity of regulatory analysis, within the broader dynamic growth-oriented perspective and the idiosyncratic reflexivity or self-referentiality of national styles, commands some respectful constraints on drawing too bold theoretical conclusions on a purely functional-deductive basis. Both theoretical and methodological arguments have been listed to indicate that regulatory redesign of complexly organised industrial systems can only at best hope to represent improvements or second best solutions, and never a dynamically changing and elusive optimum. At a general regime level, therefore, regulatory design of dynamically developing industrial systems must largely remain a heuristic process-oriented exercise, with considerable scope for experimentation.

Normative conclusions

We have seen, from the previous discussion, that the dilemma of choosing between a variety of regulatory approaches cannot be resolved substantively/deductively, because of a theoretical irreducibility problem in dealing with two partly irreconcilable theoretical paradigms. The complexity that is added on when moving from a static to a dynamic efficiency perspective further precludes strong deductively-based regulatory policy conclusions.

However, procedural rationality here stands out as an alternative bridging approach. By anchoring complex regulatory decision-making not only to internal theoretical logic, but also to implications and practice, or in semiotic analogy to link syntax to semantics and pragmatics, it becomes possible to reach higher-level regulatory conclusions even under considerable uncertainty and theoretical diversity. Procedural rationality at higher levels does not preclude, however, substantive rationality applied to more specific issues. As pointed out by Delorme (1994) there is an asymmetry between substantive and procedural rationality on this point. While the former excludes consideration of the latter, procedural rationality allows the possibility of applying substantive rationality to more limited partial problems. For complex problems, substantive rationality must therefore be 'contextualised' by an over-arching procedural design which subsumes the substantive/analytical approach thanks to its greater generality and relevance.

Path dependency may constitute one of the procedural elements that provides analytical closure at an over-arching level. In so far as cultural and institutional predispositions strongly favour one development path over another, there may remain little need for investigating analytical alternatives that lie outside this possibility-span. Given implicit and explicit choices made at the over-arching level, room is given for more specific analytical approaches to partial problems. The over-arching regulatory problem-reduction, provided by cultural and institutional constraints, thus provides 'niches' for more limited deductively rational analysis.

Given a certain over-arching procedural delineation of the regulatory regime, further analytical headway may be made by breaking down the regulation problem into sub-problems. Splitting up the value chain of a given industrial sector into subsets of commercial activities may, for instance, allow for specific regulatory measures to be applied to specific activities. As already mentioned, for grid-based production systems, the natural monopoly problem and regulatory measures to tackle it may only apply to a limited part, whereas other parts may be governed by more normal commercial regulation.

Nevertheless, a certain ambiguity may still remain as to the efficiency of various organisationally-based and hierarchy-based regulatory measures. The theoretical complexity still leaves us with an analytically unresolved dilemma in selecting between market-based and hierarchy-based governance, which in turn forces us to take extensive recursion to procedural rationality. Furthermore, ambiguity about optimal regulatory solutions arises as regulation must remain open to constant challenge and reconsideration in response to the dynamics of industrial development, as new technologies and new industrial strategies create new regulatory problems. This analytical ambiguity indicates considerable need for experimentation and learning, where playing on the pluralism of existing national variety of regulatory models and letting them challenge each other, seems to be of just as much importance as the deductive search for functional analytical solutions.

Notes

1. We shall here treat regulation and governance as synonomous and hereafter, for the sake of simplicity refer to both concepts by 'regulation'. We are, thus, using the term 'regulation' in a broad sense, encompassing both market-based and hierarchy-based governance, somewhat inspired by the French regulation school (Boyer, 1988)

2. Scott finds this approach exemplified by the work of Udy (1959), Woodward (1965), Pugh and colleagues (1969). However, the element of rational selection of formal structure in response to organisational environments is more explicitly represented in the work of design theorists like Galbraith (1973) and Swinth (1974), but also characteristic of the work of Thompson (1967).
3. Scott sees this position represented by the work of such theorists as Hickson et al. (1971), March and Olsen (1976) , Meyer and Rowan (1977) and Pfeffer and Salancik (1978).

Bibliography

Barnard, C. (1938) *The Functions of the Executive*. Cambridge (Mass.): Harvard University Press.

Barney, Jay, B. and William G. Ouchi (1986) *Organizational Economics*. Joseey-Bass Publishers: London.

Baumol, W.J., E.E. Bailey and R.D. Willig (1977) 'Weak Invisible Hand Theorems on the Sustainability of Multiproduct Natural Monopoly'. *American Economic Review 67*: 355.

Berger, Peter L. and Thomas Luckman (1967) *The Social Construction of Reality: A Treatise in the Sociology of Knowledge*. London: Penguin.

Blaug, Mark (1992) (ed.) *Frank Knight, Henry Simons, Joseph Schumpeter*. Aldershot: Edward Elgar.

Boyer, Robert (1988) 'Formalising Growth Regimes' in Dosi, G.C. Freeman, R. Nelson, G. Solverberg and L. Soete (eds) *Technical Change and Economic Theory*. London: Pinter.

Campbell, John, L. , Roger Hollingsworth and Leon N. Lindblom (1991) *Governance of the American Economy*. New York: Cambridge University Press.

Clark, James V. (1960): 'Motivation in Work Groups. A Tentative View' in *Human Organization* no. 4.

Crozier, Michl (1964): *The Bureaucratic Phenomenon*. Chicago: University of Chicago Press.

David, P.A. (1993): 'Path Dependence and Predictability in Dynamic Systems with Local Network Externalities: a Paradigm for Historical Economics' in Dominique Foray and Christopher Freeman (eds) *Technology and the Wealth of Nations*. London: Pinter Publishers.

Delorme, Robert (1994) 'From First Order to Second Order Complexity in Economic Theorizing' *Working Paper, University of Versailles*.

Demsetz H. (1968): 'Why Regulate Utilities'. *Journal of Law and Economics* 11: 55–65.

Downs, A (1967) *An Economic Theory of Democracy.* New York: Harper and Row.

Fayol, Henri (1949) *General and Industrial Management.* London: Pitman.

Galbraith, John Kenneth (1973) *Designing Complex Organizations.* Reading (Mass.): Addison Wesley.

Goshal, Sumantra and Peter Moran Insead (1996) 'Bad for Practice: A Critique of the Transaction Cost Theory'. *Academy of Management Review.* January.

Hannan, Michael T. and John Freeman (1977) 'The Population Ecology of Organizations'. *American Journal of Sociology* no. 72.

Hayek, Friedrich A. (1948) *Individualism and Economic Order.* Chicago: Chicago University Press.

Hernes, Gudmund (1978) (ed.) *Forhandlingsøkonomi og blandingsadministrasjon.* Oslo: Norwegian University Press.

Hickson, David J., C.R. Hinnings, C.A. Lee, R.E. Schenck and J.M. Pennings (1971) 'A Strategic Contingencies' Theory of Intraorganizational Power'. *Administrative Science Quarterly* 16, June, pp. 216–29.

Ioannides, Stavros (1992) *The Market, Competition and Democracy.* Aldershot Hants: Edward Elgar.

Kirzner, Israel (1973) *Competition and Entrepreneurship.* Chicago: Chicago University Press.

Laffont, Jean-Jacques and Jean Tirole (1993) *A Theory of Incentives in Procurement and Regulation.* Cambridge (Mass.): MIT Press.

Lane, Jan Erik (1993) *The Public Sector, Concepts, Models and Approaches.* London: Sage.

Littlechild, S.C., K.G. Vadya and M. Carey (1982) *Energy Strategies for the UK.* G. Allen & Unwin.

Lysgaard, Sverre (1967) *Arbeider kollektivet: En studie i de underordnedes sosisologi.* Universitetsforlaget Oslo.

March, James G. and Olsen, Johan P. (1976) *Ambiguity and Choice in Organizations.* Bergen: The Norwegian University Press.

Martin, Joanne, and Peter Frost (1996) 'The Organizational Culture War Games: a Struggle for Intellectual Dominance'. *Handbook of Organization Studies.* London: Sage.

Mayo, Elton (1945) *The Social Problems of an Industrial Civilization.* Boston: Graduate Scool of Business administration, Harward University.

Merton, R.K. (1957): *Social Theory and Social Structure.* Glencoe (Il.): Free Press.

Meyer, John, W. and Brian Rowan (1977) 'Institutionalized Organizations: Formal Structures as Myth and Ceremony'. *American Journal of Sociology*. 83: 340–63.

Musgrave, R.A. (1959) *The Theory of Public Finance*. New York: McGraw Hill.

Musgrave, R.A. and Peacock A.T. (1967) (eds) *Classics in the Theory of Public Finance*. New York: St Martins Press (now Palgrave).

Niskanen, W.A. (1971): *Bureaucracy and Representative Government*. Chicago (Il.): Aldine-Atherton.

Norman, Michael and Barry Stoker (1991) *Data Envelopment Analysis: the Assessment of Performance*. Chichester: Wiley.

Orrù, Marco (1994) 'The Faces of Capitalism'. Paper presented at the Sixth Annual International Conference on Socio-Economics. HEC. Paris.

Perrow, Charles (1970) *Organizational Analysis: A Sociological View*. Belmont (Ca.): Wadsworth.

Perrow, Charles (1974) 'Is Business Really Changing?' *Organizational Dynamics*. Summer 31–44.

Pfeffer, J., and Salancik, G.R. (1978) *The External Control of Organisations*. New York: Harper & Row.

Piore, and Sabel (1984) *The Second Industrial Divide*. New York: Basic Books.

Porter, Michael (1990) *The Competitive Advantage of Nations*. London: Macmillan (now Palgrave).

Powell, Walter W. (1981) 'Neither Market Nor Hierarchy: Network Form of Organization'. *Research in Organizational Behaviour* vol. 12 pp. 295–336.

Pugh, D.S., D.J. Hickson and C.R. Hinnings (1969) 'An Empirical Taxonomy of Structures of Work Organizations'. *Administrative Science Quarterly* 14 March 115–26.

Roethlisberger, F.J. and William J. Dickson (1939) *Management and the Worker*. Cambridge (Mass.): Harvard University Press.

Samuelson, P.A. (1954) 'The Pure Theory of Public Expenditure'. *The Review of Economics and Statistics* vol. 40, pp. 387–9.

Savas, E.S. (1987) *Privatization: the Key to Better Government*. Chatham, N.J: Chatham House Publishers.

Schein, E. (1985) *Organizational Culture and Leadership*. San Francisco: Jossey-Bass.

Schleifer, A (1985) 'A Theory of Yardstick Competition'. *Rand Journal of Economics* 16:319–27.

Schneider, B. (1990) (ed.) *Organizational Climate and Culture*. San Francisco: Jossey-Bass.

Schumpeter, Joseph (1943) *Capitalism, Socialism and Democracy*. London: George Allen & Unwin Ltd.

Scott, Richard (1981) *Organizational, Rational, Natural and Open Systems*. Englewood Cliffs. New Jersey: Prentice Hall.

Selznick, Philip (1949) *TVA and the Grass Roots*. Berkeley: University of California Press.

Simon, Herbert A. (1957) *Administrative Behaviour* (2nd ed). New York: Macmillan (now Palgrave).

Simon, Herbert A. (1976) 'From Substantive to Procedural Rationality' in S. Latsis (ed.) *Method and Appraisal in Economics*. Cambridge.

Simon, Herbert A. (1991) 'Organisations and Markets'. *Journal of Economic Perspecives* 5 (2) 25–44.

Smirchich, L. (1983) 'Concepts of Culture and Organizational Analysis'. *Administrative Science Quarterly* 28: 339–58.

Spulber, Daniel (1989) *Regulation and Markets*. Cambridge (Mass.): MIT Press.

Stigler, George. J. (1968) *The Organization of Industry*. Homewood, Il.: Irwin.

Stigler, George. J. (1988) (ed.) *Chicago Studies in Political Economy*. Chicago: Chicago University Press.

Stinchcombe, Arthur L. (1984) 'Contracts as Hierarchical Documents', Work Report No. 65, Institute of Industrial Economics, Bergen.

Swinth, Robert L. (1974) *Organizational Systems for Management: Designing, Planning and Implementation*. Columbus, Ohio: Grid.

Taylor, Fredrick W. (1911) *Principles of Scientific Management*. New York: Harper.

Thompson, James D. (1967): *Organizations in Action*. New York: McGraw-Hill.

Trist, E.L., G.W. Higgin, H. Murray and A.B. Pollock (1963) *Organizational Choice*. London: Tavistock.

Udy, Stanley H. Jr (1959) 'Bureaucracy and Rationality in Weber's Organization Theory'. *American Sociological Review* 24. December 791–95.

Weber, Max (1964) *Social and Economic Organization*. Collier Macmillan Publishers: London.

Weick, Karl (1969) *The Social Psychology of Organising*. Reading (Mass.): Addison-Wesley.

Whitley, Richard (1992) *European Business Systems: Firms and Markets in their National Contexts*. London: Sage.

Williamson, Oliver, (1975) *Markets and Hierarchies: Analysis and Antitrust Implications*. New York: Free Press.

Williamson (1979) 'Transaction-Cost Economics: The Governance of Contractual Relations'. *Journal of Law and Economics* vol. 22, pp. 233–61.

Williamson (1993) 'Opportunism and its Critics'. *Managerial and Decisions Economics*, 14: 97–107.

Woodward, Joan (1965) *Industrial Organization: Theory and Practice*. New York: Oxford University Press.

6
A Modern Austrian Approach to Economic Regulation

Karen I. Vaughn

Introduction: the Austrian perspective

The last 20 years have seen a flourishing of work in the Austrian tradition; one of the most important fruits of this work has been a more precise locating of the difference between Austrian and neoclassical economics. At the most fundamental level, Austrians differ from neoclassical economists in the assumptions that they make about the nature of the economic problem. Whereas neoclassical economics views the human predicament as attempting to maximise satisfaction of unlimited wants in the face of limited resources, Austrians add to that description the observation that human beings pursue their projects and plans in the face of scarcity of resources, the forward progress of time and limited information about the world around them. Hence, Austrian economics is the economics of wants and scarcity and also of time and ignorance.[1]

By refusing to abstract from time and ignorance in human life, Austrians offer a different perspective both on the nature of markets and on the fundamental subject-matter of economics. To Austrians, limited information is one of the necessary characteristics of all human action; it is not a 'market imperfection' so much as a fundamental aspect of human life. Markets are institutions that permit individuals to act upon their limited information in ways that lead both to learning and to the spread of knowledge in society. Imperfect information is one of the basic reasons that market interaction is useful. But the fact that people continually learn from their market dealings implies that markets are ongoing processes in time where no discernible end point is implied in the data. Every act in the market changes the constellation of human knowledge in such a way as to make new plans and new goals operative. To Austrians, then, 'solving' for equilibrium conditions is something of a pointless exercise. The continually changing circumstances of and knowledge about market phenomena render even the possibility of arriving at an equilibrium beyond the pale. To Austrians, the central problem of economic analysis is to understand how finite and partially ignorant human beings use markets to cope with their limitations and inadvertently create an orderly (and increasingly wealthy) economy.[2]

As we shall see, this Austrian refusal to abstract away from time and ignorance implies not only a positive theory of market processes, but also a critique of governmental intervention into market activities. This critique, which has emerged from over one hundred years of writings in the Austrian tradition, is best articulated in the writings of four twentieth-century Austrians: Ludwig von Mises, Friedrich Hayek, Murray Rothbard and Israel Kirzner.

Ludwig von Mises and the theory of interventionism

The Austrian attitude toward government involvement in the economy has been developed almost exclusively in opposition to would-be interventionists: first Marxists and then neoclassical planners and regulators. In the early Austrian school, Böhm Bawerk was known for his opposition to Marxism and, in general, for his liberalism. Menger himself wrote little about economic policy, but it appears from recent research that he was also politically liberal.[3] However, the Austrian whose name is most associated with economic liberalism was the second-generation Austrian, Ludwig von Mises. Indeed, it was Mises who set the course for future Austrian views of economic policy.

Mises's ideas on the relationship between government and the economy grew directly out of the critique of socialism that he began in 1920. In his now famous article, 'Economic Calculation in the Socialist Commonwealth', his target was naive Marxists who believed one could eliminate all property, all market transactions, all money, and still make rational allocation decisions in a complex economy (Vaughn, 1980). In his critiques of socialism (1920,1922, 1963), Mises contrasted what he called a pure market economy with a pure centrally planned economy. A pure market economy was one in which the role of government was limited to enforcing rules of property and contract while a pure planned economy was one in which private property and private exchange were completely eliminated. Mises argued that pure planning was impossible because without private property and market exchange there would be no market prices to aid in economic calculation. While eventually his point was acknowledged by socialist economists (although the acknowledgment served only to intensify their efforts to solve the problem of central planning), his extension of that argument to economic interventionism, or 'the hampered market economy' (1963, part 6) was less well received.

Mises argued that economic intervention – or the 'mixed economy' – was also an irrational construct because it was fundamentally unstable. Any one government intervention would set up a response by individual actors that would tend to create some other unforseen problem. Hence, an intervention that was meant to solve a particular economic problem would itself cause other problems that would require further intervention. The successive introduction of new interventions to solve problems set up by previous interventions would ultimately result in an economy that was so hampered by regulation that market prices would cease to convey useful market information and rational profit and loss calculation would be impossible.

Mises's argument was part of his larger positive theory about the importance of monetary calculation in co-ordinating a complex advanced economy (1963). To paraphrase and perhaps amplify his argument, he seemed to be saying that comparisons among competing alternative strategies could only be assessed at the moment that real alternatives became known in the market place. Assessing costs is really a process of ranking foregone desirable alternatives. Preference rankings do not exist apart from the act of choice, however. It is only in the process of weighing alternatives that individuals can balance what is preferred against what is less preferred and make rational choices. This process cannot take place in the realm of the hypothetical. It requires knowledge of real market alternatives to be authentic. But, the more alternatives, the more complex the dimensions of choice, the more important is monetary calculation for providing a common denominator for comparison. The implication was that government intervention would make prices less and less useful as measures of real alternatives and hence hamper economic calculation.

Obviously, interference with monetary calculation would have systemic negative effects. Money and money prices are the only tools available for entrepreneurs to gauge if they are using resources effectively. If prices can not be relied upon to accurately reflect a consensus of buyers' and sellers' opinions of the value of goods and resources, profit and loss become less reliable as indicators of good and bad economic judgement. Government intervention in the private trades of individuals would by necessity distort prices and hamper market activity in inefficient ways. That coupled with his view that the unintended consequences of regulation would elicit even more legislation to compensate for the inevitable regulatory failures led Mises to claim that the choice was between free markets or chaos (1963, p. 861).

Hayek and knowledge

Mises's protégé, Friedrich Hayek, learned his scepticism of government economic intervention under Mises's tutelage. And, like Mises, Hayek's analysis of the relationship between government and market also grew out of his critique of central planning. In particular, Hayek's work in the economic calculation debate led him to explore the nature and role of knowledge in the market process (1948, chs 2, 4). He emphasised the detailed, local and often tacit nature of economic knowledge and argued that it took the trial and error of market experiments to generate the kind of knowledge economists took for granted in their models. Information was by nature decentralised and imperfect: market competition was necessary to mobilise and make public this decentralised information. Competition, Hayek argued, was a discovery procedure that allowed human beings to test out new ideas and practices in a system that provided accurate feedback (1978).

In the same context, Hayek examined the nature of competition and argued that it was far more complex and robust than conventional models of perfect competition implied (1948, ch. 5). Real competition, he argued, involves many more dimensions than simply price and quantity; firms compete on the basis of product qualities and accompanying services with the result that consumer demand is met not only by increasing quantities of goods, but also by increasing heterogeneity among goods offered for sale. While Hayek never addressed the problem of economic regulation per se in his scientific work,[4] his ideas inspired Mises's other important American student, Israel Kirzner, to develop a theory of market processes that could be used to launch an important critique of the neoclassical theory of regulation.

Murray Rothbard and Austrian welfare economics

Both Mises and Hayek criticised government intervention on the pragmatic grounds that it is counterproductive. Economic policy leads to unintended consequences that make everyone, including the interventionists, poorer. Murray Rothbard, one of Mises's two most prominent students in the United States (and next to Mises, the Austrian who is most associated with free market advocacy) also believed that government intervention is counterproductive. However, his primary critique of intervention rested on the distinction he drew between voluntary and involuntary action. Market transactions are both peaceful and voluntary. Government regulation, on the contrary, is backed up by guns and jails and is, therefore, 'the economics of violent intervention in the market' (1962, ch. 12).

This distinction that Rothbard drew between voluntary and violent action formed the basis for a version of welfare economics he called 'demonstrated preference' (1956). Following conventional economic theory, Rothbard argued that since people only trade when they expect to gain, two-party trades must always be welfare enhancing. However, government intervention always has the effect of thwarting or altering the terms of certain two-party trades, so government intervention must always reduce welfare. Notice that this is a welfare economics that makes no reference to long-run competitive prices, deadweight losses to monopoly or, even more prominently, to externalities or third-party effects of any kind. To Rothbard, as to Mises, such theoretical fictions were irrelevant to assessing the market process.[5] Neither Mises nor Rothbard ever conceded that there might even in principle be a case in which economic transactions might be improved by government intervention. I believe that most Austrians today would agree with that assessment.

Kirzner and the entrepreneurial market process

The neoclassical case for economic regulation is largely based on the supposed welfare effects of monopoly. Welfare is maximised in long-run perfectly competitive equilibrium. Since the existence of monopoly elements will prevent the attainment of the perfectly competitive position, economists generally regard monopoly as ripe for some kind of regulation. Most regulatory theory concerns finding ways to limit natural monopoly and prevent firms with monopoly power from engaging in anticompetitive practices. While there is also an important literature assessing the relative costs and benefits of monopoly regulation, there is little doubt that monopoly is inefficient and when it is possible and where the costs of monopoly are big enough, it should be discouraged or regulated.

In his 1973 book, *Competition and Entrepreneurship*, Israel Kirzner built on Hayek's work to develop an entrepreneurial theory of the market process that called the conventional theory of monopoly into question.

In Kirzner's view, at any moment in time, there were innumerable opportunities for profit that were left unexploited because no one had noticed them. Entrepreneurs were in the business of noticing such opportunities and profiting from their exploitation. In so doing, they made previously hidden knowledge known to market transactors, thereby spreading their discovery throughout the system. Each entrepreneurial act served to reveal a previous disequilibrium and to increase the degree of co-ordination in the market. This simple description of an entrepreneurial process was distinctly at odds with conventional static definitions of monopoly as either a single seller or as a seller who faces a downward-sloping demand curve. Kirzner argued that in the dynamic context that he assumed, many if not most firms would be single sellers at their inception. This was simply the first stage of a competitive process where subsequent stages would bring out the imitators of the initial enterprise. On the other hand, in a competitive market, it is also likely that even long-established firms would face less than perfectly elastic demand curves. As Hayek had argued, real competition was about product differentiation, not reproducing homogeneous goods. Far from reflecting a welfare loss, such 'monopoly power' was a sign of a vigorous competitive process. The only monopoly that Kirzner was willing to admit could limit competition was a resource monopoly, but even resource monopolies are subject to erosion through discovery of substitute products and techniques.

The arguments in *Competition and Entrepreneurship* only indirectly addressed questions of regulation, mainly by undercutting its neoclassical justification. However, in a later essay, Kirzner addressed regulation head-on from a largely Hayekian perspective. In an essay entitled 'The Perils of Regulation' (1979), Kirzner argued that a significant danger of government regulation was that the intervention could impede the discovery procedure that corrects market errors. Even if some current market deficiency could be accurately identified by government, attempting to impose a solution could itself be counterproductive:

> After all, the very problems apparent in the market might generate processes of discovery and correction superior to those undertaken deliberately by government regulation; deliberate intervention by the state not only might serve as an imperfect substitute for the spontaneous market process of discovery, but also might impede desirable processes of discovery the need for which has not been perceived by the government. (p. 13)

The fact that a problem might exist, then, is not a sufficient argument for developing some interventionist strategy to correct it. The problem may be a temporary phenomenon whose very appearance leads to market correctives.

Notice that Kirzner's argument focuses on the relative capabilities of markets and government to solve problems where knowledge only emerges in a dynamic process of discovery. Government may perceive an economic inefficiency, but it is by no means certain (and probably unlikely) that the remedy it designs will be any better than what will eventually emerge from the market itself. What is certain, however, is that the remedy that it designs will skew the rest of the market discovery process in unanticipated ways. Further, the different incentives between market and government are such that regulatory agency bureaucrats will not be motivated to continue to discover better remedies for market deficiencies. That is, without profit and loss to personally guide them, regulatory agencies will not be able to discern what kind of solution will best enhance economic efficiency. Hence, while it is not always certain that economic regulation will do more harm than good, there are good reasons to be very wary of using it except in extraordinary circumstances.

Regulation and the market process

Several important components of an Austrian theory of (or critique of) regulation emerge from this short doctrinal history. First, the on-going, time-consuming nature of market competition requires that regulation itself be a process rather than a once and for all solution to a perceived market failure. As Mises argued, any one regulation such as a price ceiling or floor, rules for mergers and acquisitions, direct control of natural monopolies, will set up incentives for market participants to avoid the undesired consequences of the regulation. This means that the unintended consequences of regulation will be to create further problems that regulators will have to address in order to try to achieve their original goals. We are then forced to ask not simply what change in policy can eliminate the market failure; rather we must compare the incentives, knowledge properties and likely long-run consequences that flow from unrestrained market versus some specified process of political decision-making and implementation.

While the comparison between market and political processes is paramount, Austrian analysis also leads to the conclusion that identifying a problem to be corrected through regulation is also problematic. In a dynamic market, it is difficult to identify a practice that has inefficient consequences apart from the market process itself.

What might appear to an outsider a market inefficiency might rather be a necessary step in a time-consuming process of discovery, or it might be the case that the outside observer does not know all the constraints facing market actors. What appears to be an inefficient arrangement might be the best solution to a complex but partly hidden problem. Regulators are left with little guidance as to what should be regulated.

Finally, even if a regulator could identify a market institution or market practice that might in principle be improved upon by imposition of a new rule, it would be difficult for the regulator to know how to design a better rule or institution to improve upon the market. The market process itself is relatively efficient in responding to unmet consumer demands and solving supply problems.

Even more important, markets are good at tailoring response to particularly situated problems in a way that leaves room for readjustment and change. Market solutions are often tentative and flexible while regulations are rule-bound and difficult to change. In other words, decentralised decision-makers with relevant local knowledge can better identify problems and tailor solutions to local circumstances than can remote bureaucrats who must make general rules of universal application.

Assessing the Austrian argument

The Austrian anti-regulatory position is not unique in many of its conclusions. Many economists argue for free markets and minimal regulation from a strictly neoclassical position. Indeed, Mises's insight into 'creeping interventionism' has an exact counterpart in the neoclassical economists' analysis of the consequences of price controls of any kind. Most economists, arguing from partial equilibrium-comparative static models, are able to predict perverse consequences to the imposition of price ceilings and floors (although the similarity exists primarily because the mainstream analysis in fact uses dynamic reasoning to make the case). On the other hand, the issue of monopoly regulation demonstrates some real differences between mainstream views and Austrian arguments, even when the conclusions tend to be similar.

Recently an important literature has developed questioning the usefulness of monopoly regulation (Demsetz, Peltzman, Bork, Posner). In this neoclassically-based literature, it is argued that the costs of monopoly tend to be very small while the costs of regulation tend to be larger. On purely pragmatic grounds, monopoly regulation is not worth the effort. The Austrians, on the other hand, go beyond the usual pragmatic arguments by challenging the very logic of the monopoly construct itself based on their belief in the importance of economic processes which imply a constantly changing constellation of market knowledge.

If we deny the equilibrium conditions any role in describing a possible state of the world, we have little grounds for trying to duplicate the consequences of competitive equilibrium states through regulatory policy. In a growing, dynamic economy, monopoly indeed could well be a necessary stage of development.[6] Further, even if some monopolies persist over time, it is not clear either that an alternative market structure is viable or that monopoly results in any welfare loss. To persist in an open market, a monopoly must be more efficient than any potential competitor and pass on enough efficiency gains to consumers to keep potential competitors from entering the market. Any so-called welfare loss that engenders could well be swamped by welfare gains from a growing economy. For instance, information that price may exceed marginal cost for a particular firm, far from indicating market failure could well be the symptom of a healthy, growing economy. Hence there is little theoretical guidance for even identifying a real monopoly let alone regulating it.

Regulation of monopoly is only one form that government intervention into markets can take, however. There are any number of other kinds of economic regulations and interventions that now affect businesses in Western market economies. In particular, an increasingly dominant form of regulation concerns consumer protection issues: product health and safety regulations, labelling requirements and disclosure laws are some of the more obvious illustrations. What these have in common is a prior assumption that there are information 'failures' in the market that result in consumers being undersupplied with relevant information to guide their purchases. Austrians have paid relatively little attention to such regulations, yet information-based regulation should provide an especially interesting challenge to Austrian theory since it is justified by pointing to a kind of market imperfection that Austrians themselves tend to emphasise: knowledge imperfection. If market knowledge is imperfect and markets take time to adjust to new information, is it not possible that consumers are in fact undersupplied with relevant information, and is it not in principle possible that regulation might improve economic efficiency? While Austrians have not yet devoted much time to this issue, there are several lines of argument that the Austrian approach suggests to answer this question.

An Austrian response to consumer regulation

Information imperfections in the market can be divided into two kinds: information asymmetries between producers and consumers, and what Kirzner might call 'sheer ignorance', information that no one possesses or recognises that they possess. Information-asymmetries occur when some economically relevant qualities of a good are not obvious from inspecting the good before purchase: consumers would prefer to have more information about the characteristics of the good than producers are making available. It may be the case that producers have the knowledge that consumers desire and have chosen not to reveal it, or it may be that they are able to discover the relevant characteristics at a lower cost than consumers would incur were they to try to discover the characteristics on their own. For instance, in purchasing a new car, many consumers might like to know the average fuel consumption they can expect from the model they are interested in purchasing. This is information either that the manufacturer knows, or that he can find out through relatively low-cost testing, while individual consumers can only discover the information by purchasing and driving the car over an extended period of time. Clearly, where this characteristic is important to consumers, having the information in advance of purchase is preferable to learning it at some cost after the fact.

In so far as asymmetries are presumed to be widespread, one might consider this a reasonable case of government regulation: require producers to disclose all relevant information to potential consumers before purchase. While it is also true that the regulations will increase the cost of the product (after all, the economics of information teaches us that information is not free) it still could be the case that the increased cost of providing the information is offset by the reduction in purchasing errors made by misinformed consumers. But is the case really so clear?

While no Austrian would ever claim that consumers are perfectly informed (to the contrary, Austrians argue that consumers, along with everyone else, are relatively ignorant about almost everything), the question to be addressed is how can consumer ignorance best be overcome? To answer that question requires that one must compare the market response to consumer ignorance to the likely consequences of regulation designed to accomplish the same task.

Austrian analysis predicts a systematic market response to perceived consumer demand for more information: if knowing more about specific features of a product is important to consumers, there is a profit opportunity that is available for entrepreneurial exploitation.

Entrepreneurs who perceive the opportunity will begin to provide the relevant information as part of their efforts to out-compete their market rivals. The necessity to keep up with one's rivals will then force others to offer the same information about the products they sell as well.

To continue our example, once auto manufacturers understand that consumers want to know about average fuel consumption, that information becomes a variable in the competitive process. Producers will attempt to attract customers by advertising the fuel consumption of various models, especially if it is unusually low. While it is true that makers of cars that are inefficient users of fuel might want to conceal the relative unattractiveness of their fuel consumption, it is likely that they will be driven by competitive forces to make that information known in any case.

Notice the language I use: 'it is likely', not 'it is certain'. In fact, it is also likely that not all manufacturers will advertise fuel mileage on all models of cars. However, this is not a criticism of the market process so much as a reflection of the variation in consumer demand. Not everyone cares about the same things. Markets tend to cater to differences in demand. Indeed, one of the central aspects of market competition is the 'fit' that emerges between consumers and products.

To illustrate, consider another kind of information consumers presumably would like to have: the safety features of the automobile they are considering purchasing. There is a trade-off between safety and price of automobiles: more safety features require more resources. Airbags cost more than seat belts; reinforced doors cost more than unreinforced doors. One would expect that higher-priced cars would tend to be safer than lower-priced ones, and one would expect that safety features would not be advertised to the same degree by all automobile manufacturers. Indeed, that is in fact the case. Volvo makes safety a major part of its advertising campaign because it recognises that there is a market for safe, relatively expensive cars. Volvo has been successful in its advertising strategy, yet many people still choose to purchase less safe, but cheaper Huyndais. Also, as one would expect, Huyndai focuses its advertising strategy on low cost and fuel economy. In some cases there is also a trade-off between style and safety.

Convertible automobiles are less safe than sedans, yet some people prefer to consume the styling of convertibles rather than the safety of a hard roof. Advertising for convertibles, predictably, focuses on the subjective state of the consumer while driving rather than on safety or economy. Different consumers want different bundles of characteristics in the goods they purchase. Firms tend to provide an assortment of characteristics to meet a wide spectrum of consumer preferences.

One might argue, however, that the incentives for entrepreneurs to offer consumers the information they want still doesn't guarantee the 'right' amount of information provision on the market. While it is true that there are incentives for sellers to compete through the provision of relevant information, it may take a long process of trial and error for them to discover what it is that consumers want to know, and, in the interim, consumers would be making purchases based on less information than they would have if they could make their demands effective.

This argument cannot be ignored by Austrians who argue that equilibrium positions are unattainable in real life. Any market innovation (such as competing on the basis of disclosing product information) depends upon entrepreneurs to discover the opportunity to profit from an action and for others to be alert enough to follow. The most one can confidently argue is that where there is a profit opportunity to be grasped, entrepreneurs have an incentive to discover it. But one might also point out that it is not a common complaint that entrepreneurs fail to notice profit opportunities! From automobile specifications to amenities of resort hotels to the flight schedules of airplanes, the economy is rife with examples of competitive disclosure of information in action. Moreover, when it comes to providing information about products, consumers have not had to rely simply on manufacturers to provide it for them. Independent testing organisations have emerged specifically to provide consumers with information that they might find difficult to discover on their own. In the US, Underwriters Laboratory and Consumer Reports are two institutions that have arisen to supplement the market process. But, one must concede that there is no iron-clad guarantee that any one particular profit opportunity will be noticed and acted upon at any particular time, including potential profits from information provision.

This leads us to the most important policy-relevant question: if market entrepreneurs don't perceive that consumers want a particular kind of information and are willing to pay for it, is it likely that government would be able to recognise the opportunity before the market does? Of course, bureaucrats may think they know what consumers want, but without a market test to judge whether or not they are correct, is it not more likely that regulators will mandate disclosure of what they believe consumers should want rather than what they in fact want? Perhaps this explains why in the United States there are regulations mandating the listing of nutritional content on all processed foods that consumers routinely ignore.

However, let us assume that some government bureaucrat, responding to pressure from a consumer group, happens to discern that the market is slow to respond to consumer demand for product information and mandates its provision. There are reasons to believe that the information required by government will be less efficiently provided than what would emerge in the market process.

Regulations are of necessity uniform for all similar manufacturers. Regulations are rules, and rules must be applied equally to all sellers. This means that even if the regulator is correct that some (or even many) consumers demand the mandated information, the regulation will mandate the same information disclosure for all manufactures including those whose market segment is uninterested in the information. The regulation will then have the effect of oversupplying information to some market segments at some increased cost beyond what consumers would be willing to pay in an unregulated market. Instead of tailoring the supply of information to the appropriate market, regulations impose uniformity, increasing costs beyond what is efficient to meet consumer demand. Hence, even if a government official were correct in his belief that there are significant and correctable information asymmetries between manufacturers and consumers, that is not a sufficient argument for imposing a regulation on everyone.[7] A more difficult case is where the product has health and safety implications. There are several ways in which the market might be said to undersupply health and safety: through information failure when a supposedly benign substance could cause harm (such as a severe allergic reaction) to a subset of population that unknowingly purchases the offending product, or when a new product has certain defects or long-term effects that are unknown to either buyer or seller when it is first introduced. In these cases, market processes should eventually provide information either through entrepreneurial competition or through liability litigation. However, this is not done immediately, and the delay in providing information may have significant, even disastrous, consequences. While there are systematic incentives for good products to be produced and for products to be improved over time, in the meantime, the consequences of a mistake might be judged too costly to risk. By mandating certain health and safety standards, government reduces the likelihood of unhealthy or unsafe products being purchased. By mandating certain labelling or disclosure features, government reduces consumer error. This is the argument that a 'consumer advocate' might provide, but it overlooks yet another important consideration. It is certainly true that market discovery takes time, and during this discovery period, there are likely to be cases of consumer disappointment or even injury. But is consumer disappointment or injury entirely avoidable? Is it not the case that every disappointment and/or injury that affects consumers is the event that alerts entrepreneurs to the need for change?

In other words, the problem may not be one of informational asymmetries so much as sheer ignorance. No one, neither producer nor consumer, may know that a problem exists; for example, that the design of an automobile has a flaw that makes it unsafe in certain conditions. The unfortunate occurrence of a pattern of accidents might be a necessary part of the discovery process. But if that is the case, it is not clear that government regulation can make consumers better off. Government will have less knowledge about the characteristics of products than the manufacturer and less incentive to correct the defect. It is no surprise that health and safety regulations usually follow rather than precede product accidents. But if that is the case, why do we need the regulation? Government is unlikely to know about a defect before the manufacturer does, and once a product defect is known, liability law disciplines the offending producer. Government regulation would appear to be superfluous, and where the regulation is very specific, it may prevent firms from discovering even better ways of addressing the design flaw that caused the problem.[8]

One way that regulation tries to deal with these questions of sheer ignorance is by mandating certain testing procedures prior to the sale of the product. The best example of that in the US is the Food and Drug Administration. While this is an attractive solution to some, economists generally recognise the inherent difficulty in the prior testing scheme. Agencies such as the FDA substitute rules for producer discretion and judgement. Because the agency is criticised when a substance it approves causes harm but suffers little effect if it fails to approve a benign or helpful substance, they have an incentive to oversupply safety. This is likely to lead to over-testing to meet the agency standard, uniformity of testing procedures for disparate problems with varying risks, and cessation of innovation in the testing process itself. Agencies like the FDA become the sole judges of how much and what kind of testing takes place. It is well known that the FDA has become something of a scandal in that by minimising type I errors of approving unsafe drugs, they maximise type II errors of failing to approve beneficial substances.

While it still may not be convincing to argue that there should be no governmental oversight for product health and safety, it should be recognised that there are market alternatives that avoid some of the disadvantages of regulation. For example, in the past, voluntary testing agencies and certification processes have emerged in unregulated markets to overcome informational inadequacies. Such institutions would be likely to flourish in a regime where government is not expected to be the sole guarantor of a perfect world. The crucial difference between government regulation and market-certifying institutions is that the voluntary nature of market institutions will neither oversupply information and safety, nor will the discovery process be hampered by mandated standards or disclosure laws.

Conclusion

Given their doctrinal history, Austrians have spent more time developing theories of markets than they have analysing the theory of and costs of regulation. They have provided generalised insights into the relative workings and limitations of market and government that can usefully be applied to analysing real-world regulatory issues. Their emphasis on both process and knowledge in human affairs could prove extraordinarily fruitful in understanding both the history and the potential gains and losses from regulation. Now, if Austrians wish to be useful to contemporary debate, it would make sense for them to carry their abstract insights into more empirical studies of market processes and of government 'intervention' in those processes. Since Austrian theory does not support the contention that markets are perfect in any substantive way, Austrian policy analysis cannot be avoided. But with no theory of market perfection to attempt to duplicate with carefully designed regulation, Austrian policy analysis can only be an exercise in comparative institutional analysis. If the market is to be superseded by some governmental rule or decree, what is the likely consequence of government activity versus the likely consequences of no government? What are the systematic tendencies in political versus market orders and how do these tendencies contribute to wealth creation and the satisfying of consumer demand?

Others have also argued for policy to be the product of comparative institutional analysis, but the Austrian contribution is that in making the institutional comparisons, it is important to take not only incentive structures into account, but also the epistemic character of both markets and government. The knowledge problems in markets and in government could well swamp some incentive problems. This kind of comparative institutional analysis would of necessity be very contextual.

The modern Austrian view of market process is not, as some might hold, necessarily anti-government. It is anti 'productive state' – that is, it implies that when government tries deliberately to create economic value by bypassing or interfering with the market, it is likely to do more harm than good. However, Austrian analysis is perfectly consistent with (indeed, depends upon) a government that punishes criminal violence and fraud, and that supports property and contract.[9] While these functions of government of course add economic value, their primary purpose is not economic in the narrow sense. They are rules of justice that permit markets to flourish. Hayek saw the important connection between economic and political values, and his major work, *Law, Legislation and Liberty*, was his attempt to bring the economy and the polity under one disciplinary umbrella. Austrians would do well to follow Hayek's lead and continue to develop the new principles of political economy.

Notes

1. The articulation of this main difference between Austrian and neo-classical economics was first offered by O'Driscoll and Rizzo (1985).
2. For a fuller exposition of the Austrian approach to economics, see Vaughn, 1994, especially chapters 1 and 8.
3. Erich Streissler's recent discovery of Menger's lectures to Crown Prince Rudolf (Menger, 1994) shows that Menger stressed the importance of low taxes, minimal government interference in private economic activity, and efficient government administration. His message to the future monarch was for government to do no harm to the economy.
4. However, *The Road to Serfdom* (1944), a work Hayek regarded as polemical rather than scientific, does examine some related issues in his attack on economic planning. There, building on Mises's argument about creeping interventionism, Hayek took up the political as well as the economic consequences of government planning. He came to the conclusion that even benign attempts to introduce economic planning will lead to a cumulative process of more and more controls that would finally resolve itself in total authoritarian control of the economy and in political despotism.
5. In Rothbard's case his neglect of externalities in his welfare economics is backed up by his natural rights view of property. The right to property is absolute. Any trespass upon one's property is a legal offence that is best remedied by a court of law. Hence, third-

party effects that deprive someone of lawful use of his property is not so much an economic as it is a legal problem, and should be handled on a case-by-case basis (*Man, Economy and State*).

6. In fact, this was Menger's claim (1981). He argued that the progress of economic development was a process of moving from monopolies to more and more competitive markets as the extent of the market expanded and as knowledge grew.

7. Consider nutritional labelling once again. There undoubtedly was a market segment in the United States demanding nutritional labelling on packaged foods, evidenced by the increasing number of food suppliers who labelled their foods voluntarily before it was required. However, after the nutritional labelling became mandatory, everyone, including people who sold food at farmers' markets and those who provided speciality foods prepared in their own homes, were required to have their products analysed for nutritional labelling. This was a costly regulation to those small and often sporadic producers while the benefit to the public was minimal (and the demand close to non-existent).

8. While this line of argument suggests that in most cases (except, perhaps, where there are overwhelmingly urgent public safety factors at stake) mandated standards are either superfluous or counterproductive, this does not exclude some information-gathering role for government. Again, one might ask why private information agencies would not respond to consumer demand, but it is possible that in some cases, there is an important public goods component to product knowledge. In any case, one could imagine government providing product or producer information via voluntary certification processes or via some variation of the chamber of commerce.

9. Obviously, the interaction of property and contract law with the market economy is a complex and difficult issue. This suggests that a full Austrian approach to economic regulation dig deep into law and economics.

Bibliography

Demsetz, Harold, 'Information and Efficiency: Another Viewpoint', *Journal of Law and Economics*, 12, 1, March 1969, 1–22.

Hayek, Friedrich A. (1944) *The Road to Serfdom*. Chicago: The University of Chicago Press.

—— (1948) *Individualism and Economic Order*. Chicago: The University of Chicago Press.

—— (1978) 'Competition as a Discovery Procedure', in *New Studies in Philosophy, Politics and Economics*. Chicago: University of Chicago Press.

—— (1973, 1976, 1979) Law, *Legislation and Liberty*. 3 vols. Chicago: University of Chicago Press.

Kirzner, Israel (1973) *Competition and Entrepreneurship*. Chicago: University of Chicago Press.

—— (1979) *The Perils of Regulation: A Market Process Approach*. A LEC Occasional Paper. Coral Gables, Fla: Law and Economics Center at University of Miami School of Law.

Menger, Carl (1981 [1871]) *Principles of Economics*. Translated by James Dingwall and Bert F. Hoselitz. New York: New York University Press.

—— (1994) *Carl Menger's Lectures to Crown Prince Rudolf of Austria*. Edited by Erich W. and Monika Streissler. Translated by Monika Streissler and David F. Good. Hants, England: Edward Elgar.

Mises, Ludwig von (1935 [1920]) 'Economic Calculation in the Socialist Commonwealth', in F.A. Hayek, *Collectivist Economic Planning*. London: George Routledge and Sons pp. 87–103.

—— (1981 [1922]) *Socialism*. Indianapolis: Liberty Classics.

—— (1963 [1949]) *Human Action: a Treatise on Economics*. New Haven, Conn.: Yale University Press.

O'Driscoll, Gerald P. and Mario J. Rizzo (1985) *The Economics of Time and Ignorance*. Oxford: Basil Blackwell.

Posner, Richard A. 'The Social Cost of Monopoly and Regulation', *Journal of Political Economy*, August, 1975, 807–27.

Rothbard, Murray (1956) 'Toward a Reconstruction of Utility Theory', in Mary Sennholz, ed. *On Freedom and Free Enterprise: Essays in Honor of Ludwig von Mises*. Princeton: D. van Nostrand Company. pp. 224–62.

—— (1962) *Man, Economy and State*. 2 vols. Princeton: D. Van Nostrand Company.

Vaughn, Karen I., 'Economic Calculation Under Socialism: the Austrian Contribution', *Economic Inquiry*, 18, October 1980, 535–54.

—— *Austrian Economics in America: the Migration of a Tradition*. Cambridge and New York: Cambridge University Press, 1994.

7
The Politics of Regulation

Lutz Mez and Atle Midttun

Regulation of economic activity and industrial sectors has both the scale and scope to figure prominently in politics as well as in the political science debate for a number of reasons.

Firstly, many industrial sectors under reregulation are *core infrastructure*, upon which both private and industrial users rely heavily. Industrial sectors like electricity, gas, railway and other transport sectors, telecommunication, postal services and so on, were generally organised as utilities to provide a secure, cheap and reliable public service. It was indeed seen as a core task for any modernising industrial economy to make such infrastructure services available to all end-user segments throughout the nation.

Secondly, regulation of core infrastructure affects some of the *largest capital stock invested*. The utilities thus administrate immense economic assets. Economic power also often translates into political power and we regularly find infrastructure industry capturing determinant positions in the policy arena from where it is frequently able to control its political environment.

Thirdly, many industrial sectors involve development and employment of *advanced and controversial technologies* which often attracts environmental opposition and local protest. The energy sector is a good example. In many countries the anti-nuclear movements brought energy issues prominently onto the national political agenda and blocked many of the ambitious nuclear programmes. In a later phase more general questions of environmental pollution have been at the top of the political agenda.

Fourthly, regulatory intervention in the economy often requires collective action orchestrated by political institutions. *The competence and capacity of the political government to orchestrate collective action* is therefore also of central concern in industrial regulation. The highly political character of regulation is illustrated by the fact that regulation in many cases is regarded as constitutive of the political state itself. According to Wittfogel (1962), all ancient high cultures became states by water regulation, the water supply civil servants were the first state administration, and the bureaucracy as a special class appeared in this context.[1]

For these and other reasons regulation is generally not only a simple optimisation problem to be left to regulation experts, but also a set of issues with high symbolic content, large vested interests and extensive public attention. The shaping of technological choices and regulatory regimes is therefore likely to be strongly influenced by political forces, and a political science analysis should, therefore, supplement technical and economic regulation theory both in spelling out normative solutions and analysing future developments.

This chapter elaborates on some of the most important themes and issues in regulation that confront political decision-making and administrative implementation, as seen from a political science perspective. The following discussion is focused on four points.

Firstly, recent discussions in political science and political sociology have raised the theme of *complexity* to the forefront of the regulatory debate. With the increasing complexity of society, some writers discard the possibility of rational regulatory intervention altogether. Others take a less absolutist position and assume that rational policy intervention is possible although in a modified form. The chapter therefore starts out by highlighting some of the relevant politological issues and positions on complexity and political governance through regulation.

Secondly, as one of the core functions of politics is to legitimate *collective, regulatory action* when faced with societal needs that cannot be fulfilled individually, the chapter also takes up the classical issue of legitimation. This issues is central whether collective action is taken by traditional public authorities or by regulatory intervention. Referring to the extensive political science debate on democratic and corporate legitimation, the chapter focuses on legitimation both *vis à vis* the general public and organised interests.

Thirdly, generating collective action at the societal level involves capacity-building to *efficiently and effectively implement collective public policies*. A major issue, closely related to the two former points is therefore the question of operative state capacity, when confronted with regulatory needs. The chapter, therefore, also discusses the implementation capacity involving the mechanisms of internal governance.

In a final section, the chapter presents some concluding reflections on the implications of the political science approach to regulation.

Regulation and complexity

The move away from direct operative political intervention in infrastructure-systems to more indirect regulation of competitively exposed infrastructure companies in Europe can in many respects be seen as a response to the increased complexity of modern society. Governance, regulation and complexity is not a new theme in political science, however. The notion that modern society is becoming more and more complex and that this will have severe influence on the role of the State was already discussed in sociology and political science at the change of the century (for example Simmel, 1900; Weber, 1947), and has more recently been followed up by Parsons (1964) and Luhmann (1989).

The political science literature discusses complexity under several headings such as: *functional differentiation* of the economy and society; *innovation and dynamic growth under uncertainty*; and *internationalisation, transnationalisation and globalisation* of the economy.

Regulation and functional differentiation

The theme of functional differentiation of society has been a fundamental theme in modern sociology, ever since classics like Weber (1947) and Simmel (1900). Simmel's distinction between 'Gemeinschaft' and 'Gesellschaft' captures the depersonalising of personal relationships in modern society, which was again a precondition for modern functional differentiation (Simmel, 1900). Weber's conceptualisation of fundamentals of formal organisation through his analysis of bureaucracy highlighted the preconditions for modern complex organisation of both public regulation and firms (Weber, 1947).

Taking as a point of departure Parson's definition of regulation as a combined specification of rights to facilities and to system access, the late modern challenge of regulation of complexity can be addressed at two levels. At the economic level, the focus is on the process of allocation of resources and balancing of advantages and costs within a given institutional role-structure. At the political level, Parsons focuses on power relations within the institutional system, including the broader aspect of settlement of terms. At both levels, complexity and uncertainty pose extensive challenges to modern regulation.

Building on Parsons, Luhmann (1989) argues that each society, especially modern society, is based on the increase of diversity at both levels, and therefore per definition defies regulation. Faced with society's increase of diversity, regulation and control, as Luhmann sees it, we run into two problems: simultaneousness and differentiation.

The simultaneousness problem has to do with the fact that during regulation in one area, billions of other events take place simultaneously. The relationship between all these factors is unknown and the regulator is therefore unable to intervene in a rational manner. The differentiation problem has to do with the fact that regulation has to reproduce differences between the system and the environment, to guarantee an 'open' future.

Luhmann does not, however, argue for abolishing regulation, but for developing regulatory approaches which are capable of mapping evolving complexity and interacting adequately with continuously differentiating systems. Most probably, self-regulatory and communicative forms of regulation would here have a central place.

In reply to Luhmann's critique of regulation, Fritz W. Scharpf has taken a modified rationalistic position. Scharpf (1989, p. 22) argues that political regulation is possible due to constellations of collective or corporate actors, who control a certain share of regulatory resources. The capability of taking the other actors' interests into consideration here plays a decisive role. Some direction is given to the outcome of negotiations by firstly the state's own participation, and secondly by the threat of authoritative regulation if negotiations fail. Scharpf's (1992) negotiated model – in the shadow of hierarchy – therefore in practice may come close to traditional regulation.

A number of authors take a middle position in this debate, stressing possibilities of mediation between centralistic societal regulation and self-regulation of autonomous subsystems. Schuppert's (1995) concept of the state as a moderator is one example. Renate Mayntz's (1987) term of the co-operative state and Willke's (1983) approach of decentral contextualisation are other examples.

As a concrete example of increasing complexity that challenges modern governance, we can today observe functional broadening of companies' activities across sectors following the deregulation of European infrastructure sectors. This tends to create an asymmetry between commercial and regulatory organisation, which is traditionally mono-sector oriented. One regulatory response to cope with increasingly broader strategic configuration may be to broaden the regulator's mandate. The emergence of new broader multi-sector regulators (for example the British regulator for electricity and gas) is a case in point. Another possible solution may be to lean back on general competition regulation.

However, even abandoning sector regulation to competition regulation is no easy way out. The multi-sector complexity of advanced strategic business configuration challenges even competition-regulation to assess the strategic interaction-effects of cross-sector engagements. Furthermore, regulation must remain 'light' as it might otherwise become a cost-burden as well as an unnecessary limitation on commercial experimentation. In highly technologically complex sectors like telecommunication, technical complexity has led to a 'negotiated' type of regulation, where regulatory authorities act more and more on a casuistic basis after informal hearings. However, this may, from a political point of view create a new form of 'super corporatism' which threatens to undermine basic decision-making and role allocations in constitutional democracies. The management of post/late modern functional complexity thus raises fundamental challenges when it comes to balancing commercial and political concerns.

Regulation and dynamic configuration

The need for strategic, dynamic reconfiguration raises extensive challenges both at the firm and regulatory authority levels. At the firm level the challenge is to achieve organisational, functional and techno-logical innovation to be dynamically efficient in the long run and at the same time secure cost efficiency in an increasingly competitive market economy. Balancing the short-run cost efficiency against the long-run dynamic innovation is also a challenge at the regulatory level, as it implies basic uncertainty about the effects of regulatory strategies and striking a balance between two seemingly irreconcilable theoretical worlds.

On the one hand, regulation designed to enhance static efficiency thus means establishing incentives to push companies as far as possible in productivity within given resource and technological constraints. Under such conditions, rule-based arms-length regulation may be a highly efficient regulatory form.

On the other hand, as implied in the very concept, dynamic efficiency focuses on a dynamically shifting sequence of optima resulting from new technological and organisational knowledge, where these theoretical optima cannot possibly be fully defined. In Schumpeter's (1943) perspective, economics and economic regulation with a dynamic focus, should therefore be more concerned with disequilibrium and creative destruction than with marginalistic equilibrium analysis. With their rejection of the equilibrium concept and concentration on a dynamic process perspective, the Austrian understanding establishes a fundamental indeterminateness of economic activity that defies any concept of equilibrium and thus of optimality (Ioannides, 1992).

The radical uncertainty and the dynamic focus make the Austrian approach process-oriented and concerned with innovation and learning. As dynamic innovation presents the economic actors with radical uncertainty, the Austrian tradition is therefore less willing than neoclassics to take up strong deductively-based normative positions. This acknowledgement, for many Austrians, leads to a rather restrictive position on regulation as illustrated by Vaughn (this volume). To the Austrians the process perspective and the derived indeterminateness assumption imply that the market systems constitute a self-regulating order which does not require specific economic regulation, except for the institutional arrangements of the liberal state.

Referring back to Parson's distinctions, economic and political science theory here play complementary roles. Economic theory, although ambiguously, seeks to understand firm behaviour and effects of regulatory strategies on firm behaviour. Political science, on the other hand, seeks to specify adequate institutional/organisational forms that facilitate the chosen regulatory strategy. Clearly the institutional/organisational form will differ extensively if the task shifts from regulating static to dynamic efficiency. Under dynamic efficiency, the institutional set-up must probably be more procedural and learning-oriented (Delorme, 1996).

Regulation and internationalisation

Internationalisation and transnationalisation imply that the scope of commercial activity expands beyond the regulatory competency of the nation state. This undermines the state's ability to set authoritative regulatory boundaries for commercial activity as it must engage in complex negotiations with other states over intern.

The major driving forces behind internationalisation of regulation come from globalisation of industry and consumption. As argued by Kenichi Ohmae (1985, 1995), industry, investment, individuals and information at the end of the twentieth century flow relatively unimpeded across national borders. In this situation he argues, the strategies of modern, multinational companies are no longer shaped and conditioned by reasons of state, but rather, by the desire – and the need

– to serve attractive markets wherever they exist and to tap attractive pools of resources wherever they sit.

Ohmae here advances a general functional argument, which draws on classical market-selection principles in combination with classical scale and scope arguments, where international trends and opportunities override the influence of national regulation. Ohmae claims that the driving forces towards globalisation are financial, technological and commercial. As he sees it, the global orientation of financial sources will tend to favour globally converging firms. Furthermore, the global markets for technology, investment and consumers favour companies that can establish global presence. The rapid innovation necessary to keep pace with advanced technical opportunities favours companies that can distribute technological development costs over global sales. Similarly, world-scale presence may also make it easier to support the enormous marketing and branding costs that are seen as necessary to differentiate high-quality products.

A competing path dependency and national styles literature argues that national differences in strategic orientation may reproduce themselves even under international competitive conditions (Whitley, 1992; Campbell, Hollingsworth and Lindblom, 1991; Orrù, 1994). However, they do not necessarily support the idea of sovereign national regulation.

Paradoxically, while national industrial 'milieus' draw on specific traditions and competence in their national surroundings, the nation state may increasingly be losing sovereign regulatory power. As trade barriers are removed under international deregulation and negotiations, even the sectors that base themselves heavily on national resources and traditions may find themselves competing internationally, and regulatory authorities will have to take international repercussions into consideration, thereby undermining their sovereignty.

As argued by Majone (1996) governance at the international level is likely to be indirect and market- rather than direct and plan-oriented. The reasons for this, he argues, lie in the limited legitimacy carried at the federal or EU level compared to the nation state. The EU has neither the cultural capital nor the taxation possibilities of the national state. Given this governance deficit, strong interventionist governance from the European level would quickly lose legitimacy and inevitably run into conflict with the diverse interests of the European nation states. A European regime must, in other words, be liberal, because this is the minimum common denominator which European states may, at most, agree upon.

The European Commission has learnt, through painful retreats in the case of the energy directives (Midttun, 1997) that it can only reach control through indirect market-forces. However, by gradually exposing European industry to European market competition, the European Union is de facto expropriating the interventory power of the nation state and eroding its control over the electricity sector.

Companies spreading out across national boundaries in Europe support the process of Europeanisation of the economy by stimulating the transfer of de facto regulatory power to the European level. By doing this they acquire some sheltering from national regulation, and come under a more general European regime. As argued by Jurewitz (2001), this is quite parallel to US practice, where energy companies are divesting within states and investing across states to come under federal regulation.

The strong interventionist and even operative nation state is in other words not likely to reproduce itself at the international level. Internationalisation therefore implies a move from stronger and more directly governed nation states to weaker federal-like indirect governance. Governance, for example at the European level, is therefore critically dependent on the success of regulatory and not etatist intervention. If market-oriented regulatory intervention fails, then Europeanisation will easily run into 'state failure', since there is no European etatist alternative in sight.

Regulation and political legitimation

In terms of Parsons' previously quoted distinction between economic and political aspects of regulation, the latter concerns establishing the institutional context and mobilising the power behind regulatory intervention. Industrial regulation often involves large investments in core infrastructures with controversial technologies. Mobilising political legitimation behind regulatory intervention is therefore often conflictual and the establishment of regulatory authorities with sufficient mandate to act efficiently on society's behalf is not a trivial matter, seen from a political point of view.

Besides legitimating regulatory intervention as such, striking a balance between general and specific interests also poses a major legitimation dilemma, particularly as these interests have unequal organisational capacity with respect to influencing regulatory decisions. We shall therefore discuss the challenges to political legitimation of regulation both with respect to the general public and specific stakeholders, as well as the difficult trade-off between them.

Democratic and corporatist legitimation of regulation

Democratic legitimation of regulatory intervention, under parliamentary democracy, fundamentally falls back on the principle that regulatory authorities or their supervisory department are responsible to the elected assembly for their actions. Parliamentary government is 'responsible government' in so far as ministers may have to resign if they are judged by parliament to have taken regulatory measures that imply mishandling of their departments (Birch, 1964).

However, it has been argued that formally democratically mandated regulation of (for example) complex infrastructure requires highly specialised skills and detailed knowledge of, and intimate involvement with, the regulated activity. These requirements support rather autonomous regulatory agencies that enjoy a certain freedom from immediate political supervision to pursue independent expert-driven strategies.

Evidently, some of the arguments for preferring independent regulatory bodies go against direct democratic answerability. However, the proponents of independent regulatory bodies argue that the separateness from government departments is necessary to free them from party political influence. This again provides greater continuity and stability than cabinets because they are one step removed from election returns (Majone, 1996). In the US, where regulation has a longer history than in Europe, there is, accordingly, a tendency to see 'the regulatory branch' developing as a fourth branch of government (besides the executive (government); the rule-making (Parliament) and the courts).

In order to compensate for the 'democratic deficit' implied by expert-dominated regulation, regulatory practice in the US has favoured public participation and given opportunity for consultation by means of public hearings. The involvement of multiple agencies with mandates and interests related to various sides of the issue is also seen as a guarantee against biased decisions. Gormley calls this the 'surrogate representation model' (Gormley 1982, p. 299). In the late 1970s many state governments set up proxy advocacy offices in order to represent consumer interests in regulatory commission proceedings. Proxy advocates work for the government, but represent the needs of citizens.

However a large literature on regulatory capture casts doubt as to whether these measures are sufficient to secure public interests. Capture theory, which was developed in the 1950s and 1960s, explains 'administrative and regulatory decisions as responses to external pressure, exerted primarily and sometimes exclusively by regulated industries'

(Gormley, 1982, p. 298). This literature argues that industrial sectors expect government to set framework conditions, where profits can be maximised, and points out that in return, the regulated industry provides votes and campaign resources for political candidates and parties.

The neocorporatist literature, which also focuses on interest intermediation through close industry–government relations, puts greater emphasis on the role of interest organisations and deeper societal and political conflicts when explaining industrial regulation (Streeck and Schmitter, 1985). The main thrust of the neocorporatist literature has been concerned with negotiated economic governance at the macrolevel, however, later work within the neocorporatist tradition (Cawson, 1985) has also shown greater interest for sectoral arenas. In both cases the argument is that industrial regulation tends to create internal policy-arenas where the main actors are organisations that represent, regulate and defend sectoral interests (for example Mayntz, 1996, p. 151).

The result is seen to be a functional fragmentation of societal governance to relatively autonomous sectoral decision-making arenas, where market-based, politically-based and administratively-based institutions are sectorally oriented in their decision-making and tend to overrule general societal interests (Olsen, 1988).

Legitimation and organisation of interests

One of the reasons for the strong position of vested interests is that such interests are often organised with specific reference to the field of regulatory action. They are also strongly motivated to bias the regulation because as employees, special clients or as specialised interest groups, they have large stakes in the regulation outcomes (Figure 7.1). Vested interests are, in other words, not only specifically organised to voice their interests, but also often specifically affected. For this reason, policy-legitimation *vis à vis* vested interests is often more specific in character, and is usually conducted through extensive negotiation, partly through informal and rather specific channels. In spite of pluralistic attempts to make up for the 'democratic imbalance' by postulating interventory opportunity for all affected interests, the fundamental payoff matrix in Figure 7.1, therefore still remains, and gives the various interests very different payoffs and hence motivation and ability to put resources into influencing regulatory decisions.

The result from bias in favour of vested interests is that democratic regulation according to parliamentary–constitutional rules suffers from the fact that only very seldom do broad societal 'majorities' have the resources and time necessary to compete with organised vested interests

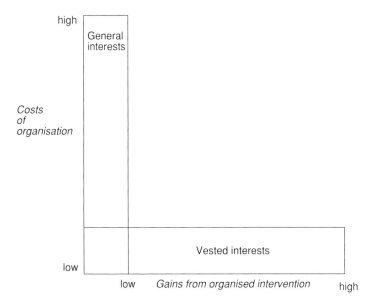

Figure 7.1   Costs and Gains from public regulation for vested interests and the public at large

over particular regulation policies. Their situation with respect to gains and costs of active participation is generally more or less the inverse of that of the vested interests (Figure 7.1). Their organisational costs are large, and their gain from favourable sector regulation for each carrier of the societal interest is very small.

The situation may, however, change if general interests succeed in defining regulatory intervention in general policy terms. Through policy escalation, regulatory issues may, in such cases, be brought up on the national political arena, implying that problem-definitions and implications will be drawn at a higher level and related to generalised political preferences, as expressed in party policies and general political ideologies.

Although regulation will often primarily be legitimated at the sectoral level, with a dominant influence of vested interests, there is always a potential threat that democratic–constitutional intervention may be reinforced through symbolic escalation. In this way, 'low politics', which tends to be channelled through specialised channels, may be transformed to 'high politics' where general interests come more into focus in the general political arena.

In such processes mass media often have a crucial role in influencing 'public opinion' which in the next round may become an important resource of power. Beside the traditional check and balance system of a democratic society by three divided powers: government, parliament and courts, the mass media have been characterised as the fourth power. By taking on a disputed regulatory decision media may increase the transparency of decision- and policy-making and serve to strengthen public control of elected personnel in administration and state apparatus. The media thereby limit the closure of corporate decision-making and may be instrumental in bringing issues to the democratic arena.

Regulation and implementation

While legitimation concerns support for the general thrust of a policy or regulatory strategy, implementation concerns the instrumentation and detailed operative procedures implied in putting the regulatory policy or strategy into practice. Like legitimation, implementation of regulation is confronted with the complexity problem both in terms of functional and dynamic complexity. However regulatory implementation is also confronted with the internal complexity of the State apparatus itself. When technologies are changing, and/or social conditions and/or opinions are being radically reshaped, traditional instruments and regulatory strategies may miss their targets or even worse, have negative unintended consequences. This has caused several German scholars to talk about 'State failure'.

Implementation and state capacity

As already mentioned, implementation fundamentally involves a discussion of state capacity as the conditions for operative regulation are highly dependent on the state's ability and capacity for regulation. A large German literature therefore addresses the regulatory challenge with a central focus on the state, and thereby relates industrial regulation particularly to public institutions. The so-called 'state discussion' (see Schuppert, 1989; Luhmann, 1989; Hartwich, 1989) has in the late 1970s come to focus on the phenomenon of state failure. The term 'state failure' was coined by the political scientist Jänicke (1979 and 1990), the economist Recktenwald (1978) and the constitutional lawyer von Arnim (1987), mainly as a response to the inability of the state to deal with environmental problems in industrialised countries.

Notably Jänicke (1990) distinguishes different forms of state failure:

- The renunciation of political shaping and preventive intervention towards societal challenges and problems which he calls 'political failure of the state'
- The diseconomy of the excessive price of public goods which he terms 'economic failure of the state' and
- Missing effectiveness of state activity, which he calls 'the functional failure of the state'.

It follows from this literature that it is either necessary to develop strategies for reducing or neutralising political, economic and societal resistance, in order to empower the state or, in situations where unilateral strong state intervention is unfeasible, to develop implementation by negotiation and mediation. In spite of a certain belief in a moderate restoration of the state (Evans et al., 1985) the strongest emphasis in today's international economy seems to be on negotiation and mediation. As already mentioned, Fritz W. Scharpf (1989, p. 22) put forward the thesis that political regulation is only possible today if one recognises that in most situations constellations of collective or corporative actors dispose over a certain share of regulatory resources. Mediation, and the capability of taking the other actors' interests into consideration are therefore decisive. Similarly Renate Mayntz (1987, p. 22) has pointed out that without taking the subjects of political action into consideration, political regulation can hardly be expected to lead to purposeful social change.

Implementation tools

At a more specific level, the allocation of implementation tools to regulatory tasks is a core issue in the political science literature, but authors make different typologies of implementation strategies and implementation tools.

Theodore Lowi (1964) distinguishes between four sets of general policy-orientations or 'tool bags': distributive, regulative, redistributive and constitutive policy. Lowi's classification scheme is based on the mode of enforcement.

Schneider and Ingram (1990, p. 514) worked out five policy tools: authority tools, incentive tools, capacity tools, symbolic and hortatory tools, and learning tools.

According to Ayres and Braithwaite (1990, p. 39), the enforcement strategies of the state include: command regulation with nondiscretionary punishment; command regulation with discretionary punishment; enforced self-regulation; and self-regulation.

All typologies indicate that regulatory authorities are faced with a fairly rich repertoire of regulatory tools and need to make some fundamental choices in their implementation strategy. Some of those choices can be grouped along a familiar market–hierarchy axis: authority tools (hierarchic-oriented) versus incentive tools (market-oriented). However other tools are also grouped around other dimensions. Schneider and Ingram's symbolic tools, learning tools as well as Braithwaite's self-regulation, point at autonomous regulatory processes, more or less outside the domain of public authorities altogether. These tools may in principle be administered by private hierarchies such as industrial associations, or by direct signalling in the market.

As shown by Midttun (1999) it may be argued that 'softer' self-regulation in practice may be more efficient than strong authoritative governance, particularly in international transactions where diverse national interests only leave room for very limited authoritative intervention. Yet, it is perhaps the interface between 'strong' authoritative and 'soft' voluntary regulation that provides some of the most promising perspectives on regulation. A case in point is what Ayres and Braithwaite call the enforced self-regulation model which focuses on negotiation occurring between the state and individual firms to establish regulations that are particularised to each firm. Each firm in an industry is required to propose its own regulatory standards if it is to avoid harsher (and less tailored) standards imposed by the state. Seen from the point of view of the individual firm, self-regulation is 'enforced' in two senses. First, the firm is required by the state to do the self-regulation. Second, the privately written rules can be publicly enforced (Ayres and Braithwaite 1990, p. 101). However, the possibility of tailoring the regulation specifically to each firm, if successful, provides a promise of stronger regulatory performance at lower costs than by other means.

Implementation as a learning process

The complexity of regulation, particularly under limited state capacity, has motivated some political scientists to look at implementation as a learning process. Early proponents of this approach took an explicit systems-theoretical point of departure. Norbert Wiener (1948, 1961) was apparently the first to introduce the term cybernetics for the analysis of regulation and control processes in society. He here drew on a general conceptual apparatus which was developed as a comparative scientific approach to explain regulatory processes in biology, technology and sociology. Following Wiener, Karl W. Deutsch (1966) conceptualises governance and regulation as a learning process in an explicit systems-theoretical perspective. Deutsch's basic hypothesis was that a social system, hereunder also regulation, can only survive by possessing a certain social learning capacity. Social learning of a political or regulatory system is the precondition for reaching adequate solutions to regulatory problems. More specifically, Deutsch sees learning processes, understood as communication, as being dependent on the structure of information flow, that is the capacity of information channels and the efficiency of regulation and control mechanisms. With inadequate information channels and inefficient regulatory and controlling mechanisms, he argued that the learning process becomes pathological and the regulatory body will not be able to adequately fulfil its tasks.

More recently Sabatier (1986, 1993) has followed up on the learning approach, with a focus on 'advocacy coalitions', where public policy is constituted by the state administration and/or other relevant policy mediators. The distinguished features of this framework are (1) its explicit use of policy subsystems as the aggregate unit of analysis, (2) its focus on advocacy coalitions, and (3) policy-oriented learning as a critical factor in understanding subsystem dynamics (Sabatier, 1987, p. 654).

More specifically, a policy subsystem is defined as the set of actors who are involved in dealing with a policy problem such as air-pollution control, mental health or energy (Sabatier, 1987, p. 659). 'Advocacy coalitions' are people from a variety of positions (elected and agency officials, interest group leaders, researchers) who share a particular belief system – that is, a set of basic values, causal assumptions, and problem perceptions – and who show a non-trivial degree of co-ordinated activity over time (Sabatier, 1987, p. 660).

Policy-oriented learning, in Sabatier's terms, is the process of seeking to realise core policy beliefs until one confronts constraints or opportunities, at which time one attempts to respond to this new situation in a manner that is consistent with the core. Although exogenous events or opponents' activities may eventually force the re-examination of core beliefs, the pain of doing so means that most learning takes the core for granted and directs the learning to the secondary and more pragmatic aspects of a belief system or governmental action programme (Sabatier, 1987, p. 675).

Both with respect to policy development and implementation, the advocacy coalition approach seeks to transcend regulatory obstacles by staging learning co-ordination and consensus-building processes across institutional barriers. As far as co-ordination and consensus-building are concerned, there are clear links between the policy learning perspective and earlier mentioned perspectives that emphasise the importance of negotiation and intermediation in policy implementation.

Concluding remarks and reflections

As we have seen in our previous discussion, taking a political science perspective on regulation implies adding an institutional dimension to the analysis, which allows a parallel discussion of the operative/instrumental and the institutional levels of regulation. Co-ordination between these two levels may prove to be crucial to regulatory efficiency, in so far as the use of certain types of regulatory instruments may only work efficiently within a given institutional context. Or, in other words, the institutional context may predispose for use of certain types of instruments and vice versa.

A case in point, as we have already noted, is the problem of state failure which focuses on the problems of weak or incomplete institutional anchoring of regulatory strategy. In this context, several authors (notably Scharpf, 1989 and Mayntz, 1997, 1998) argue that 'strong' regulatory instruments/strategies may be misplaced and have to be replaced by 'second best' instruments that are more robust to imperfect institutionalisation. Negotiation and learning models and the like belong to this category and exemplify a move into somewhat unclear regulatory terrain, in order to mutually optimise on regulatory instrumentation under weak institutionalisation, given state failure conditions.

We have also shown that in a wider context, the political science perspective is basic to the fundamental reflection about constitutional and democratic dimensions of regulation. The political science perspective here offers an approach to systematic reflection on political legitimation and analysis of implications for political democracy. As a major tool in economic governance, regulation must be evaluated up against basic constitutional and democratic norms. We have already previously noted that regulation is vulnerable to 'democratic deficit' given that there are powerful structural drivers that impede representation of the general public interest in decision-making. From a democracy-theory point of view, a major question is therefore: will regulatory strategies lead to further segmentation and neocorporatist bypass of parliamentary processes, and hence contribute to the democratic deficit? Or do regulatory models create policy-arenas that can substitute for parliamentary political debate? Although it may be difficult to arrive at strong conclusions on these issues, they remain fundamental to the development of democracy under internationalisation and commercialisation.

The political science perspective, however, also has methodological implications for regulatory analysis. Introducing a wider institutional context into the discussion of regulatory instruments increases complexity and makes it more difficult to apply simple analytical techniques. The political science discussion, therefore, tends to move the discussion from a relatively precise analytical level which allows a considerable degree of quantitative optimisation, to a more heuristic level where the analytical approach is subsumed under a larger framework. The greater generality and comprehensiveness of the integrated analysis presumably makes the regulatory decision and/or intervention more relevant and robust, and seems to be in line with new policy research, which has stressed that intended policy outcomes in general are not the outcome of a single optimal instrument, but the result of a mix of different policy instruments (OECD 1997).

Note

1. Damming up water, and the water pipes and lines of Romans and Assyrians, are often mentioned in technology history. But the most prominent case was the well-regulated water economy of China. The construction and building of a channel system, to regulate the water flow and irrigate huge parts of the country and cultivate rice on artificial marshland, created a bureaucracy, the Chinese state as such. This model of political government, based on a technocratic alliance of water supply civil servants and a hierarchy of the bureaucracy under despotic leadership still underlies political governance in many Asiatic countries, and also has been fundamental in shaping European states, and has partially survived in all states.

Bibliography

Arnim, H. von (1987): Staatsversagen: Schicksal oder Herausforderung?, in: *Aus Politik und Zeitgeschichte* B48/1987.

Ayres, Ian and John Braithwaite (1990) *Responsive Regulation: Transcending the Deregulation Debate*, New York: Oxford University Press.

Birch, Anthony Harold (1964) *Representative and Responsible Government, an Essay on the British Constitution*, London: Allen and Unwin.

Campbell, Hollingsworth and Lindblom (1991) *Governance of the American Economy*, Cambridge: Cambridge University Press.

Cawson, Alan (ed.) (1985) *Organized Interests and the State: Studies in Meso-Corporatism*, London: Sage.

Delorme, Robert (1996) 'From First Order to Second Order Complexity in Economic Theorizing' Working paper, University of Versailles.

Deutsch, Karl W. (1966) *The Nerves of Government: Models of Political Communication and Control*, New York: The Free Press.

Evans, Peter B., Dietrich Rueschemeyer and Theda Skocpol (1985) *Bringing the State Back In*. Cambridge: Cambridge University Press.

Gormley, William (1982) Alternative Models of the Regulatory Process: Public Utility Regulation in the States, in: *Western Political Quarterly*, vol. 35, 297–317.

Hartwich, Hans-Hermann (ed.) (1989) *Macht und Ohnmacht politischer Institutionen, Tagungsbericht*, Opladen: Westdeutscher Verlag.

Ioannides, Stavros (1992) *The Market, Competition, and Democracy: a Critique of Neo-Austrian Economics*, Aldershot: E. Elgar.

Jänicke, Martin (1979) *Wie das Industriesystem von seinen Mißständen profitiert*, Opladen: Westdeutscher Verlag.

Jänicke, Martin (1990) *State Failure. The Impotence of Politics in Industrial Society*, Cambridge: Polity Press.

Jurewitz, John (2001) Business Strategies Evolving in Response to Regulatory Changes in US Electric Power Industry, in: Midttun, A. (ed.) *European Energy Industry Business Strategies*, London: Elsevier.

Lowi, Theodore J. (1964) American Business, Public Policy, Case Studies, and Political Theory, in: *World Politics*, vol. 16, 676–715.

Luhmann, Niklas (1989) Politische Steuerung: Ein Diskussionsbeitrag, in: H.-H. Hartwich (ed.): *Macht und Ohnmacht politischer Institutionen*, Opladen: Westdeutscher Verlag, 12–16.

Majone, Giandomenico (ed.) (1996) *Regulating Europe*, London: Routledge.

Mayntz, Renate (1987) Politische Steuerung und gesellschaftliche Steuerungsprobleme – Anmerkungen zu einem theoretischen Paradigma, in: Thomas Ellwein et al. (eds): *Jahrbuch zur Staats- und Verwaltungswissenschaft*, Bd. 1, 89–110.

Mayntz, Renate (1996) Politische Steuerung: Aufstieg, Niedergang und Transformation einer Theorie, in: Klaus v. Beyme, Claus Offe (eds) *Politische Theorien in der Ära der Transformation*, Opladen: Westdeutscher Verlag, 148–68.

Mayntz, Renate (1997) *Soziale Dynamik und politische Steuerung. Theoretische und methodologische Überlegungen*, Frankfurt/M.: Campus.

Mayntz, Renate (1998) New Challenges to Governance Theory, *Jean Monnet Chair Papers* 50, Florence.

Midttun, Atle (ed.) (1997) *European Electricity Systems in Transition.* London: Elsevier Science.

Midttun, Atle (1999) 'The Weakness of Strong Governance and the Strength of Soft Regulation: Environmental Governance in Postmodern Form', in: *Innovation* vol. 12, no. 2.

OECD (1997) *Regulatory Reform in OECD Countries*, Paris: OECD.

Ohmae, Kenichi (1985) *Triad Power: the Coming Shape of Global Competition*, New York: Free Press.

Ohmae, Kenichi (1995) *The End of the Nation State: the Rise of Regional Economics*, New York: Free Press.

Olsen, Johan P. (1988) 'Administrative Reforms and Theories of Organizations', in: Campbell, Colin, B., Guy Peters (eds): *Organizing Governance – Governing Organizations*, Pittsburgh: Pittsburgh Press.

Orrù, Marco (1994) 'The Faces of Capitalism' Paper presented at the Sixth Annual International Conference on Socio-Economics. HEC. Paris.

Parsons, Talcott (1964) *The Social System*, New York: The Free Press.

Recktenwald, H.C. (1978) Unwirtschaftlichkeit im Staatssektor. Elemente einer Theorie des ökonomischen Staats'versagens', in: *Hamburger Jahrbuch für Wirtschafts- und Gesellschaftspolitik*, Tübingen, 155–66.

Sabatier, Paul A. (1986) Top–down and Bottom–up Approaches of Policy Implementation: A Critical Analysis and Suggested Synthesis, in: *Journal of Public Policy*, 6, 21–48.

Sabatier, Paul (1987) Knowledge, Policy-Oriented Learning, and Policy Change – An Advocacy Coalition Framework, in: *Knowledge: Creation, Diffusion, Utilization*, vol. 8, no. 4, June 1987, Sage Publications.

Sabatier, Paul and Hank Jenkins-Smith (1993) *Policy Change and Learning: An Advocacy Coalition Approach*, Boulder, CO: Westview Press.

Scharpf, Fritz W. (1989) Politische Steuerung und Politische Institutionen, in: H.-H. Hartwich (ed.): *Macht und Ohnmacht politischer Institutionen*, Opladen: Westdeutscher Verlag, 17–29.

Scharpf, Fritz W. (1992) Die Handlungsfähigkeit des Staates am Ende des zwanzigsten Jahrhunderts, in: Beate Kohler-Koch (ed.): *Staat und Demokratie in Europa*, Opladen Leske + Budrich, 93–115.

Schneider, Anne and Helen Ingram (1990) Behavioral Assumptions of Policy Tools, in: *Journal of Politics*, vol. 52, no. 2, 510ff.

Schumpeter, Joseph (1943) *Capitalism, Socialism and Democracy*, London: Allen & Unwin.

Schuppert, Gunnar F. (1989) Zur Neubelebung der Staatsdiskussion: Entzauberung des Staates oder 'Bringing the State back in?' in: *Der Staat*, 28. Band, H. 1, 91–104.

Schuppert, Gunnar F. (1995): Rückzug des Staates? Zur Rolle des Staates zwischen Legitimationskrise und politischer Neubestimmung, in: *Die öffentliche Verwaltung*, no. 18, 761–70.

Simmel, Georg 1900, *Philosophie des Geldes*. München: Duncker & Humblot.

Streeck, Wolfgang and Schmitter Philippe C (eds) (1985) *Private Interest Government: Beyond Market and State*, London: Sage.

Weber, Max (1947) *Wirtschaft und Gesellschaft*. Tübingen: J.C.B Mohr.

Whitley, Richard (ed.) (1992) *European Business Systems: Firms and Markets in their National Context*, London: Sage.

Wiener, Norbert (1948) *Cybernetics or Control and Communication in the Animal and the Machine*, New York and London: Technology Press.

Wiener, Norbert (1961) *Cybernetics*, Cambridge, Mass.: MIT Press.

Willke, Helmut (1983) *Entzauberung des Staates. Überlegungen zu einer sozietalen Steuerungstheorie*, Königstein/Taunus: Athennäum.

Wittfogel, K.A. (1962) *Die orientalische Despotie*, Berlin (German edition).

8
Regulatory Reforms in Areas with Multi-level Politicisation

Per Ingvar Olsen

Introduction

Since the neo-liberal wave of the mid-1980s, regulatory reform of the public utility sectors has been put on the agenda in industrialised as well as third-world countries. The main reason for reform can be found in the disapproving economic performance and lack of dynamics in these systems compared to private sector industries and of course in the strength of the ideological wave itself.

One of the sectors that has been put up for reforms is the electricity sector. Some governments are heading for privatisation as the core of their planned reforms, whereas others leave public ownership untouched while reregulating in order to establish a market-based system for electricity supply. In this case, the market is seen as a tool for efficiency improvements within the frameworks of a publicly owned and controlled system. Britain is a prominent example of the privatisation approach, while Norway represents just as clearly the public sector market – or socialist rivalry – alternative.

The two modes of reregulation: privatisation and socialist competition, pose some intriguing challenges to the architects of the new liberal order and to economic theorising. A system based on socialist rivalry, at first glance from the point of view of standard market theory, looks like an anomaly, where the assumed hierarchical control and social welfare preferences of the government within the public sectors is contradicted by the equally assumed atomistic behaviour and profit maximising preferences of firms in competitive markets. Because efficiency by the standard theory is assumed to follow from the profit-oriented attitude of private entrepreneurs, these accordingly ought to hold the position as the residual claimants to the firms' net earnings. Based on this argument, privatisation of ownership becomes a core issue for efficiency improvements.

The polarisation into a public hierarchy with a planned economy and a private market with a competitive economy, is however, challenged by both empirical studies and theorising within fields such as institutional economics, sociology, politology and organisation theory. It has become prevalent to acknowledge that the public sector, to a large extent, is marked by split regulatory and control rights and separated ownership at multiple levels of politicisation, and that public sector resource allocation is subject to negotiated as well as commercial economic rivalry and co-ordinated structuring. This real separation of powers and control rights at multiple levels of politicisation and of multiple sectors within the public part of the economy, seems a necessary precondition for a market to work within a publicly dominated area.

Markets, on the other hand, apart from being marked by atomistic rivalry, have been shown to contain more or less subtle and elegant co-ordinating institutional structures, usually with a distinct hierarchical order and even with the execution of managerial leadership at a sectoral or even cross-sectoral level. In a number of countries, important commercial markets are deeply involved and partly controlled by government or public sector bodies in highly complex interactions ranging from outright public ownership to integrated industrial and commercial co-ordination to R&D integration and funding. The strict duality of standard theory in this respect becomes frustratingly insufficient as an approach to these more complex systems.

Usually, there are convincing arguments for the privatisation of most of the productive sectors in a society. In the case of the utility sectors however, the issue is not obvious. Both the supply side, which is marked by capital intensity, sector specificity of investments and elements of natural monopoly, and the demand side, which is usually specifically domestic and hence vulnerable to national political interventions, raise substantial problems in establishing long-term credible contracting between the privatised utility sectors and their political environments.

These structural features of utility sectors radically address the issue of institutional safeguarding for privately owned firms, who otherwise are likely to be subjects for political hold-ups and undermining of ownership control rights or outright re-expropriations if political conditions are changed. Such safeguarding institutions would typically be partly constitutional and partly international, by, for instance, subscribing to international conventions or agreements like the EU common market law or through international integration of the deregulated markets. Establishing long-term political commitment through the establishment of specific safeguarding institutions, is basically opposed to the political interest in keeping future political options open. The resulting limited political credibility poses important problems on the privatisation alternative.

Faced with a broader menu of structuring alternatives along a continuum of co-ordination–rivalry relationships and with the specific character of the utility systems, the concept of socialist rivalry represents an alternative that potentially might be better able to manage the complexity of challenges raised by the efforts to increase efficiency in these kinds of sectors.

The theoretical approach to socialist competitive markets

At the theoretical level, the concept of socialist rivalry will be approached from the perspectives of economic theories. Leaving aside the simplistic instrumentalist position of neo-classical theory, the perspective is distinctly that of realism. Such economic theories are typically framed within the area of institutional economics – or the efficiency branch of institutional theory – and more narrowly within evolutionary economics. Theories of public sector structures and behaviours typically belong to the non-efficiency branch of institutional theory within areas like sociology, politology and organisation theory – theories that cannot be touched upon here. Of particular interest, is perhaps the public choice theories that can be seen as an extention of neo-classical rational choice theories of market behaviour into a positive theory of public sector behaviours. The public choice perspective, however, will primarily be approached from a diffferent angle, namely that of the selection argument in evolutionary economics.

The evolutionary economic theories are typically concerned with the explanation of dynamics in private markets like, for instance, the classical Chicago School, the various Theories of the Firm and the Austrian economic theories. The ambition of this chapter will be to apply these theories that basically deal with private market systems, the public sector competitive market context, in order to characterise the conditions for, and obstacles to, economic dynamics and efficiency improvements in such a system.

One essential contribution of the classical Chicago school is the application of the Darwinian natural selection argument to economic theorising. According to this idea, efficient firms displace less efficient firms and are permitted to grow by the selective forces of the market, through the allocation of profits. The coupling of natural selection with efficiency however, presupposes that success in tems of survival and growth cannot be achieved by other means than through increased profits from competitive markets, as, for instance, through legislative sheltering or access to tax funding. This raises important considerations on institutional structuring and separation of roles for market selection to be credible within markets where the equity owners, the legislators and the tax monopoly of the state are somehow hierarchically subordinated to the government.

Theories of the firm can be seen as theories that expand the concept of market selection to the organisational level of analysis. In this case, selection is not seen as working upon organisations, but on individuals, routines, structures and so on. The various theories of the firm seem to hold that prevailing routines, structures and individuals within competitive markets are efficient, because otherwise they would have been superseded by more efficient ones. Once again this presupposes that the legislative and tax monopoly of the state is excluded. In a more complex environment, competitive markets, legislative authority and the tax monopoly can all be seen as representing selective elements that work upon the organisation, its individuals, routines, structures and so on. Which of these is most powerful towards given organisations and their individuals, routines and structures clearly depends on the institutional structuring and demarcations of the particular field. Access to the various areas of selection will typically be unequally distributed to institutions as well as to holders of various roles. Given that particular individual incentive structures are simple functions of the sources of selection, this permits us to deduct different incentive structures applied to roles such as managers, public owners, professionals and employees, from the institutional structuring of access to such success-generating sources as the market, legislation and public taxation.

From these arguments, the traditional individual rational choice approach of public choice theories can be reviewed and applied. According to public choice, individuals taking decisions in markets are of equal type to those within public sectors and indeed everywhere else. The selection argument focuses this problem differently. What matters to the individual is to behave so as to be selected by the market, by the legislators and/or by the tax monopoly. To be successful is more at the core of it than to be profit-oriented, even though the ultimate result of success in any case is the accumulation of resource control. A great number of issues matter in this more complex situation, as, for instance, the creation of and maintenance of political legitimacy, the development of professional normative and cognitive powers, the participation in social networks and the creation of powerful lobby organisations.

The solution offered by public choice theorists to the existence of success without efficiency, has been to propose a radical separation with strong safeguarding of institutional borders between legislation and taxation on one hand and any type of economic activity on the other. An important part of this is the need for further specifications of private property rights. Even though I do not hold with the individual rational choice concept in general, suffice to note that for efficiency to be realised in both the selection and the rational choice perspective, an exclusion of the possibility of legislative sheltering and advantageous taxation treatments is necessary.

The socialist rivalry concept in this perspective is, of course, a pragmatic approach to conflicting political objectives. Even so, the cost-efficiency issue is essentially that addressed by public choice theory: How can a sufficiently credible separation of markets from legislative and taxation powers be established within the public sector itself?

The Norwegian electricity market reform experiment

Empirically, the issue will be illustrated by the presentation of a single case: the Norwegian electricity market reform in 1991. The reform introduced competition in generation and supply and a regulated natural monopoly in the transmission and distribution system, without touching upon the ownership issue. The sector has about 70 generating firms and more than 200 suppliers. Most of these are vertically integrated with parts of the grid system: the national grid, regional grids or local grids. The competitive parts of the system are separated from the monopoly part by regulated internal divisionalisation of each electricity firm. Only a very few firms are private. The others belong to the state, the counties or the municipalities.

In accordance with standard economic theory, the normative and cognitive approach to electricity system governance after the Second World War has been that of the integrated public service sector.

Efficiency was expected to follow from state-led co-ordination and public ownership of the electricity companies. Through the representation of social welfare preferences on the side of the owners, and top–down internal structuring and co-ordination, an efficient system was expected to emerge.

Several attempts by the state to centralise and restructure the industry, however, met fierce opposition from local interests, which claimed that their local companies were comparably more efficient than the larger units. The economic model with one integrated public sector turned out not to be compatible with the strong sense of local communalism, local entrepreneurship and local political control rights established in the area from the start of the electrification of the country. Hence, the situation before the new market reform was one of both state-led co-ordination and rivalry between a top–down structuring approach and a bottom–up co-operative approach.

By the late 1980s an intensified effort to integrate and orchestrate an integrated public hierarchy was politically wiped out by the neo-liberal wave. Later to be characterised as an outright revolutionary takeover, a change of paradigms was introduced and a new institutional order was added to the regulative structure. The unfortunate situation of a large number of generating and supply companies, now turned out to be a structural advantage, as the normative focus turned from co-ordination to atomistic rivalry.

The market selection arguments in public sector contexts

The combination of market-oriented regulatory reforms and the maintenance of a dominating public ownership, raises interesting questions related to the conditions under which rivalry, co-ordination and efficiency are related; to the basic structures of situations that rule and govern the interaction of agents in a given field of economic activity. In order to come to grips with these kinds of issues, it is necessary to achieve some understanding of how markets function in a more realist sense, and in particular of what can be said to distinguish private and public sectors as subjects for market reforms and economic regulation and control. In order to do so, I will shortly review some of the classical arguments of evolutionary economics.

The selection arguments of the Chicago School

The selection argument of early evolutionary economics can be said to reveal basic background beliefs of marginalist economists about the way market economies function. It developed partly as a response to critiques by anti-marginalists, who claimed that economic agents do not rationally calculate their actions in terms of marginal analysis, and, therefore, marginal theory is unwarranted as a tool for analysis of real world economies. The neo-classicist answer to this claim is that marginal analysis need not be rejected. It can hold even if entrepreneurs are not rational profit maximisers because the theory is primarily a theory about markets and industries, not of individual firms or individual behaviour.

A.A. Alchian (1950) was the first to argue that marginalist economics is not a theory about the behaviour of individual firms. The contemplations of entrepreneurs are held to be unimportant if not irrelevant in assessing the usefulness of marginalist theory. Alchian argues that rational intentional actions may serve very well to explain behaviour when there is certainty. When there is uncertainty, however, due to imperfect knowledge and incomplete information, profit maximisation fails to be a guide to action. In Alchian's view, uncertainty is pervasive; it is impossible to trace economic efficiency back to deliberate rational actions. What matters is not the deliberations of businessmen, but the profits (or losses) they realise. Impersonal market forces see to it that those who realise positive profits are the survivors; those with losses disappear. In this respect, Alchian proposes to focus directly on results rather than on rational choice. Alchian's selection argument is a process of adoption: the environment (market) adopts survivors whose behaviour turns out to be appropriate. Individual motivation and foresight are sufficient for efficiency to be realised, but are not necessary conditions. However, Alchian does not claim that marginal analysis necessarily holds. He rather takes the position that it may hold, but that we cannot be certain that it does.

M. Friedman (1953) takes a rather similar but to some extent a more radical defence position towards neo-classical marginal analysis. In Friedman's view, the more significant the theory, the more unrealistic its assumptions. This expressive methodological instrumentalist position seems primarily to reflect a personal belief in the usefulness of standard marginal analysis rather than something that is really an outcome of his theories.

Friedman's selection argument is similar to that of Alchian: individual profit maximisation is of no real help in explaining the behaviour of individual firms. The market selection mechanism is a force operating on firms from the outside. The individual intentional forces working inside firms, the motives and contemplations of businessmen, may lead individual firms astray. But this will be corrected in due course by the external force that favours firms that manage to make maximum positive profits over firms that fail to do so. In the long run, the average behaviour of the firms in the industry will approximate the behaviour that is predicted on the basis of the profit maximisation hypothesis. This is a necessary condition for the neo-classical marginal theory to hold.

Friedman seems to hold that natural selection eliminates all firms that do not succeed in making maximum profits. Contrary to Friedman, Alchian does not assume that unbeatable firms will be among the competitors. To him, only tendencies in industry evolution will be similar to the predicted outcome of marginalist theory, whereas Friedman holds that indeed the actual outcome is similar to those predictions. Every individual firm is consistent with that theory. Whether firms are engaged in profit maximising or not, economic natural selection sees to it that each surviving individual firm displays behaviour that is consistent with maximisation.

G.S. Becker (1962) is a third neo-classical economist who set out to defend marginal theory from the position of market selection theory, and to provide a better validation of the market selection argument of Alchian. He argues that the theorems of marginal theory hold also when individuals exhibit irrational behaviour. The generating principles underlying neo-classical theorems are taken by Becker to be shifts in opportunities of individuals. Households and firms are forced to respond to changes in opportunities in the way that is asserted in the theorems of modern economics, regardless and independent of the decision rule they use. However, the decisions of irrational firms are restricted by budget constraints. The opportunities to behave irrationally are, accordingly, limited. From this position, Becker argues that changes in resource constraints alone can account for the rational market responses that are predicted by the neo-classical theorems. Firms that happen to make positive profits gather the means to expand, whereas firms that confront losses cannot but contract. In competitive markets, this process of selection, according to Becker, takes place regardless of the motives, deliberations and the like, of individuals.

Market selection in the public sectors

From the perspective of the various market selection arguments of Alchian, Friedman and Becker, the fundamental distinguishing difference between the private and the public sector seems to be the public sector's tax monopoly on the private sector and the legislative monopoly of the state. The success criteria within the public sector differ in the sense that expansion can be achieved in more than one way: by increases in profits from the activities of the organisation or by increased transfers from the tax monopoly.

The public ownership efficiency problem does not seem to contain the problem that public organisations are not exposed to selective forces that are external to the firms. Rather, the distinguishing problem seems to be that the influences of state legislation and taxation tend to pervert existing market selection mechanisms and accordingly the incentives of the publicly owned organisation to expand by being efficient and thereby generating larger profits. It can indeed be argued that increased profits might reduce the ability to generate funds from the tax monopoly and/or the legitimacy needed to secure monopoly rights, so that the efficient organisation might be, overall, less successful than the inefficient.

Taken as an outside force that works upon economic organisations, the market selection argument can be directly applied to the public sector. The ability of any government to increase its revenues can be seen as dependent on a market selection process, where geographically separated taxation areas (federal states, states, counties, municipalities and so on) compete to increase their tax bases by means of industrial policies, tax policies, public sector efficiency and quality, and the like. Just as in private markets, those who succeed in this process will gain profits (taxes) that will permit a growth in public sector activities. Those who do not, will be forced to contract public spending and hence public sector activities. At this overall public sector level of analysis, it is hard to see that the selection arguments of Alchian and Becker do not apply to the public sector. This kind of selection between nations is well known and addressed as national competitiveness, balance of trade and the like, whereas rivalry between public sector organisations and between local governments within the national state seems much more foggy. Again this seems to be an effect of the absence of external legislative and taxational powers at the national level. States, like private firms in competitive markets, have no choice but to compete in order to be selected for by markets for money, goods and services. Public organisations and local governments have the option to be selected for by the state rather than by the markets.

Seen in this perspective, it becomes evident that the claim that expansion follows from success in external selection processes, has a tautological character. It is ultimately true for any kind of economic activity in society. The interesting distinguishing feature is accordingly not whether or not selection forces are present, but rather how strongly they influence organisations and decision processes, and how public sectors can be structured in order for market selection processes to work more efficiently.

From the perspective of a government that seeks to increase the efficiency of public sectors, the selection argument points to a few overall guidelines to public sector market regulations. Firstly, the ability to obtain resources from tax transfers should be strictly limited and separated from the management of competitive publicly owned firms. Secondly, market protection by law or regulations should be equally restrictive and credible. Thirdly, powers and control rights ought to be allocated to separated levels of politicisation and to different public sector institutions so that legal ownership, public purchases and regulation are sufficiently separated from one another. Fourthly, public sector firms should be permitted to expand their activities freely if the expansion is based on profits. In the opposite case, resources would not be reallocated efficiently.

The selection arguments of the theories of the firm

Dating back to an article by R. Coase (1937), a theoretical tradition has emerged that is usually called the theory of the firm, or the efficiency branch of organisational theory. In general, the different theories subscribed to this bulk of science hold the position that prevailing organisational forms in competitive markets are efficient. Basically, they all seem to be referable to some version of the strong selection claim of Friedman, at an analytical level of analysis that seeks to explain the behaviour of the individual firm in terms of the behaviour of individuals. The theories, however, hold no assumption that all participants have the same interests as the entrepreneurs. The transaction costs, the agency costs and the property rights variants of the theory of the firm rely fundamentally on the efficacy of market selection processes. In this sense, these theories can be seen as extensions of the neo-classical evolutionary theory to the firm-level of analysis.

The intriguing question raised by Coase, was: why do firms exist at all if markets are efficient? His, and later Williamson's answer to this, is that firms exist because organisational co-ordination has cost-saving advantages over markets. There are substantial costs related to market transactions such as search and negotiating costs. The organising of legal relationships between the employer and the employee serves to reduce this kind of cost. The most efficient organisational forms are selected in competitive markets, which implies a link between organisational form and cost minimisation. This is clearly a variation of Friedman's strong selection argument that connects the selection mechanism to the marginal theory also at the level of the internal organisation of firms. Where the old neo-classical theory is concerned with technologies, output and prices, the new theory of the firm is concerned with organisational and contractual aspects of the firm as the subject of selection.

Again, it seems obvious that the tax and legislative monopoly of governments is potentially destructive to the link between economic success from some objectified external selection process and efficiency in terms of cost-minimising. Some organisational forms and contractual arrangements might rather be intended to secure tax revenues or legal protection, whereas others are selected for, by, for instance, capital markets.

In the Norwegian electricity market, there is an isomorphic tendency of organisational change from the public bureau to the publicly owned joint stock company. In a variant of Williamson's selection claim, one could argue that this is not an effect of the market selection process as such, but follows from the shift from legislative sheltering to market orientation.

The Property Rights variant of the theory of the firm is in particular referable to Alchian and Demsetz (1972). In their view, firms are basically production teams with some party holding a controlling position in the contractual arrangements. The problem of the team is that shirking is attractive to individual team members. The efficient solution to this is to introduce property rights that make the owner the residual claimant with title to the net earnings of the firm. The owner will then have a sufficient individual incentive to monitor the monitor of the team. This construct is a representation of the classical capitalist firm with well-defined property rights.

Property rights theorists emphasise that different property rights assessments lead to different penalty–reward structures and possibly to different outcomes. More complete specification of individual property rights is seen as tending to promote the efficient allocation of resources because defining property rights has the effect that economic externalities are internalised.

In the public sector however, property rights are less clearly interpreted than in private markets. One interpretation would be that public ownership is a representation of the general public, in which case every citizen within the relevant geographical area has a stake in the ownership. In this case, the political ownership is a representation of collective co-operative interests. This variant becomes almost similar to no ownership at all. Another interpretation would be that the public owner is a separated judicial entity which in reality is self-governed with its own interests separated from that of the voters.

In the Norwegian electricity system, both interpretations are represented. One is seeing the equity of the electricity company as owned by the consumers. In this case, the profits of the firm should be transferred back to the consumers rather than to the local government. The other sees the local government as the actual owner with the right to the equity of the firm. The problem with the first interpretation is that co-operative ownership is a weak ownership concept with only weak incentives to the individual owner to engage in increasing the profits of the company. The problem with the second seems primarily to be referable to the taxation and legislative issues discussed above.

A third interpretation would be that the electricity company itself to an important extent is self-governed. In this case, the firm becomes its own residual claimant. Dividends to the owners tends to be treated as equal to other duties in fixed, stable and predictable numbers. Here, the publicly owned company approaches a public foundation in its governance, power and control rights system. The individuals taking the position of the monitor of the monitors of the production teams in this case, are those with organisational control of the company: those with the actual authority to allocate resources and to execute strategies on behalf of the company.

This openness to interpretation illustrates the potential separation of formal ownership and real control. This is not a special public sector phenomenon, but reflects a widespread observation throughout private markets as well. The separation of ownership from organisational control implies that the property rights approach might be misleading as the main approach to the governance problem.

This theme is further elaborated on by the agency cost variant of the theory of the firm, advocated by Jensen and Meckling (1976). In their view, the dominating type of modern firm is the corporation, which is characterised exactly by a separation of ownership and control. This induces a potentially serious agency problem to the owners where agency costs have to be incurred. Although the value of the firm is not maximised in the corporation, in the standard rational choice interpretation, due to the lack of direct controls of management, agency costs theorists regard the corporation as an efficient ownership structure – based on the market selection argument. It has outperformed other firm structures and is accordingly more cost efficient than any of its alternatives.

From the owner's point of view, they argue, there is no loss at all, because the agency cost is borne solely by the agents (the managers).

The basic argument here is that the equity market is competitive. Because managers are assumed to have some interests in attracting financial funds, managers themselves become interested in being monitored. In this sense, managers are not really monitored by the owners, but by the efficient equity market. Agency costs theorists argue that there really are no owners of the modern corporation. There are only owners of factors of production. Share owners are the owners of equity capital that is diversified over several assets. Managers are owners of human capital and have a stake in the success of the corporation as such as it affects their future market salary.

In the agency cost perspective, the problem within public sectors would not be that property rights are not well defined. The problem is that the equity market is not competitive but regulative and dominated by the tax monopoly. However, if there is a credible separation of managerial control from access to preferential funding and legislative influences, and an open-market regulatory structure with publicly owned joint stock companies that make each company dependent on a market for equity, it is hard to see that there will not be a market-like rivalry between public sector firms for the attraction of equity just as in any other market.

Whether or to what extent the public companies are exposed to the competitive equity market depends on the legislative system and the organisation of ownership. What we find in the electricity sector, is a process towards separation of the public firms from the public bureaus of which they used to be part, and an increased flexibility in ownership where different local governments own electricity company shares that are tradeable. This means that not only governments can engage in equity trade in the electricity sector, but also the electricity companies, private industries and investors. On the other hand, concessionary laws still have substantial restrictive influences on free trade with electricity company shares and still discriminate against private ownership.

Nevertheless, the agency costs approach seems to represent the most promising entrance to the public ownership problem as judged from the perspective of the theories of the firms. Unlike both transaction costs and property rights theory, the focus of selection processes is not primarily on the owners, but rather on management. With such a view, solutions to the separability of production from legislation and taxation appear closer. In this case, separation is not a matter of separating roles of politicians, but the roles of politicians from the roles of managers of joint stock companies where politicians at multiple levels and areas of politicisation are shareholders.

The convergence of a socialist rivalry system towards a politically safeguarded private-like competitive market

Outright privatisation of utility systems (like for instance, the electricity system), is faced with substantial problems of building safeguarding institutions in order to solve long-term contracting problems between the private companies and their political environments. An efficient socialist rivalry system, on the other hand, seems to be faced with specific problems of public sector sophistications. There is a need for real separation of powers and control rights at multiple levels of politicisation, for specific organisational forms, for clear-cut separations of taxation, regulation/legislation and controls of production companies, and for the institutional safeguarding of competitive equity markets within the public sectors.

In real terms, these claims convert the socialist rivalry system into a private-like competitive market with public ownership serving as the political safeguarding system for long-term contracting between the firm as represented by its management, and the political environment. Seen from this perspective, the organisation of markets within public sectors has dramatic impact on organisational forms, the separation and allocation of roles and so on, that in a longer perspective seems likely to represent an evolutionary process towards semi-privatisation.

On the other hand, the agency cost approach illustrates that the ownership issue might not be the most important for the efficiency of modern firms. It might rather be that the markets for managers, equity and other factors of production should be the focus for the architects of the public utility liberal order.

Bibliography

Alchian, A.A. (1950): 'Uncertainty, evolution and economic theory', *Journal of Political Economy* 58: 211–21.

Alchian, A.A. and Demsetz, H. (1972): 'Production, information costs, and economic organization', *American Economic Review* 62: 777–95.

Becker, G.S. (1962) 'Irrational behavior and economic theory', *Journal of Political Economy* 70: 1–13.

Coase, R.H. (1937): 'The nature of the firm', *Economica*, 4: 386–405.

Friedman, M. (1953): 'The methodology of positive economics', in *Essays in Positive Economics*, Chicago: University of Chicago Press.

Jensen, M.C. and Meckling, W. (1976): 'Theory of the firm: managerial behavior, agency costs, and ownership structure', *Journal of Financial Economics* 3: 305–60.

9
Deregulation is not Reregulation

Jan-Erik Lane

Introduction

The traditional theory of public regulation, focusing upon entry regulation, employed licences which government would issue to firms, either private or public, that stated the conditions under which they were allowed to operate in a sector. Such licences would lay down prices and quantities, which the firm had to respect in order to receive the sole permission to be active in this regulated sector of the economy. Sometimes quality standards that had to be met were also specified.

Traditional public regulation thus conceived of some degree of reciprocity between government and the firm, the latter accepting being regulated against receiving a legal monopoly, based upon the licensing power of the state as part of its legal authority. However, the occurrence of asymmetric knowledge undoes the reciprocity, when public regulation is approached as a principal–agent relationship.

Once the difficulties in creating a reciprocity between government as regulator and the regulated firms were realised, there followed a search for deregulation. But here the key question becomes: how far should or could deregulation go? Is there perhaps a fundamental need for reregulation, that is the invention of new forms of regulation that could successfully supplant traditional regulation? One may examine the argument by G. Majone (1996) suggesting that Europe needs a new regulatory state and that the European Union is very much a response to this need. Before we discuss the need for a new regulatory state in general and for Europe in particular, we examine the argument against the old regulatory state.

Three types of regulation

We need to reflect first on why traditional public regulation could not make this reciprocity work. One may distinguish between three types of regulation: competition regulation, entry regulation and product regulation. Since the aim of public regulation is to promote socially useful ends, one may identify the different standard objectives of entry regulation on the one hand and of product regulation on the other. Finally, there is competition regulation, or anti-trust policy-making (Tirole, 1993).

First, when government issues licences, stating the conditions for entry into a sector of the economy, then the objective is to promote economic efficiency. Licences and entry regulation have been used in relation to infrastructure and capital intensive industry. Traditional entry regulation is considered a policy tool to undo the occurrence of monopoly in the market, when contestation is not naturally forthcoming due to economies of scale or scope. The rationale of entry licenses is the economic theory of economies of scale or scope, which argues that one sole producer minimises unit costs.

Government, it was argued, could undo private monopolies by regulating them. Thus, there was, strictly speaking, no need for the use of a public enterprise, because government could interact with a private firm, using its power to legislate in order to lay down the conditions for the operation of the firm. Thus, firms would accept rules of how to be socially useful, receiving from government as a reciprocity the licence to be the sole active in a sector. Private firms acting upon such a trade-off between accepting regulation and receiving entry protection would constitute the so-called public utilities.

Traditional public regulations theory models government as the active part in setting up regulatory schemes, supervised by a public board of some kind. Yet, the criticism of public regulation portrays government regulation as a so-called endogenous phenomenon, that is it is determined by the market and it is not determining the market, i.e. it is not exogenous.

Second, product regulations target risk, or the reduction of the probability of the occurrence of accidents. Thus, such regulatory policies consist in the specification of product standards about quality. During the last decade, the amount of product regulation has increased considerably as measured by the number of new rules about the quality of products or how they are to be handled. The rationale of product regulations is consumer vulnerability or the search for safety (Wildavsky, 1988).

Third, there is anti-trust policy-making, which is directed towards the regulation of competition and market structure. Whereas traditional regulation aims at limiting entry into markets, anti-trust regulation has the opposite goal, namely of increasing the potential number of players who wish to enter markets. Thus, the logic of anti-trust policy-making is entirely different, but it remains the case that it is a form of intervention into the market economy, based upon discretionary decision-making by bureaucrats or regulators.

Traditional regulation and rent seeking

Public regulation may become the target of so-called rent seeking, which benefits the regulated firms first and foremost. Regulation is a valuable good or service in which firms are prepared to invest in order to capture the government regulators (Stigler, 1975). Governments creating licenses become captured by the firms seeking favourable public regulation of the market, limiting competition.

Since licenses can be extremely lucrative, there is a plentiful supply of money available for rent seeking. Moreover, product regulations may enter into rent seeking, as much of regulation may favour certain producers. Figure 9.1 shows the standard model of rent seeking, as developed within the public choice school.

The potential gain from rent seeking is the entire consumer surplus in Figure 9.1. If a private firm can receive favourable regulation from government, then it could restrict the quantity supplied and engage in price discrimination. Thus, the quantity supplied would be less than the optimal quantity – Q, and the price would be raised, allowing the private firm to receive an economic rent, or excessive profits. If the price is raised from Pe to Pm, then the firm takes a huge chunk away from the consumer surplus, or the shaded area in Figure 9.1 (Sherman, 1989).

To the private firm, the legal monopoly offers the possibility of a huge rent, which would be transformed into a capital gain for the shareholders of that firm. If a public enterprise is operating a similar legal monopoly, then the windfall profits will either be used up in the form of X-inefficiency or they will be handed over to the owner of that enterprise, namely the state. Let us mention a few things about the public enterprise and how it is affected by vast deregulation.

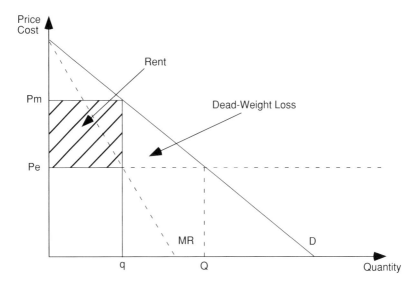

Source: Tollison, 1982

Figure 9.1   Rent seeking model

In the case of entry regulations, it has been argued that governments should employ a double strategy, using not only public regulatory schemes but also their own people, that is the public enterprise form. But will public enterprises really refrain from rent seeking?

Deregulation and the public enterprise

The traditional public enterprise has almost ceased to exist in many countries. Governments have chosen another governance form for their business activity, namely the public joint stock company. In addition to its advantages for running business activity it offers to the government, as the owner, also the possibility of privatisation, partially or completely, by simply selling out the equity.

The basic difficulty with public enterprise is the occurrence of X-inefficiency (Leibenstein, 1966). It destroys the entire argument about the social usefulness of the public enterprise. Even if public enterprise uses cost plus prices, there is no guarantee that it will minimise costs. On the contrary, public enterprise has no self-interest connected with being X-efficient.

The key problem concerns who is to gain from increased X-efficiency in the public enterprise: the principal (government), the agent (the enterprise) or the client (the customers)? The transformation of the enterprise into a public joint stock company (incorporation) implies that government has won, at least over the public as consumer/customer. Incorporation entails higher user fees, fewer employees and larger profits, to be partially repatriated to the state.

Government may try to promote X-efficiency by means of two strategies: (a) monitoring the enterprise and (b) affecting the reputation of managers. Monitoring is not cost-less. Transaction costs may start running high after a certain minimum level of monitoring has been accomplished. And reputation is not strategy-proof, meaning that both government and managers of the public enterprise may invest in strategies that impact upon reputation, which would actually be a form of rent dissipation.

Governments have turned to another institutional mechanism, the public joint stock company replacing the public enterprise form. The advantage of the public joint stock company for the public or the citizens is that subsidies and losses are easily discovered. Thus, they may also be eliminated. Public joint stock companies live in an entirely different environment, where rules about third-party access, the levelling of the playing field and mutual recognition reign.

Who takes the rent in regulatory games?

Under traditional public regulation there will be legal monopolies. Monopolies, whether public or private, present two allocative problems. First, there is the dead-weight loss in Figure 9.1, which concerns both the producer and the consumer, implying that the quantity allocated must be Pareto inferior. Second, there is the economic rent that the producer captures in the form of an excessive price, cutting deep into the consumer surplus. This is a distributional matter which is outside Paretian considerations. What, if anything, should government do?

Enter the mechanism of a public enterprise. Government could look upon the public enterprise as a tool for removing the private monopoly, which is embarrassing from the viewpoint of efficiency as well as distribution. There are two possible solutions, both involving the public enterprise achieving a Pareto-improvement. Either the public enterprise is instructed to supply the optimal quantity, government covering the loss to the firm by means of a subsidy over the budget. Or government orders the public enterprise to choose a so-called second-best solution, that is failing to reach a Pareto-optimal or first-best solution, one tries something as close as is feasible to that, i.e. where price equals average cost. The standard second-best solution using a public enterprise to remove private monopoly is to employ so-called Ramsey prices, which would be a price where average costs are covered but not more (Spulber, 1989).

Public enterprises exist because they are socially useful – this is the implication of the analysis above. Public enterprises could dramatically lower the cost to the consumer, allocating the Pareto optimal quantity or close to that quantity Q. This is all theory though, as we must discuss the implementation of such an ideal solution.

In practice, the public enterprise will move close to the monopoly point, because it is the best solution for the enterprise, because at this quantity it may maximise its X-inefficiency. The government may argue that it could accept this solution on the condition that it receives the excessive profits, that is the rent is transferred from the enterprise to the state. But why would the enterprise do that? In reality, there will ensue a struggle between government, the enterprise and the public over how the consumer surplus is to be divided.

Three solutions are conceivable:

(1) The Private Enterprise Takes All: If the private enterprise can use a scheme of perfect price competition over the entire quantity allocated, then it would maximise its profits, the producer rent seizing the entire consumer surplus.

(2) The Public Enterprise Takes All: If the public enterprise could engage in a maximum amount of successful price discrimination, then it could operate with considerable X-inefficiency, to the benefit of its employees.

(3) The Government Takes All: Government could require that the public enterprise transfers all of its excessive rent to the state, for instance stating that the enterprise should pay a high dividend on the capital that the state has placed with the enterprise.

The likely outcome of these three possibilities is that the public enterprise takes the huge part of the gain, due to the occurrence of asymmetric information. The public enterprise will capture this rent by the use of strategies that entail running up X-inefficiencies.

A private enterprise would benefit from a monopoly position by having windfall profits. Thus, it would still be interested in running costs as low as possible, because the profits can be transferred to the owners of the enterprise. However, a public enterprise would have a somewhat different incentive structure, as the potential profit would go to the public, that is, to each and everyone. The difficulty involved is typically analysed by means of principal–agent theory (Stiglitz, 1987).

However, the capture of government comes with a cost to the private firm. It must engage in lobbying in order to get the favourable regulation. This rent-seeking behaviour can become very costly, as government must be paid attention to in many ways – the firm accumulating transaction costs. These costs for rent seeking can run as high as dissipating the entire consumer surplus, that is, the shared area in Figure 9.1.

Thus, traditional public regulation may not only cause a huge burden to the economy (dead-weight loss, abnormal profits), but it may actually result in no gain whatsoever for anyone. If that is the case, the entire producer surplus being dissipated, then entry regulation is only socially wasteful.

Legislative markets for public regulation and procurement

If governments creating regulation are not acting exogeneously, that is, independently, in relation to the economy, then how is public regulation forthcoming? Widening the concept of public regulation to cover any kind of state intervention into the economy, the model of rent seeking must be developed to take into account the possibility of competition for legislation that regulates the economy. Besides regulatory decision-making, there are all the government contracts. Government is not simply captured by firms.

Not only entry regulation is interesting for the players in the economy. Lots of other kinds of state intervention have economic consequences. Thus, private as well as public firms, interest organisations or consumer groups seek to influence the making of state intervention by framing legislation to their advantage. There will be competition in the demand for state intervention or government contracts from various players.

How about supply of state intervention? One may argue that the initiative does not rest entirely with the players seeking state intervention, but that one should also take into account the willingness of politicians to supply state intervention in the form of licenses or product standards.

One may generalise the analysis of government creating regulatory schemes to cover not only entry regulation or product regulation but all kinds of state intervention in markets, including also public procurement, or government purchasing things by means of state contracts. Such a generalisation should include both supply and demand, with the result that we arrive at a model of legislative markets for state intervention (Peltzman, 1988).

Government contracts may be subsumed under the general model of the demand for and supply of state intervention. Such contracts favour certain groups, firms, regions, employees and consumers, and disfavour others in the same manner as legislation works to the benefit of some and brings about costs for others. In all countries, rich and poor, government contracts tend to be of substantial size and quite lucrative for some.

Government contracts used to be mainly concerned with the purchase of equipment and the construction of buildings and roads. However, with the advent of contractualism in the entire public sector, government contracts are omnipresent. Here, we deal with so-called public procurement.

Once one opens up for competition in the demand and supply for state intervention, then the losses from rent seeking can be substantially reduced. Politicians stand to gain from allocating legislation, if they can establish a quid pro quo for the services that they provide, that is the legislative acts or the contracts, receiving votes or money.

On the other hand, politicians may lose in a grim fashion if they supply state intervention that the electorate does not want, resulting in loss of votes. Evidently, there is both push and pull in legislative markets. A general way of modelling legislative markets is outlined in Figures 9.2

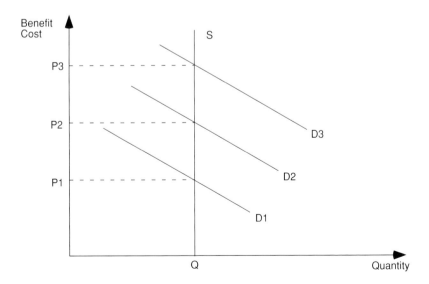

Figure 9.2   Legislative markets 1

and 9.3. Suppose first that the same kind of regulation can be supplied to three different firms with varying demand for legislation.

Figure 9.2 depicts how three firms are prepared to pay differently (DI, D2, D3) for a certain amount of regulation, depending upon how much benefit they derive from legislation at the quantity Q. Politicians may wish to cash in on the willingness of the three firms to pay the prices for the legislation, PI + P2 + P3.

Suppose instead that regulation can be supplied differently to various firms or that different kinds of legislation can be enacted in response to firm demand. Figure 9.3 shows how politicians may adjust to the different demand of three firms for different amounts of regulation.

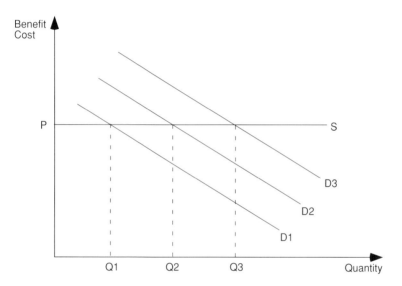

Figure 9.3   Legislative markets 2

In both Figure 9.2 and Figure 9.3, politicians are not merely captured by firm interests, but supply legislation in such a manner that at least their costs are covered.

The theory of legislative markets covers any and all forms of state intervention in the economy, from entry regulation to anti-trust as well as government procurement. If traditional public regulation does not work, then perhaps politicians can gain little from supplying it. How about anti-trust policy-making? Does it really work?

Anti-trust regulation

Regulatory reform has been initiated and completed in many countries. It has been a cornerstone in public sector reform in all countries with an advanced economy, as deregulation has been accomplished in a number of sectors of the economy.

Based upon the analysis of public regulation within the Chicago School of Economics (Stigler, 1988), there has been widespread agreement that traditional public regulation was counter-productive. It focused upon so-called entry regulation, which creates a legal monopoly through the mechanism of the licence. Deregulation has targeted the enhancement of contestability in various sectors of the economy, especially in the infrastructure part where traditional public regulation earlier loomed large.

Deregulation is to be seen as a practical response to the challenges of globalisation. When national boundaries are taken away, and the playing field is levelled between public and private players regionally or globally, then traditional public regulation has no rationale. The key question then becomes: what is to replace traditional public regulation?

The concept of deregulation entails only that rules that frame economic activity are eliminated. Although few doubt the positive contribution of deregulation for economic growth and world trade, many underline that no economy can operate without rules or regulations. Thus, deregulation can never work one hundred per cent. Even a deregulated economy with open borders and with equal conditions for public and private firms must have some sort of basic regime, laying down the rules of fair competition and the regulations concerning contractual honesty and fulfilment.

Since deregulation is only the abolishion of rules, but any economy is in need of a regulatory framework of some sort, many have concluded that deregulation is only a first step and not the end result. After deregulation comes reregulation, it is argued. After negative regulation there must come positive regulation. If deregulation is closely connected with reregulation, then perhaps the choice is never: 'Deregulation versus Regulation', but it is a matter of alternative regulatory regimes: 'Weak Regulation versus Strong Regulation'.

New Public Management is clearly linked up with regulatory reform, as it accepts the critique of traditional public regulation set out above (Lane, 2000). NPM endorses the basic principles of a deregulated economy: (1) denationalisation of the economy; (2) levelling the playing field between public and private players; (3) regional competition mechanisms; and (4) the world regulation of public procurement. What is contested, however, is the extent to which the implementation of these principles requires more than deregulation or negative regulation. Could NPM also endorse massive reregulation or positive regulation?

Thus, when it comes to replacing old-style entry regulation with a new form of regulation, then the consensus breaks down, some arguing that deregulation is enough but others looking for a new kind of regulation. What would positive regulation amount to? If traditional regulation did not work, then one may argue that there are limits to reregulation, as strong state intervention will not work. Or is reregulation to be done taking into account the lessons from the failure of traditional public regulation?

The adherents of reregulation or strong positive regulation often envisage a need for competition regulation, that is the making and implementation of so-called antitrust policy. We must ask: is there really a need for reregulation after deregulation? Can anti-trust policy-making work? Let us examine the Majone argument for reregulation.

At other times, the adherents of reregulation focus upon welfare state provisions, stating that the denationalisation of the economies together with the establishment of regional market and trading regimes create a need for the harmonisation of not only basic economic regulations but also welfare state provisions (Scharpf, 1999).

The case for reregulation: anti-trust?

Let us now return to the argument that traditional regulation is irrelevant but that the economy would need a substitute in the form of strong reregulation. Majone develops this argument in relation to the European Union, stating that the EU is basically a new regulatory state along the American model of public utilities regulation – see his *Reregulating Europe* (1996).

A number of EU institutions could be seen in the light of public regulation. Such a perspective could embrace not only the Court of Justice and the European Central Bank but also the Commission with its 20 Commissioners. Often one focuses upon the competition regime, contained in the EU constitution (Gowder, 1995). But if entry regulation fails, then maybe competition regulation or anti-trust policy-making also is questionable?

Economic activity is in need of institutions, but how far should the institutionalisation of the economy proceed? What Majone has in mind as a model for European regulation is actually the old American combination of public utilities regulation and anti-trust policy-making.

When European governments dismantle their public enterprises and move towards levelling the playing field in various sectors of the economy, then one could claim that they should also start regulating prices and quantities or conduct anti-trust policies. One must, however, ask whether or not the regulators in such new schemes of regulation could also become captured by special interest groups.

Majone replies that reputation will guarantee that public regulation is honest and efficient. This is basically again a principal–agent problem, where the agents – the regulators – may choose from different types of rewards from the principal, the government, one of which is reputation. There is no guarantee that reputation will be the most important consideration of the agent or that it constitutes a strategy-proof mechanism.

Against the Majone argument, one may state the Demsetz conclusion that anti-trust policy-making does not work. Governments appear very hesitant in stopping firm mergers due to firm pressures. But the key point is that it is not worth doing it, because there are no natural monopolies. Contestation is always forthcoming in an economy with open entry. Government need not stimulate competition by forcing efficient companies to break up (Demsetz, 1991).

If anti-trust regulation is not necessary, then perhaps most kinds of regulation of prices and quantities are also superfluous? What is important is that there is a basic framework of institutions that safeguard honest market operations with few limitations on the free movement of goods, services, labour and capital. This has been accomplished in Western Europe through negative regulation by the EU. The erection of a new and strong regulatory state in excess of that seems, strictly speaking, not a well-founded proposal.

The quest for reregulation appears unfounded to a large extent. What has happened in many European countries is that the traditional public enterprises have been transformed into public joint stock companies and in some cases privatised. At the same time, these new players have become the target of new regulation, aiming at the traditional American system of sector boards with strong independent regulators. But if the critique of public utilities regulation is correct, then it should not be tried in the European context.

Is the EU a super regulator?

If one asks the question: what is the EU?, then there are so many alternatives: 'co-operative federalism without a state', 'specific Community Methods', 'decision-making with variable geometry', 'convergence in public policy or on a European political model', 'mutual recognition versus harmonisation', 'European public sphere', 'partnership', 'common sphere of mediation at the European level', 'regulatory state' (Meny, Muller and Quermonne, 1996, pp. 1–22). If one describes both the Union itself and its interaction with member countries as characterised by 'uncertainty', 'openness', and 'opacity', then there may not exist any single label to be employed as an overall description. Perhaps it is more fruitful to focus upon what the Union does – the pragmatic approach. The EU is a regulatory mechanism.

What stands out is that the Union is something very firm – as with the rules of the common market and its adjacent legal orders. But the EU is also something very loose as in the interaction leading up to policy-making either in the form of norms or the allocation of money. This very double nature of Union transparency versus complexity probably cannot be eradicated by any realistic institutional reform.

The European Union has been seen as involving a conflict between legal integration and policy-making integration, which could be coupled with the distinction between negative and positive regulation (Scharpf 1999). If one takes the position that there is too little positive integration in the Union framework, then that is seen as a result of this conflict between the legal order and the political institutions. European integration in terms of the existing institutions implies that negative integration at the Union level blocks national policy-making at the same time as the intergovernmental nature of the Union restricts positive integration at the Union level.

Does European integration really need more positive regulation to tame 'capitalism'? One should not underestimate what has been achieved by means of negative regulation in counteracting market-deviating behaviour. The call for more public intervention at the Union level contradicts the lesson of why positive regulation has been so difficult to achieve within the EU. If positive regulation is so difficult to arrive at, especially when capitalism is international and trade unions national, then maybe the whole idea of extensive positive regulation is not worthwhile? One seldom speaks about the consumers, who may actually be the real winners from extensive negative regulation.

The Union is very much about regulation. Much has been achieved in terms of regulatory reform by the Union despite its implementation deficit. There is a logic to EU regulation in that European integration has been done thoroughly with regard to basic regulatory tasks. However, one must not underestimate both the amount of income redistribution that has taken place by means of the regional funds and the macroeconomic convergence that is already apparent with the advent of Monetary Union.

The Union focus on regulation far ahead of other kinds of government intervention is to be understood as a rational adaptation to the situation. Given the vast legal resources of the Union and its systemic lack of other kinds of state attributes than law and money, as well as the needs of the member states to create common rules without free-rider problems, the EU concentration upon regulation is understandable.

In fact, European integration has proceeded where and in a manner that makes sense. It is when one confuses regulation with welfare policy that the risk of policy failure increases. Social regulation includes the many directives of the Union targeting the environment, consumer protection, product safety, health and safety in the workplace as well as equal rights of men and women. Welfare policies would be much more demanding.

How would positive regulation be achieved in the Union? Following the theme of rent seeking, one could examine the decision-making process from the point of view of the influence of organised interests. The informal status of much of the EU lobbying by Euro-groups and national organisations is a fact, but many would have liked to see some kind of corporatist regime for the Union (Streeck and Schmitter, 1996). At the same time the attempts at EU corporatism were defeated by the marketeers.

The risk of rent seeking appears from the discussions about the role of interest organisations within EU policy-making. There is talk about a gigantic number of so-called Euro-associations as well as of consultative committees, connected with primarily EU policy-making. However, certain decision rules – standard operating procedures – tend to emerge which express an internal logic corresponding to the power relationships within the EU institutions. The Union is basically negative regulation.

The European Union is both exchange and domination, from which constellation arises the paradoxes described as the 'joint decision trap' or the 'two-level game'. The players – public and private – involved in the 'multi-level game' in Brussels, Strasbourg and Luxembourg may engage in all kinds of coalitions, ad hoc and temporary, but once the game has been played and the decision identified, then authority prevails.

EU regulation has strongly reinforced the Europeanisation of economic rules in a broad sense. Standardisation, harmonisation, mutual recognition as well as a levelled playing field all over Europe constitute elements in a legal order that applies with state force (Craig and de Burca, 1997).

European integration is more order than chaos, where modelling the emergence of this order resorting to speaking of 'policy networks' or 'policy community', is much too vague. Only in relation to the EU projects funded with the structural funds money does the term 'network' seem appropriate. The EU makes policy by a small professional bureaucracy (the Commission) developing ever-closer relations with a complex *mélange* of other policy actors.

By employing the distinction between competition and industrial policy one may identify a characteristic feature of European governance: that is the priority given to the first kind of policy and the more or less lukewarm action in the latter. The explanation is that the Union is doing what it is best at – the introduction of common market regulation – and abstaining from what it does worse – discretionary public intervention.

The institutions of the Union are capable of resolving collective action problems in putting into place public goods such as one and the same common framework for an integrated European economy whereas they do not seem to be conducive to carrying through huge-scale single projects in the form of an industrial policy. Industrial policy-making, if feasible, is seldom successful but often very costly.

The EU regulating orders are chiefly negative regulations as with the unification harmonisation and mutual recognition of the rules of markets. The EU is hardly a super regulator, engaging in massive reregulation.

The risk of overregulation

The introduction of NPM has in a few countries been attended by a rather considerable increase in the number of regulatory bodies as well as in regulatory activities. Much evidence suggests that the number of regulators and the costs of regulation have gone up sharply, for instance in the UK (*Financial Times* 12 August 1999). This is the reregulation argument in effect, which claims that after deregulation must come reregulation. Without resources for active regulation, a competitive regime like NPM cannot operate efficiently.

There are two sides to this argument. On the one hand, it is true that NPM presupposes that a regime for competition is in place and operates with reasonable efficacy. Such a competition regime will comprise a mechanism responding to a complex world where the distinction between private and public players in the economy has been undone and where national boundaries have come down. A competition regime requires not only consistent state legislation creating the bulk of legal norms but also consistency in the application of the norms by an implementation mechanism.

On the other hand, the creation of an economy-wide competition mechanism which is also in harmony with such regimes in other countries or in agreement with a regulatory framework for the world economy could become the starting point for increasing state intervention, resulting in excessive overregulation. Reregulation may involve not only enforcement of rules about competition but also the inspection of market structure and firm behaviour. There is no limit to the number of inspectors that government can create, especially if various parts of government will each manage their own inspections. Thus, reregulation may run into the problems connected with Parkinson's Law, meaning a rapid rise in the number and size of regulatory bodies.

That there is a real possibility that reregulation may result in overregulation appears in recent UK developments. Thus, we read:

Since Labour took office two years ago, it has created almost a dozen inspectorates: one for housing; one for the health service; a benefits fraud inspectorate; a youth justice board; a training standards council to inspect publicly funded training; a 'best value' inspectorate that will cover the whole of local government. (*Financial Times*, 12 August 1999)

When the soft sector is opened for competition, then it is believed that securing a high-quality level requires regulation and inspection. However, at heart this is a contractual problem under an NPM regime, the solution to which could be found in the use of the ordinary court system (Posner, 1992). In the business sector the drive for reregulation has been strong since deregulation was initiated. Thus, we also read:

In the private sector, there has been some rationalisation of regulation. The Financial Services authority now embraces nine former regulations – a process that in theory should not extend regulation but in practice is beginning to. Electricity and gas have been merged into a single energy regulator, although a bus regulator may yet be added. (*Financial Times* 12 August 1999)

The reregulation of the business sector often extends far beyond that which is necessary for the achievement of a competition regime. The goal of reregulation is often to directly control the products that are forthcoming in order to ensure that quality is high as well as that prices remain reasonable. Reregulation is thus never only the maintenance of a competition regime but involves other and additional tasks. Again, we read that the British government wants to see a testable, measurable outcome from every extra pound of public spending it produces, and it sees the inspectorates as providing that kind of guarantee. (*Financial Times* 12 August 1999)

Yet, the so-called inspectorates come with a considerable cost, involving both the direct costs for all the inspectors and the inspections as well as the indirect cost of compliance with the complaints from inspections and the anticipated reactions to inspection. Running the inspectorates could involve increasing rent-seeking costs or the money that providers would be prepared to spend in order to soften the impact of future inspections.

If one argues that reregulation is essential to any deregulated economy, then one must reflect upon the costs of reregulation, especially inspection. Again we face the problem of finding the optimal amount of inspection, which involves setting the marginal value of another inspection equal to the marginal cost of that inspection. Any deliberations about the size of the regulatory effort cannot avoid reflecting upon the two basic alternatives for accomplishing reregulation. Either one employs a plethora of special public regulatory bodies, one for every special sector of the economy, or one relies upon regulation by means of the ordinary courts, expressed in a set of decisions with long-term effects (precedents). Whereas the first method tends to be interventionist and results in detailed regulations, the second method tends towards general rules, although with effective implementation.

Now it is argued that NPM requires a massive regulatory effort, especially of the first kind, including, as well as a competition regime, lots of inspections by a set of inspectorates. This is the argument that we wish to rebut. NPM does not entail the first method of regulation but it requires the second method discussed above.

Creating lots of inspectorates will only in the beginning improve the relation between benefits and cost, producing value for money. The marginal value of inspections is large when conducted parsimoniously, but it declines rapidly when inspections become frequent. At the same time the costs increase when inspectorates grow larger and their activities expand. At the end of the day, it is competition itself that is the most effective tool for checking quality, especially if combined with litigation and strict liability (Posner, 1992).

Conclusion

Deregulation, creating one huge market for the supply of goods and services where all suppliers, private or public, compete on equal terms is not the same as reregulation. Deregulation is based upon the philosophy that markets work well under normal conditions and that natural monopoly does not imply market failure as long as the size of the market is not artificially restricted by state intervention. Reregulation is based upon the philosophy of state intervention into markets in order to improve upon the functioning of markets.

There is a risk that the gains from widespread and far-reaching deregulation will be captured by the introduction of new and massive reregulation. The danger of overregulation is a real one, as new boards set out to intervene into the setting of prices, quantities and quality. The possibility of anti-trust policy-making has always fascinated people who prefer state to markets. However, there is no evidence whatsoever that anti-trust would be more effective than traditional regulation focusing upon entry and licenses.

The argument that state intervention tends to be ineffective has great relevance for the theory of legislative markets, where politicians offer regulation, legislation and contracts in relation to the demand for a variety of state intervention. The implication of the distrust in both traditional regulation and anti-trust regulation is that politicians stand to gain little from engaging in new massive reregulation, that is, the costs can be substantially higher than the benefits that groups searching for regulation would be willing or able to provide.

The road ahead lies not in the reregulation of the European economy, neither on a country basis nor on a European-wide basis, but in the arrival at the global level of a common market framework, covering all players – public and private.

Bibliography

Craig, Paul and de Burca, Grainne (1997) *EC Law, Text, Cases, and Materials*. Oxford: Clarendon Press.

Demsetz, H. (1991) *Efficiency, Competition and Policy*. Oxford: Blackwell.

Financial Times, 12 August 1999, Another Inspector Calls.

Gowder, D.G. (1995) *EC Competition Law*. New York: Oxford University Press.

Lane, J.E. (2000) *New Public Management, An Introduction*. London: Routledge.

Leibenstein, H. (1966), Allocative Efficiency versus X-Efficiency, in *American Economic Review*, 56: 392–415.

Majone, G. (1996), *Reregulating Europe*. London: Routledge.

Meny, Y., Muller, P. and Quermonne, J.-L. (1996) *Adjusting to Europe*. London: Routledge.

Peltzman, S. (1988) Toward a More General Theory of Regulation, in Stigler (ed.) (1988), 234–66.

Posner, R. (1992) *The Economic Analysis of Law*. Boston: Little, Brown & Co.

Scharpf, F.W. (1999) *Governing in Europe. Effective and Democratic?* Oxford: Oxford University Press.

Sherman, R. (1989) *The Regulation of Monopoly*. Cambridge: Cambridge University Press.

Spulber, D.F. (1989) *Regulation and Markets*. Cambridge, MA: MIT Press.

Stigler, G.J. (1975), *The Citizen and the State: Essays on Regulation*. Chicago: University of Chicago Press.

Stigler, G.J. (ed.) (1988) *Chicago Studies in Political Economy*. Chicago, IL: University of Chicago Press.

Stiglitz, J.E. (1987) Principal and Agent, in Eatwell, Milgate, Newman, *Allocation, Information and Markets*. Oxford: Blackwell 241–53.

Streeck, W. and Schmitter Ph. C. (1996) Organized Interests in the European Union, in Kourvetaris G.A. and Moschonas A., (eds) *The Impact of European Integration*. London: Preager.

Tirole, J. (1993) *The Theory of Industrial Organization*. Cambridge, MA: The MIT Press.

Tollison, R.D. (1982) Rent-Seeking: A Survey, *Kyklos*, 35: 575–92.

Wildavsky, A. (1988) *Searching for Safety*. New Brunswick: Transaction Books.

10
Reflections on a Research Agenda: The Explanation and Design of Economic Regulations

Eirik Svindland

Introduction

In this chapter I will present, but not develop in detail, some ideas on the analysis and explanation of the regulations concerning economic affairs. The main task is, however, to recollect and structure some of the problems associated with this kind of analysis. The analysis is restricted to some basic issues of the regulatory system, the identification of the regulations needed and the design of these regulations. That is, problems that must refer to a certain type of economic activity, are beyond the scope of this chapter. This is because it is a subject which is related to the explanation of the variety of market organisations. It would require more space than a section in this chapter, if my mental picture of the problem is correct. My guess is that the characteristics of the products determine the type of market formation, information problems, conventions, and hence also the requirements with respect to the public regulations of the market concerned.

I restrict myself in this chapter to systemic issues. The choice between public and private productions, the privatisation issue, is excluded. I skipped it. First, because our ideas on the design of auction mechanisms tell us that auction can make the choice between private and public provisions of a good/service unimportant, and hence irrelevant to my discussion. Second, because regulations in this chapter are, in principle, neutral with respect to the owners of the companies concerned. They are first of all manifestations of a politico-economic system, which is manifested in the design and operation of a constitution and a related legal system. This focus raises the question about the institutional context of the economic regulations, which constitute the theme of the next section.

Any attempt to structure the relation between this institutional context and the regulations will have to deal with the complexity of the system. This is a difficult task, but I believe that it is possible to handle the problems by sorting the elements according to their domain and place in the constitutional hierarchy of institutions (see p. 194, Regulation and Complexity).

The fourth main section (p. 197) concerns constitutional and cultural rules – that is the primary regulations applying to all agents of an economy. These primary regulations define the rules of the societal system of production and distribution of economic goods. They also comprise the laws required for division of labour and other kinds of co-operation, for instance the system of units of measurement, and they shape the setting for the special regulations that apply to a certain sector of the economy or to the allocation of a certain product. The explanation of these general regulations is a central theme. I have chosen to focus on the relation to economic efficiency, and I hope to make clear that this part of the theory of economic regulations is of vital importance for economics in general. I hold that the programme of economics – as a scientific discipline – is not realisable beyond the scope of Aristotle's treatise on household management, if it ignores how laws and other general regulations mould the system of economic affairs. Moreover, the explanation of these regulations goes beyond the narrow scope of economic theory. It relies on an interface with the explanation and modelling of political processes, which introduces a wider set of ideas on human behaviour than the standard assumptions of neo-classical economics. Appreciating the role of regulations in economic performance is therefore not only to integrate the analysis of these institutions in economics and in the study of economic history. It is also to realise that the programme of economics is necessarily a programme of a political and social science, that is, the programme of political economy.

The manifold exemptions from these general rules and the related inconsistencies of the economic system as defined by its regulations and rules constitute the issues of the fifth section (Regulations and Politics, p. 205). We have to interpret them before we can explain them as outcomes of a political process. The problem of modelling this political process brings us back to the constitutional rules that govern the introduction of regulations. A special – for our purpose important – application of these rules is the principle of organisation of the regulatory bodies that introduce and supervise the special regulations of a sector and/or a kind of economic activity (p. 211).

The economic theory applied in economists' discussions of the problems I consider in the previously outlined sections of this chapter is usually of the static type, an equilibrium model of economically rational/efficient allocations and contracts. It misses the dynamics of the relations between regulations and economic development and evolution, which I therefore will consider in the seventh section (see p. 213). But, any development of relevant knowledge of design and effects of economic regulations is related to the perception of the problems of economic regulations. The normative foundation of the economics of regulations is the subject of the last section of this chapter.

The abbreviation R refers henceforth to the singular regulation and Rs refers to the plural.

Regulations and institutional context

With respect to the scope of this theory I observe that many of our ideas about economic Rs, including complete research areas like 'Law and Economics' and 'Neo-classical Institutional Economics', are dominated by explicit or implicit references to US society. But, due to their different constitution and cultural characteristics, the other market economies have their own national style of solving regulatory problems – for instance concerning the property rights of individuals. They are thus different with respect to the

- Applied methods of regulation
- Introduction of detailed restrictions on individuals' freedom of contract
- Bureaucratic procedures etc.

A certain national system may therefore have regulatory requirements, for instance concerning hostile takeovers or abuse of market power, which are non-existent or different in a neighbouring country. Recent experiences in transformation countries have amply demonstrated the practical importance of such national characteristics. One key observation is that partial and inconsistent institution transfers have occurred, which effected additional problems instead of making economic recovery and social welfare easier (Midttun and Svindland, 1996).

If this observation that national characteristics determine the practical relevance of the prevailing academic ideas about economic Rs is correct, and if our theories on economic Rs are meant to be practical instruments for empirical analysis, the variability of national settings implies that we should

- Either develop a theory of economic Rs, which deals more explicitly with the variability of basic institutional settings, than hitherto
- Or explain why all countries should adopt the same system of economic Rs.

When the economic crisis occurred in several Asian countries the influential *Foreign Affairs* (May/June 1998) invited some American analysts to express their opinions about the export of the American style of capitalism. The questions themselves, and the answers, indicate that some people think that this export is either advisable or inevitable. And there is indeed a clear tendency for economists – all over the world – to introduce and repeat problem descriptions and conclusions which are well known due to their pertinence to the United States of America. International organisations such as the World Bank also quite often promote this export of America's unique brand of capitalism. I do not claim that this standardisation of Rs is a mistake. My problem is instead that it is not yet clear why all countries should have identical economic systems, and indeed why the American socio-economic system is considered superior to other systems. Available evidence, such as economic and social statistics, rather supports the alternative conclusion that we should accept the existence of national styles and, hence, extend the scope of the theory of economic Rs by taking more institutional settings into account. We need this perception of different systems, for instance when we want to understand how proposed new Rs fit into the existing structure of national Rs and we examine whether or not this measure requires a more extensive reform.

Having said this, I do not support the well-known allegation that 'main stream' economics is abstract, context-free, and – at best – ethnocentric. The collection of facts, descriptions of existing national Rs and the analysis of their functioning are important tasks, although still merely a matter of application of the missing systematic economics of Rs, which is the subject of this chapter. The introduction of more models and systematic variations of assumptions are needed. The development of the economics of growth that took place after the shift from the traditional macroeconomic model to a 'New Theory of Growth' demonstrates how a shift from one to several models can enrich research and its analytical results. Delorme, as well as Arentsen and Künneke are represented in this volume, which illustrates the acknowledged variety of reasonable models. Offering practical economists, especially the community of international active advisors, an analogue diversification of the theory of economic Rs would improve their understanding and help them to avoid the problems of unfitting institution transfers.

Regulation and complexity

The observation that we are dealing with a complex subject when we study the economy is my point of departure for my attempt to structure the agenda of an explanation and design of economic Rs. This complexity of the economy implies that economic regulations are a complex, diverse subject too. Characteristically, they are often discussed under other labels than the regulation of economic affairs – for example tax policy, privatisation, economic systems and so on. Moreover, the complexity of the economic system referred to in this book necessitates many analytical simplifications and, hence, a partial perception of problems. Consequently there exists a multitude of different questions and answers concerning these regulations. The recollection of diverse sources concerning economic Rs is one of the aims of the contributions to this volume.

The term 'regulation' itself is also vague. It applies to too many things. According to Merriam-Webster's Collegiate Dictionary (1994)

- to regulate means, among others, '1a: to govern or direct according to a rule b(1): to bring under control of law or constituted authority (2): to make regulations for or concerning "the industries of a country" 2: to bring order, method, or uniformity to "one's habits"'.
- a regulation is, among others, '1: the act of regulating: the state of being regulated 2a: an authoritative rule dealing with details or procedure "safety" b: a rule or order issued by an executive authority, or regulatory agency, or a government and having the force of law'.

But economists are used to such abstract descriptions. For instance Douglas C. North opens his important book *Institutions, Institutional*

Change and Economic Performance (North, 1990, p. 3) with the sentence: 'Institutions are the rules of the game in a society or, more formally, are the humanly devised constraints that shape human interactions.' With this reference we can describe regulations as the institutions created by formal organisations. And we can apply the metaphor of Chandler (1977) and say that the Rs are the 'visible hand' that controls the 'invisible hand' of the market mechanism (Adam Smith). That means: the Rs will complement the informal constraints of the economy. They are either steering the outcome of economic activities in a certain direction or preventing certain results. And they are either permissions to do something or bans on something.

Table 10.1   Forms and aims of regulation

	Directing	Preventing
Permissions	X	(y)
Bans	(x)	Y

The combinations X and Y reflect two basically different approaches to Civil Law and administrative regulations of economic affairs. X is the type of Rs, which characterised the first attempts to liberalise economic activities in the former Soviet Union – that is, the issue of permissions to do something like retail sale of milk. This type of Rs reflects an authoritarian, directing style of government, which is practical under conditions of a stationary society (and often explains the lack of developments too). Apart from the unpleasant implications with respect to human rights, the non-existing or delayed permissions for endogenous evolutionary developments – that is unexpected results of the manifold ideas of citizens – is the main drawback of this approach to Rs. It is impossible to know and specify in advance all the results of decentralised decision-making, i.e. a kind of market economic system, which will not conflict with basic goals of the government concerned. It is, however, quite easy to

1. Identify and specify the dislikes
2. Issue corresponding Rs of the type 'You shall not ...'
3. Have the result that the citizens will have workable choice sets when they develop their ideas and initiate developments.

That is the reason why I interpret the Y-combination as the basic regulatory approach of market economies. There are, however, circumstances and matters which imply

- Bans as method of the alternative, directing policy (x). This happens, for instance, when the government issues a ban on something – like the use of asbestos – in order to induce the application and development of alternatives.
- Permissions as a method of prevention (y). This happens for instance when a general ban against the sale of drugs makes special authorisations (the licence, concession) of retail pharmacy necessary.

Several organisations issue Rs. The hierarchy and complementarity of their assignments imply that the Rs should be related by means of the same hierarchy and complementarity. On top there are the constitutional and cultural rules. They define the possible set of the primary Rs that define the rules of the societal system of production and distribution of economic goods and, hence, apply to all agents of an economy. They comprise the laws required for division of labour and other kinds of co-operation, for instance the system of units of measurement, and they shape the setting for the special Rs that applies to a certain sector of the economy or to the allocation of a certain product. Delorme shows (in this volume), how this basic institutional setting directs and shapes the alternatives as regards special Rs. The explanation of the general Rs is thus a central theme, which I will come back to in the next section.

Midttun raises in his contribution a question about the possibility of designing an efficient and consistent system of regulations, which deserves special attention. His thesis, that vertical hierarchy (organisations) and markets both have specific, essential rules and problems, seems to exclude the formulation of the meta-theory, required for the analysis of alternative combinations of hierarchy and markets.

Anyhow, the numerous Rs constitute a complex system in which contradictions, unnecessary complications, redundancies, even harmful elements, are possible. The detection of such inefficiencies is a central problem of the economics of Rs. It raised the economic, organisational, and strategic questions that motivated the various types of discussions hitherto labelled the 'Economics of Regulation'. Three questions have guided the development of this special literature:

- The optimal design of a certain R
- The search for alternatives to the traditional Rs (by release of orders and costly control of their compliance)
- The societal cost and benefit, i.e. the net welfare effect, of a specific regulatory task (see the contribution of Wickström).

I do not consider the literature on these questions as a special subject of this chapter; I will deal with these questions, as they appear in relation to the topics I consider.

Economically rational regulations and economically efficient regulation

This section aims at a structuring of the analytical issues we have to discuss with reference to such Rs and I hope to make clear that this part of the theory of economic Rs is of vital importance for economics in general. Focusing on economically rational and efficient Rs I start with the need for Rs, which define property rights and govern personal inter-actions. The rationalisation of these property rights popular among economists rests on strong model assumptions, which we have to consider as a problem, when we think over the observed problems with the explanatory power of this simple, but rational approach to R design. My discussion of discrepancies between reality and economic ideals takes notice of the arguments of North (1990) and proceeds from there to the issue of not internalised costs. This return to the core of economic theory clears the way for the last part of this section where I discuss a noticeable difference between (a) the analysis of Rs with reference to their economical rationale and (b) the analysis of Rs with reference to the induced allocations of resources.

Economic theory of property rights and regulations of individual interactions

The distinction between the economic problems of the isolated Robinson Crusoe and his problems after the arrival of Friday makes evident how our ideas on resource allocation, cost and income are related to Rs of individual interactions.

Robinson Crusoe alone must deal with his restricted resources, and he knows that he can improve his future situation if he allocates some of his valuable time to the development of these resources. He is, in other words, dealing with the problems of household management, which are the subject-matter of our theory of consumption and inter-temporal allocations. He benefits from the arrival of the second person, if they co-operate (sometimes work together, specialise according to their abilities, and exchange their goods and services). But this co-operation will not take place unless they also agree on the distinction between 'yours' and 'mine', that is, on property rights, on the respect for property of others (compensate damages) and on rules for their interactions, i.e. contracts and their settlement. They have, in other words, to regulate their relations. The Mosaic Law is an illustrating case in point. These regulations are the implicit basic rules of the game when we ponder about markets and trade and apply analytical models of interactions of two or more decision-making individuals (for example 'game theory').

The subjection of Friday and his occupation thereupon as a slave constitute an extreme solution for the relations between Robinson and Friday. It illustrates that 'force' belongs to the explanation of property rights. An individual's ability and willingness to apply force is, however, in general restricted. Religious beliefs (for example a taboo), ideology (such as socialism) and other cultural variables (like the role of kinship and respect of 'human rights') are among the variables that apparently determine this restriction by influencing rules of conduct, laws, and individual expectations. They also explain why the distribution of property and the definition of the required rights are, in principle, arbitrary.

Economists are keen to identify the basic reasons for observed economic phenomena. They therefore often ignore the specific role of ideology and other cultural variables because these explanatory variables are intermediary in the sense that they are themselves products of historical processes and, hence, themselves subject to specific explanations. Their alternative explanation of property rights rests on an application of cost-benefit analysis to the following observations:

- The ability/permission to exclude is the essence of property
- Some assets are free in the sense that nobody cares about an exclusion of other users
- Some of the activities of individuals and firms conflict with property of other agents without effecting penalty, compensation for the owner or a ban on these activities.

The conclusion is simply that the benefit and cost of the necessary activities and transactions determine whether an asset is a free good, or unprotected, or exclusively used by its owner. An asset becomes property when the gain from exclusive property rights exceeds the cost of an enforcement and protection of these rights. Demsetz's 1967 paper, 'Toward a Theory of Property Rights' is the classical reference and Eggertsson (1990) is a useful source for a survey of the discussion and refinements of this basic economic approach to the explanation of Rs and property rights.

It is, with respect to the application of this hypothesis, important to remember that not only tangible assets are subject to property rights. All exclusive rights that have an economic value count in the economics of R as property – that is, also patents, privileges, contractual assignments, and the control over own labour. Law on contracts, commerce and firms is thus among the general Rs of individuals' interactions that define property rights. The explanation of property rights will hence fail if it is not able to explain this law too.

The Rs, which define and/or determine property rights, belong to the determinants of the distribution of cost and income. Revisions of Rs and additional new Rs effect redistribution with impacts on the subsequent distribution of investments as well. And these entrepreneurial decisions change the overall performance and development of this economy.

Having such consequences of the Rs in mind, we now consider the case that some Rs determine property rights, which are inefficient in the sense of the economic cost-benefit model of property rights. These other Rs do nevertheless influence economic relations and the performance of the economy. We must, hence, recognise and explain these Rs too and we must recognise their impact on the distribution of cost and incomes, if we want to understand the economy of the country concerned. This observation has important consequences for the conception of economic theory, if this theory is meant to be a device for practical analytical and political work. It is the reason why I hold that the programme of economics – as a scientific discipline – is not realisable beyond the scope of Aristotle's treatise on household management, if it ignores how laws and other general Rs mould the system of economic affairs.

Assumptions

The Rs are rational in the sense of the applied economic model, if they induce and secure that property rights correspond with this cost-benefit approach to the explanation of property rights. From an economist's point of view this reaction on expected net benefit is a good thing in itself and it is also analytically advantageous because it extends the domain of his economic picture of the world. For other people, this is a categorisation of Rs, which is more a matter of tautology. It is therefore useful to recollect two basic assumptions of this picture and to keep them in mind:

1. The Methodological Individualism applies – i.e., all economic phenomena, like the Rs of property rights, are manifestations of individual behaviour and explanations of this human behaviour begin with the individuals, not with the influence of institutions and/or collective phenomena like culture.
2. The individuals concerned – not only the entrepreneurs, but also legislators, landlords, judges, bureaucrats, and all other kinds of employees – are rational agents who independently and consequently pursue their own self-interest in the sense of utility maximisation.

Not all people will regard these assumptions as a satisfying restriction on the development and variety of the theory of economic regulations. Especially the idea that culture, political system and the notion of society are unintended results of the behaviour of individuals (which do not have significant influence on economic policy, design of property rights, individual behaviour, occurrence and handling of unemployment problems and so on), will not please everyone.

My own opinion is that the notion of Methodological Individualism itself first of all is a manifestation of culture. It is, however, also a convenient principle of modelling socio-economic interactions between independent individuals. Critics of an application of this principle should therefore first consider when, how and whether something influences the individual behaviour so strongly that the model will systematically produce wrong predictions.

Discrepancies between reality and economic ideals

North and Thomas (1973) generalised the notion of property rights as a result of their cost and benefit by arguing that the institutions of the economic systems and relative prices of products and cost items have interacted throughout history and effected constructions of economically efficient institutions. But the numerous cases in which something other than this economic value/transaction cost approach applies, especially the historical evidence on the long-term prevalence of evidently inefficient property rights, convinced North that he needed a supplementary explanation. Still sticking to the two basic assumptions of standard economics, he declared that rulers devise property rights in their own interest and ignore the efficiency problem, if it suits their interests. He applied this view of institutions in his 'Structure and

Change in Economic History' (North, 1981). It was, however, only an intermediate station on his route to the central question in *Institutions, Institutional Change and Economic Performance*: whether and how the institutions 'can explain the radically different performance of economies over long periods of time' (North, 1990, p. 7).

This relation between the Rs and the performance of an economy becomes visible when we take notice of two undisputed facts:

1. Production relies on the producer's ability to take on the cost
2. Production cost has several components.

We may, for instance, first ask where the cost arises and thereupon distinguish between internal and external cost. The latter category refers to all kinds of external effects to the disadvantage of the neighbourhood (environment/third parties). Alternatively we may ask about the finance of this cost and, hence, distinguish between the private and the socialised cost. The first category refers to the cost, which the producer covers with his proceeds from sales (or with an allocation of his assets). This producer may be a firm owned and operated by the government; 'private' has in this context only the meaning of the agent who causes something.

With this twofold classification of production cost we can work with the following scheme of the production cost of an economy:

Table 10.2   Social cost

	Private cost	Socialised cost
Internal cost	A	B
External cost	D	C

All Rs and property rights, which we associate with this distribution of production cost, may satisfy the rationality criteria of the cost-benefit model of property rights. The society (neighbours) may deem actions against external effects too costly and accept the combination (D). The Society may likewise accept that private people use public property for their private purposes, for instance as grazing land (B).

Only the Rs and property rights, which make costs internal and private (A) may, however, satisfy the efficiency conditions of the internal cost, which underlie the appreciated Pareto optimal welfare properties of a market economy described in basic textbooks. Deviations from this situation imply inefficiencies in the sense of deviations from the optimal allocation of resources, which we term Pareto Optimum.

The introduction of economically efficient property rights and the enforcement of these rights would internalise otherwise 'external cost' and thus have positive welfare effects by improvement of the allocation of resources. A lot of discussions among economists therefore centred on the construction of new markets and other regulatory devices, which will effect this 'internalisation'. Ronald Coase's two seminal papers 'The Nature of the Firm' (Coase, 1937) and 'The Problem of Social Cost' (Coase, 1960) set the path for this discussion. Coase gave us a notion of the market place and voluntary contracting as an alternative to administrative Rs, when the society has to solve problems with private economic activities. The shift from the combination (C) to (A) is the subject of this debate, and there is full agreement that the allocation and trade of property rights would effect this shift, if there were no transaction cost.

These transaction costs exist, however, and the questions 'What do transaction cost actually effect?' and 'How to deal with the consequences' are still open for discussion. One, practical and, hence, currently popular approach to this problem is to go for the introduction of Rs, which will privatise hitherto socialised external cost – that is, effect a shift from (C) to (D). The introduction of environmental taxes is legitimated by this objective.

Two approaches to economic efficiency

The theory of general economic equilibrium, which has identified the conditions of a Pareto optimal distribution of resources, cost, and income, did not take account of information and transaction cost. The information problem concerned Hayek (1937, 1945) when he raised the question of how the economy can ever approach this optimum. The transaction cost is our concern with references to Pareto optimum. Let us therefore assume the conditions of complete information, that the principle of methodological individualism applies and that the individuals are rational agents, who independently and consequently pursue their own self-interest in the sense of utility maximisation.

Consider two contracting parties, in the setting of the general equilibrium theory without transaction cost, who realise a situation, which is not in the set of Pareto optimal contracts. A comparative static analysis of this situation tells us that at least one of the two contracting parties could certainly improve his welfare without adversely affecting the welfare of the other, if we go on ignoring the transaction cost. This situation permits two interpretations:

- Either, the party, who would benefit from a revision of this contract, has evaluated the benefit and cost and refrains from this revision, because his expected improvement is less than the transaction cost
- Or, it is a new situation, which will induce adjustments in accordance with our assumptions.

North (1990) refers to the first alternative, the case that transaction cost prevents the adjustment of institutions and contracts, when he explains the persistence of economically inefficient contracts. This explanation fails, however, if we include the transaction cost in the set of cost that will explain the conditions of a Pareto optimum. It is a modelling strategy that secures the identity of Pareto efficient Rs and property rights with Rs and property rights which are efficient in the sense of individuals' cost and benefit. Much of the property rights literature – as reviewed by Alessi (1980) – refers to this theoretical setting, when emphasising the distortion of efficiency incentives associated with attenuated property rights and implicitly assuming that this cost-benefit-efficiency is a sufficient criterion. It is, however, also a strategy of modelling, which

- Makes the notion of Pareto optimality immune to critiques of the theoretical model, because every model will produce the same optimum conditions, but with different meaning of the cost considered
- Deprives the notion of Pareto optimality of much of its value as a reference for discussions of the problems of practical economies.

It is not in order to rescue North's explanation of economically inefficient institutions, but in order to keep the Pareto optimality as an ideal and a reference for discussions of the problems of practical economies, that I

- Argue as if information and transaction cost are not included in the model of Pareto optimality, i.e. not defining this kind of optimum
- Maintain that information and transaction cost can explain the persistency of situations, which are not efficient in the sense of a Pareto optimum.

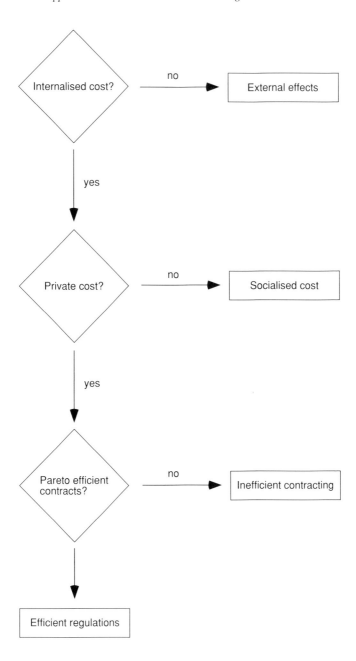

Figure 10.1   Allocation efficient and rational regulations: (a) Allocation efficiency

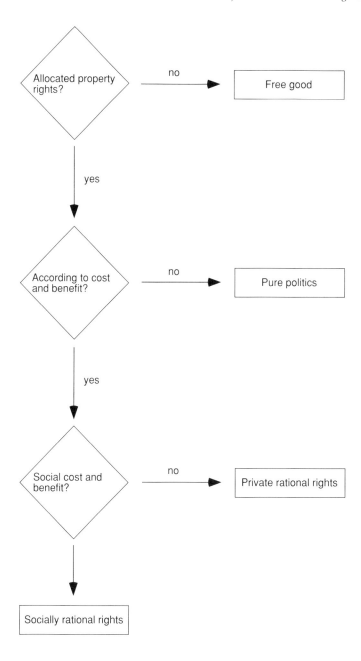

Figure 10.1 Allocation efficient and rational regulations: (b) Rational regulation

This 'realistic' view implies the existence of allocations between two contractual parties, which do not satisfy the Pareto conditions. It establishes, hence, that internalised private cost (A) is a necessary but not sufficient condition for the criteria of economic efficiency in the sense of Pareto optimum. As a methodological procedure it helps me, specifying the difference between two approaches to the perception of economically inefficient Rs and property rights. Figure 10.1 illustrates my argument.

The first part, the efficient Rs approach, stresses the importance of internalising and privatising costs and income. It makes us aware of external effects and politics as obstacles to this objective of economic policy. The figure representing the second, rational Rs approach reminds us that both problems have at least two versions. Namely, that

- External effects are either ignored (considered to be unimportant), if the environment concerned is considered to be a free good, or they are debated as the reason why social and private cost and income are different.
- Politics is either preventing economically rational Rs or it is dealing with differences between social and individuals' benefit and cost.

The common 'free rider' behaviour and our basic assumption that the individuals are rational agents, who independently and consequently pursue their own self-interest in the sense of utility maximisation, both fit with the ignorance of environmental problems. This observation complicates, however, the explanation of the case that the difference between social and private cost and benefits has effects on the formation of Rs.

In their chapter Mez and Midttun discuss the difference between the pay-off and organisational cost of pursuing vested interest of a sector or an agent compared with the pay-off and cost of pursuing the interest of the public in general (if it exists). This difference has effects on the outcome of political process. The theory must therefore explain the formation of both

1. A collective conciousness about the importance of an external effect
2. A political reaction

if it will explain Rs that correspond with the social benefit and cost.

The individual perception of their own interest and welfare renders the explanation of a majority view easy, but how do we explain that societies invent patent rights and other Rs that restrict the positive external effect of an inventions? Sure, this explanation is possible, if we argue that the individuals have a long-term orientation and wisely take account of the unknown, but possibly chance that they will benefit the next time. But, it is an application of the economic approach to Rs and property rights, which is not the standard of the literature on this basic economic approach to the explanation of Rs and property rights. Accepting this possibility of paradigm conformity, I nevertheless think that a dash of ideas about system properties (the Whole is different from the sum of its Parts) and about general societal partnership with respect to this system, will improve this part of the explanatory problem.

Regulations and politics

In this section I carry on the last argument about the explanation of Rs and property rights and apply it to the contributions of some analysts who have been especially concerned with the existence and effects of Rs, which are preventing efficient allocations of resources and rights. I therefore start with the observation that the socialisation of the cost of private economic activities is a characteristic of property rights, which have been installed by political decisions. A brief characterisation of three approaches to this problem will be illustrated by a reference to the practical case that a government establishes an agency responsible for the regulation of certain economic activities.

Consider for instance the case of a company which has smaller receipts from sales than the internal cost of its operation and receives compensating subsidies from a public budget. This company contributes to the existence of category (B) in Table 10.2. Consider now also the case that political decision-makers want to terminate this transfer of budgetary funds to the company concerned. The enforcement of this proposal requires the introduction of a hard budget constraint in combination with

- Either a product price increase, which will reduce the 'rent' of the final consumers of the provided product/service (if these consumers meanwhile benefit from a socialisation of cost of their private consumption)
- Or a rationalising reorganisation of the company concerned, which will also reduce the total income payments to the staff of this company.

As a result of this expectation, consumers as well as the employees of the company (often supported by the management) will mobilise political forces against this 'privatisation' of all cost. And quite often they succeed. This observation is a gateway to the field of political economy that focuses on the occurrence of such distributions of public funds and property rights to the advantage of a certain group of agents – namely: first, the idea that individuals and interest groups are lobbying for political decisions, which will give them additional income/valuable property rights – that is, the idea that 'rent seeking' is a major determinant of public transfers, tax exemptions and other property rights. The analytical use of this idea, which we first of all identify with the works of James Buchanan and Gordon Tullock, opened this field of economics, which is known as 'Public Choice'. The collection of essays in Buchanan, Tollison and Tullock (1980) illustrates its wide applications, i.e. the fruitfulness of this approach to political economy. Mueller (1989) is an acknowledged survey. This approach to the analysis of economic Rs, which are not efficient in the sense of the cost and benefit of property rights, is, however, limited by the restrictions on microeconomic modelling of relations between rational agents. Macroeconomic considerations, which have often effected differentiated schemes of taxation and investment subsidies, are beyond the scope of this microeconomic modelling of 'rent seeking' (see also the macroeconomic argument of Keynes (1936) in favour of the introduction of fixed (minimum) wages). And the human welfare considerations, which have protected the wages of low income groups (national minimum standard of real income, wage structure to the advantage of the low income groups) and still do so in some countries, are not captured either. The ignorance of the micro-economists' warnings since Pigou (1920) illustrates this point.

Posner (1971, 1974), Stigler (1971, 1974), and Pelzman (1976) and others launched an alternative approach to this basic policy problem, when they invented the generalised version of the 'capture theory' that R occurs as an outcome of the operation of a political market. This group, also termed the 'Chicago School', holds that regulation often occurs on demand of the regulated industry itself (hence 'capture'), and that it transfers income to the interest groups in return for votes and other contributions to the benefit of politicians. Alfred Haid (in this volume) gives more details on this approach.

The modelling of the political decision processes, which can bring forth these decisions to the advantage of a special group, is a second research area. One problem of these attempts to establish positive theories of the political process originated from the existence of a standard economic model of a democracy with competing political parties, which was initiated by the location theory of Hotelling (1929) and Smithies (1941), and popularised by Downs (1957). This model predicts that all parties will try to attract the median voter in order to maximise the group of potential voters. But if the government sticks to the interests of such an electorate, it will never cause damage to the majority by allocating rents to the benefit of special interest groups. For instance Aranson and Ordeshook (1981) and Mueller (1989) discuss this drawback of the median voter model and explain attempts to solve the problem. The Alfred Marshall Lecture of Torsten Persson and Tabellini 'The Size and Scope of Government: Comparative Politics with Rational Politicians' (Persson and Tabellini (1999) illustrates how far the development of this model of political competition has taken it away from the original contribution of Downs. Meanwhile a large literature is dedicated to this modelling of the political process. My impression is that more attention to the following circumstances would earn positive yields with respect to the explanation of why governments establish inefficient economic Rs:

- The variability of voting systems
- The role of organisational structures in politics
- The role of ideology
- The problems of spatial differentiation
- The role of personal relations etc.

Organisational structures and personal relations established in these structures, like political parties or committees, will for instance give people personal influence on political decisions, which are not recognised as being their responsibility.

A third research area is the study of ways and means to put a stop to such distributions of public funds and property rights to the advantage of a certain group of agents. This is a branch of public choice which has become so special and prominent that it carries its own label – 'Constitutional Economics'. Interest attaches to (a) the study of how society chooses the rules under which the system operates, (b) how these rules work, and the central objective of the studies is to establish operationally meaningful results about 'good political systems'. This area too is particularly associated with the ground-breaking works of Buchanan and Tullock (Buchanan and Tullock, 1962; Buchanan, 1975; Brennan and Buchanan, 1985), but the ideas of F.A. Hayek (1979) have had a great impact too. Buchanan himself has provided authoritative descriptions of this field (for instance Buchanan, 1990). The contributions to Pies and Leschke (1996) contain stimulating criticism of this economics of constitutions.

Accidental circumstances (like the composition of a committee, the imagination and bias of individual committee members, and the preferences of the constituency) determine the outcome, when a committee designs a constitution or other institutions. To this important insight I add the observations that the constituency and the selected committee normally respond to detrimental experience when they change/design a constitution and that this happened at different times and after different experiences in the countries concerned. The result is an explanation of the occurrence of the national styles mentioned earlier in this chapter, which is not dependent on the (by the way valid) argument that the constituencies have different cultural biases, which influence the style and outcome of a political process.

I value the referred approaches to the explanation of lasting inefficient economic Rs highly and I would not dismiss the established insights concerning the practice and organisation of economic Rs, but I also think that the basic assumptions of these analyses deserve special attention. Coase himself once stated: 'Modern institutional economics should study man as he is, acting within the constraints imposed by real institutions. Modern institutional economics is economics as it ought to be' (Coase, 1984, p. 231).

Indeed, these basic assumptions determine not only the results, but also the relevance of analytical instruments. In addition to the two basic assumptions mentioned before, we here also have to take account of explicit references to the Pareto optimum. Due to the well-known Second Best problem (which says that the first-best-solution to allocation problems (Pareto optimum) is not the first best reference for considering the effect of single deviation from this optimum allocation), this reference is here inadequate. The less demanding Pareto criterion, that a change is in general advantageous, if it improves the situation of at least one person without hurting anyone else, is, however, applicable. Once more my main problem, which I can only pinpoint, but not yet solve, arises from the assumption concerning the handling of the pursuance of personal interests – especially in combination with the rules of conduct concerning some professional assignments. The R, which establishes a public agency responsible for the regulation of certain economic activities, is a case in point, which illustrates my last concern.

An organisational issue: the regulatory agency

The modus operandi of this agency is my starting point. There is a general agreement that the agency shall be 'politically independent', but there is not a clear understanding, or agreement, as to what this independence means exactly.

The extensive interpretation of the term 'independence' would establish an agency outside the political system (government/ parliament). Such an agency, superior or parallel to the elected government, would be a technocrat ruler with an obligation to be independent, neutral and wise when establishing standards that will influence and define property right and rents of private investors and so on. It is a 'rule of the best' institution, which fits the Platonian concept of government, but definitely contradicts the style of modern European democracies.

In these democracies we have to distinguish three levels of regulations:

1. The law by parliament
2. The decree by a ministry (according to a legal authorisation and concerning a special subject-matter of this authorising law)
3. The decision by a regulatory agency (according to the general authorisation of the agency, which is given by a certain law, and according to the special authorisation and other instructions, which are given by a minister, who has to execute this law).

I will here follow the simplifying view that we are only dealing with the last, third level when discussing the independence of a regulatory body, but stress that we in practical work have to take account of the possibility of moving issues up or down the ladder of regulations. Moreover, the national style of R is characterised by this allocation of R in this ladder.

The 'independence' of a public agency is, in this setting, a legal, not a political matter. It is related to the accomplishment of tasks, which have been assigned to this agency by a law. The law may say something about the autonomy of its fact-finding and decisions – like the description in constitutions of the independence of public courts. This independence is, however, still the feature of a law, which has to be administered by the government. A certain ministry takes on the administration of the law including the responsibility for the work of the agency. The ministry is in other words supervising the agency in the sense that it has to

- Observe whether the agency is working in accordance with its assignment
- Act as the first resort for complaints about the activities of the agency.

The agency is politically independent in the sense that

- The responsible ministry can, if it agrees with a plaintiff, order a second hearing of the case, but not another decision by the agency
- If the second decision by the agency effects a repetition of the complaint, then the case has to be decided by the court of justice, which in this case is the first court of appeal.

The agency is usually also subordinated to the ministry in the sense that the relevant law authorises the ministry to complete the description of the tasks and procedures of the agency by issuance of orders. The legal provisions concerning the number, scope and frequency of these orders are the crucial characteristics of the 'independence' of the agency. The independence of a regulatory agency (with respect to its administration and decision-making) is in other words restricted by its legal assignment and by issued instructions. It is politically independent in the restricted sense that politicians are not allowed to interfere with individual decisions.

The problem with this construction, and the reason why I have described it in some detail, is that it is strongly at variance with the results of modern theory on the design of regulatory institutions as reviewed in Estache and Martimort (1999). This theory

- Proceeds on an even stronger assumption than the Bureaucracy model of Niskanen (1975) with respect to the effects of the self-interest of public servants, namely on the assumption that the regulator, that is the head of the regulatory agency, will sell favourable Rs against income for himself and/or his institution
- Focuses on the avoidance of such capture, on the avoidance of collusion, and the minimisation of transaction cost as the main strategic problems of organisation
- Applies game theory (in accordance with the notion of agents who pursue their own self-interest)
- Produces results that concern a system of competing regulators – for example, on the optimal number of competing regulators, information sharing versus private information of the regulators,

on the duration of the regulators' licence, conflicts between the legislative and regulators, appointment versus election.

I agree that governance problems are important and deserve special attention, that the creation of a regulatory agency establishes relations between the government and the agency and between the agency and various companies, which are characterised by diverging interests and asymmetric information. That means that the agency has a so-called principal–agent problem with respect to regulated firms and that this type of problem also occurs in the relation between the government and the agency, if the agency becomes subject to the capture of the industry (in the original sense of this term). So there are severe problems with the design of such an agency, which have no patent solutions within the described framework of European democracies. Moreover, I also think that there is a general agreement with respect to the objective that the Rs shall protect:

- Consumers from potential abuse of market power and from potential damage from dangerous products
- Investors from untidy, arbitrary political influence.

Agreement also exists with respect to the insight that there is a trade-off between the

- Credibility of the regulator that grows with the duration of his Rs
- Flexibility of regulatory policy, which is needed in order to react to occurrences that change the regulatory needs.

But, the section 'Lessons for a pragmatic approach to the design of regulatory institutions' in Estache and Martimort (1999) that summarises the theory on issues discussed by practitioners, shows that these ideas of the theoreticians are far removed from the current perception of the practical problems of R.

Regulation and economic dynamics

Regulations are either invented or grown out of the practised behaviour of people. All Rs have a function and corresponding effects. In the case of invented Rs these effects may be intended. The solution to disagreements about the purpose and evaluations of Rs is hence a central theme to the theory of Rs. The corresponding theme in the case of the other

Rs, which are not designed by somebody, is to explain how these Rs emanate. And then, of course, the theory of R should give an answer to the question of why some Rs are the result of a goal-oriented human design and others come out of unco-ordinated actions of agents. Is the set of intentionally established Rs mainly a result of politics, culture or needs? In other words: will someone else, private persons, establish some of the Rs if the elected/appointed authority refrains from doing so?

Hayek became the hero of the modern endogenous R school when he worked out his explanation of appropriate/socially efficient rules as the result of processes endogenous to the economy itself (Hayek, 1973). In fact he resumed an old theme of his – the systemic foundation of the Austrian school, which is represented in this volume by Karen Vaughn's chapter – and he ended in marked contrast to his earlier work in this subject (Hayek, 1939).

My general understanding of intentional institutional development is that constitutional Rs together with normative evaluations normally govern the feedback from individual perceptions of problems to the political design of the 'solutions' that thereupon steer the subsequent economic and regulatory developments. Stressing this political idea, my standpoint dissents with the current emphasis of economists on game theory that intends to demonstrate that institutions might evolve out of interactions between learning individuals. This game theoretic approach is to my mind not mainly due to empirical observations of endogenous, spontaneous evolution of institutions. It mainly seems to echo the methodological individualism of mainstream economics – namely the basic insight of Carl Menger that decentralised parallel decision-making by numerous individuals has unintended outcomes, which cannot be explained without reference to the actions of these individuals. Menger was, however, quite explicit about the necessity of taking account of political interference with this sort of endogenous formation of institutions. He stressed that the government always has (and often applies) the right to design property rights and other institutions and thus often modify the likely outcome of unco-ordinated actions (Menger, 1921, pp. 254–6).

Moreover, we have to observe a difference between two kinds of regulatory reforms:

1. The introduction of a new kind of R or the abolition of an existing one
2. The revision of an existing R.

The latter kind of reform raises a problem of consistency, which is known as the Arrow-Condorcet problem, that is, the possibility of intransitivity of majority voting. This problem complicates the design of consistent regulatory reforms. It is quite likely that the majority introduces special regulations, which do not fit well into the existing order and, hence, effects frictions.

Here, in this observation that political coalition-building and parliamentary voting may effect sub-optimal and even inconsistent Rs, do I detect the appropriate background for an implementation of the ideas about endogenous Rs – that is, the idea that the people concerned select the Rs.

Economic agents struggling for success react upon the design of Rs and express any complaints. Moreover, if an R is ill-designed, the collected statistics, also international comparisons, and the observed strategy of the agents concerned, will indicate a damage to the economic performance of the nation and provide arguments. In open economies we likewise observe reallocations of activities that become political arguments. Governments confronted with such evidence must react and either repair mistakes or explain why they stick to this R in spite of its criticised effects. Thus, there exists, in democracies, a selection mechanism with respect to its economic Rs that resembles the endogenous selection of species (Darwin, 1888) and firms (Alchian, 1950). According to my knowledge, Darwin was inspired by the economists' ideas about competition when he formulated his application of the principle known as the 'survival of the fittest'. Frameworks, which are easily supplemented with the operation of a political selection system and thence give more details to the idea expressed here, were provided by, for instance, Opp (1979) and Gäfgen (1981).

In Europe this principle of survival of the fittest Rs applies to the harmonisation of Rs within the European Community. The members have tried but failed to negotiate a unification of their regulations. They therefore agreed to issue standards for national Rs and to let each member country have the obligation and right to implement a consistent national R, which takes account of its national preferences (the principle of subsidiarity). The related idea is that forces of the common market shall select the winners among the national approaches and enforce accommodating adaptations in other countries. This notion of a harmonisation process corresponds with the political feedback process of regulatory reforms just outlined.

Imagine the case of a consistent national system of Rs that includes a restriction on the convertibility of the national currency and imagine also that this system hitherto was appropriate. The government now decides to abolish this convertibility restriction. Either a national consolidation or an external influence on the government (for instance an international agreement) motivates this decision. The second possibility shows that in the current world the openness of national economies enables external circumstances and their change (shocks) to interfere with national politics; they restrict the national autonomy (sovereignty). This means with respect to the notion of endogenous institution formation that this idea

- Is a matter of isolation of the system concerned
- Permits the existence of external influence and negotiations, with external parties in which the parties express ideas on collective cost and benefit.

Hence, it is more a matter of adherence to ideologies than of substantial differences, if we interpret the discussion between representatives of regions or (by analogy) between representatives of other interest groups as evidence for or against the idea that endogenous processes determine the Rs.

This thesis refers to the short and medium term of the current European society. But, of course, in a retrospection of the long run all the regulatory developments will appear as endogenous. Moreover, the reference to Western Europe indicates that the constitutional and legal system matters. The US system, for instance, has a design that leaves many more details to settlement by endogenous economic process. As a consequence of this element, the operation of the economic system contributes more to the explanation of the economic development than in our European case. This difference is probably the basic reason why current economics, dominated by Americans, stress the endogenous approach to the explanation of regulatory development. The German liberals developed instead a concept of ideologically determined political decision-making on Rs, which aims at establishing and securing a certain operation of the economic system – that is, 'Ordnungspolitik' (see for instance Vanberg, 1988).

It is still an open question, deserving more attention, as to how far openness makes a harmonisation of particular Rs necessary. Imagine the case of a very pronounced harmonisation within a group of sovereign countries. Which selection mechanism picks the standard? Is it an EU-like regulatory competition, expert advice, or the choice of a dominant economy? The answer contributes not only to our insight in international economic integration, but also – by analogy – to the explanation of national processes that determine/change Rs.

The size of the country and the sector of the economy respective to the kind of regulated activity are two of the factors influencing the measure of openness of an economy, which may explain the strength of market forces towards a regulatory harmonisation. Evidence on the strength of this harmonisation drive gives hints about the sustainability of the national styles of Rs that were stressed in the introduction to this chapter. National styles of Rs are still evident, but experience in areas like banking shows strong tendencies to adopt international standards. The formation of a European electricity market is another example. Market forces recently demonstrated a strong harmonising impact on the key rule concerning the Third Party Access to the grid.

The example, that the local government abolishes a convertibility restriction, also illustrates the problem of systemic interdependencies and consistence. The assumed measure increases the international mobility of capital and so changes the conditions and business of domestic financial institutions. Such changes usually effect the need to revise other domestic Rs (like the rules concerning accounting, reporting, capital, liquid reserves, restrictions on types of business and so on) and these reforms take place by amendments of special laws. The problem now is that these amendments should not contradict the system of more general, basic laws and that they may require adjustments of these more general Rs too.

The status of a normative theory of regulation

Any development of relevant knowledge of design and effects of economic Rs is related to the perception of the problems of economic Rs. The normative foundation of the economics of Rs, is the subject of this relation. We are, like other scholars, not only searching for answers to special questions, but also for robust results. Therefore, it seems appropriate to consider the following question too: do we discuss problems of a normal research area or of normative opinion-building?

Figure 10.2 illustrates the reason for this question: a research agenda normally refers to a set of positive questions and to the demand for corresponding theoretical and empirical analysis. Our interest in problems of economic Rs, however, often emanates from normative interpretations of information about economic circumstances.

The lower part of Figure 10.2 elucidates such a relation between the positive research and its inevitable normative orientation.

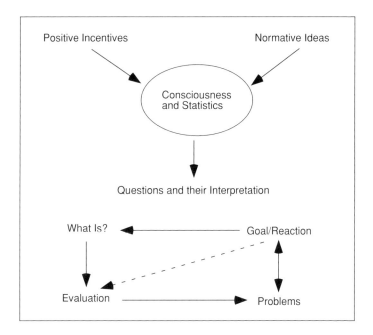

Figure 10.2   Normative orientation of research

Questions about 'what is' often results from ideas about 'what should be' – that is, either the goal of the political activity concerned or the expected current situation. They induce analysis first and then evaluations of the evidence. Such evaluations serve more purposes than the mere test of expectations, which we associate with empirical work concerning theories. If they conflict with the notion of 'what should be', they bring about a new consciousness of the current situation, its problems, and sometimes also with respect to the goal (revision of aspirations). This result sometimes also affects reactions in the sense that it shapes new ideas and induces additional questions about the current situation and its alternatives. But generally this loop of analysis means that

- The normative, reference system of evaluations, is inevitably an element of the idea of any current state
- The conciousness with respect to the definition, registration and evaluation of problems of economic Rs is not explainable without reference to the ideas about the goal.

Prejudices like ideology therefore contribute to the shaping of the subjective mental constructions which are in use when people interpret the world around them and select alternatives. They thus also shape ideas about regulatory needs and problems. Such dependencies make it difficult, probably virtually impossible, to keep the normative and positive issues of research rigorously apart. Recently Galbraith (1999) named it an 'innocent fraud' and Samuelson (1999), on the same occasion, spoke about ignored dangers of ideology. Midttun, in his contribution to this volume, points to the influence of the current situation – based on the experience of a marked economy we understand relations and problems in a different manner from in the context of a system of central planning. The communication problems, which we had discussing matters of economic policy and institution-building with colleagues from transformation countries shortly after the dismissal of the Soviet economic system, illustrates this point.

As a methodological problem this influence of normative ideas is mainly a concern of 'empirical research'. The required economic theory is still possible, if authors make their assumptions explicit. The empirical issue, that normative ideas influence the design and application of economic Rs, is, however, a problem and a guideline which we cannot ignore when we reflect on the explanation and design of economic Rs. It affords arguments for a political economy of Rs, which is methodically and ideologically more comprehensive than the current state of the art.

Bibliography

Alchian, Armen A. (1950) 'Uncertainty, Evolution and Economic Theory', *Journal of Political Economy*, 58, pp. 211–21.

Alessi, Louis De (1980) 'The Economics of Property Rights: A Review of the Evidence', *Research in Law and Economics*, 2, pp. 1–47.

Aranson, Peter H. and Peter C. Ordeshook (1981) 'Regulation, Redistribution, and Public Choice', *Public Choice*, 37, pp. 69–100.

Brennan, Geoffrey and James M. Buchanan (1985) *The Reason of Rules – Constitutional Political Economy*, Cambridge: Cambridge University Press.

Buchanan, James M. (1975) *The Limits of Liberty – Between Anarchy and Leviathan*, Chicago: Chicago University Press.

Buchanan, James M. (1990) 'The Domain of Constitutional Economics', *Constitutional Economic Economy*, 1, pp. 1–18.

Buchanan, James M., Robert D. Tollison and Gordon Tullock (eds) (1980) *Toward a Theory of the Rent-Seeking Society*, College Station, Texas: Texas T&M University Press.

Buchanan, James M. and Gordon Tullock (1962) *The Calculus of Consent – Logical Foundations of Constitutional Democracy*, Ann Arbor: University of Michigan Press.

Chandler, Alfred (1977) *The Visible Hand*, Cambridge, MA: Harvard University Press.

Coase, Ronald H. (1937) 'The Nature of the Firm', *Economica*, 4, pp. 386–405.

Coase, Ronald H. (1960) 'The Problem of Social Cost', *Journal of Law and Economics*, 3, pp. 1–44.

Coase, Ronald H. (1984) 'The New Institutional Economics', *Zeitschrift für die gesamte Staatswissenschaft / Journal of Institutional and Theoretical Economics*, 140, pp. 229–31.

Darwin, Charles (1888) *The Origin of Species*, London.

Demsetz, Harold (1967) 'Toward a Theory of Property Rights', *Journal of Political Economy*, 57, pp. 347–59.

Downs, Anthony (1957) *An Economic Theory of Democracy*, New York: Harper & Row.

Eggertsson, Thráinn (1990), *Economic Behavior and Institutions*, Cambridge: Cambridge University Press.

Estache, Antonio and David Martimort (1999) 'Politics, Transaction Cost, and the Design of Regulatory Institutions', *World Bank: Policy Research Working Paper*, No. 2073.

Foreign Affairs, May–June 1998.

Gäfgen, Gérard (1981) *Institutioneller Wandel und ökonomischer Erklärung*, Universität Konstanz: Volkswirtschaftliche Beiträge, Serie A- Nr. 161.

Galbraith, J.K. (1999) 'The Commitment to Innocent Fraud', *Challenge*, September–October 1999.

Hayek, Friedrich A. von (1937) 'Economics and Knowledge', *Economica*, 4, pp. 33–54.

Hayek, Friedrich A. von (1939) *Freedom and the Economic System*, Chicago: Chicago University Press.

Hayek, Friedrich A. von (1945) 'The Use of Knowledge in Society', *American Economic Review*, 35, pp. 519–30.

Hayek, Friedrich A. von (1973) *Law, Legislation and Liberty (Vol. I: Rules and Order)*, London: Routledge & Kegan Paul.

Hayek, Friedrich A. von (1979) *Law, Legislation and Liberty (Vol. III: The Political Order of Free People)*, London: Routledge & Kegan Paul.

Hotelling, H. (1929) 'Stability in Competition', *The Economic Journal*, 39, pp. 41–57.

Journal of Economic Growth, various issues.

Keynes, John Maynard (1936) *The General Theory of Employment, Interest and Money*, London: Macmillan & Co (now Palgrave).

Menger, Carl (1921) *Grundsätze der Volkswirtschaftslehre* (1871), 2nd edn. Wien: Hölder Picheler-Tempsky A.G., Leipzig: G. Freytag G.m.b.H.

Merriam-Webster's Collegiate Dictionary, electronic media edition, 1994.

Midttun, Atle and Eirik Svindland (1996) 'The Political Economy of Economic Transition', *Emergo*, Winter/1996, pp. 16–33.

Mueller, Dennis C. (1989) *Public Choice II, A Revised Edition of Public Choice*, Cambridge: Cambridge University Press.

Niskanen, William A. (1975) 'Bureaucrats and Politicians', *Journal of Law and Economics*, 18, pp. 617–43.

North, Douglas C. (1981) *Structure and Change in Economic History*, New York: Norton.

North, Douglas C. (1990) *Institutions, Institutional Change and Economic Performance*, Cambridge: Cambridge University Press.

North, Douglas C. and Robert P. Thomas (1973) *The Rise of the Western World: A New Economic History*, Cambridge: Cambridge University Press.

Opp, Karl-Dieter (1979) 'The Emergence and Effects of Social Norms. A Confrontation of Some Hypotheses of Sociology and Economics', *Kyklos*, 32, pp. 775–801.

Ostrom, Elinor (1986) 'An Agenda for the Study of Institutions', *Public Choice*, 48, pp. 3–25.

Pelzman, S. (1976) 'Toward A More General Theory of Regulation', *Journal of Law and Economics*, 19, pp. 211–48.

Persson, Torsten and Guido Tabellini (1999) 'The Size and Scope of Government: Comparative Politics with Rational Politicians', *European Economic Review*, 43, pp. 699–735.

Pies, Ingo and Martin Leschke (1996) *James Buchanans konstitutionelle Ökonomik*, Tübingen: J.C.B. Mohr (Paul Siebeck).

Pigou, A.C. (1920) *The Economics of Welfare*, London: Macmillan & Co. (now Palgrave) (fourth edition, 1932).

Posner, R.A. (1971) 'Taxation by Regulation', *Bell Journal of Economics and Management Science*, 2, pp. 22–50.

Posner, R.A. (1974) 'Theories of Economic Regulation', *Bell Journal of Economics and Management Science*, 5, pp. 335–58.

Samuelson, P.A. (1999) 'Two Gods that Fail', *Challenge*, September–October 1999.

Smithies, A. (1941) 'Optimum Location in Spatial Competition', *Journal of Political Economy*, 49, pp. 423–39.

Stigler, G.J. (1971) 'The Theory of Economic Regulation', *Bell Journal of Economic and Management Science*, 2, pp. 3–21.

Stigler, G.J. (1974) 'Free Riders and Collective Action: An Appendix to Theories of Economic Regulation', *Bell Journal of Economics and Management Science*, 5, pp. 359–65.

Vanberg, Viktor (1988) '"Ordnungstheorie" as Constitutional Economics – The German Conception of a "Social Market Economy"', *Ordo-Jahrbuch*, 39, pp. 17–31.

Index

Compiled by Sue Carlton